Unearthed

A Lost Actress, a Forbidden Book, and a Search
for Life in the Shadow of the Holocaust

Unearthed

Meryl Frank

hachette
BOOKS

New York

Hachette Books
Hachette Book Group
1290 Avenue of the Americas
New York, NY 10104
HachetteBooks.com
Twitter.com/HachetteBooks
Instagram.com/HachetteBooks

First Edition: April 2023

Published by Hachette Books, an imprint of Perseus Books, LLC, a subsidiary of Hachette Book Group, Inc. The Hachette Books name and logo is a trademark of the Hachette Book Group.

The Hachette Speakers Bureau provides a wide range of authors for speaking events. To find out more, go to www.hachettespeakersbureau.com or call (866) 376-6591.

Books by Hachette Books may be purchased in bulk for business, educational, or promotional use. For information, please contact your local bookseller or Hachette Book Group Special Markets Department at special.markets@hbgusa.com.

The publisher is not responsible for websites (or their content) that are not owned by the publisher.

Print book interior design by Amy Quinn.

Library of Congress Control Number: 2022951956

ISBNs: 978-0-306-82836-2 (hardcover), 978-0-306-82838-6 (ebook)

Printed in the United States of America

LSC-C

Printing 1, 2023

To Haadi and Naomi,
I pass this memorial candle, with tenderness, to you.

CONTENTS

I wasn't one of the six million who died in the Shoah,
I wasn't even among the survivors.
And I wasn't one of the six hundred thousand who went out of Egypt.
I came to the Promised Land by sea.
No, I was not in that number, though I still have the fire and the smoke
within me, pillars of fire and pillars of smoke that guide me
by night and by day. I still have inside me the mad search
for emergency exits, for soft places, for the nakedness
of the land, for the escape into weakness and hope.

—Yehuda Amichai, "I Wasn't One of the Six Million"

A Note on Proper Names

In Eastern Europe during the early part of the twentieth century, shifting geopolitical currents forced international borders to change, constantly. These shifts, along with the movements of displaced populations, entangled languages and alphabets, muddling names and terms, and presenting a challenge in a book like this to both writers and readers. A single road—German Street, for example—might have different names in Polish (ulica Niemiecka), Yiddish (Daytshe gas), and Lithuanian (Vokiečių gatvė).

The city at the heart of this story was Wilno to the Poles, Wilna to the Germans (who occupied the city during each of the two world wars), and Vilne or Vilna to the Jewish population, and, starting after World War II, it became widely known by its Lithuanian name, Vilnius.

People's names are also subject to the whims of different transliterations from the Hebrew or Cyrillic alphabets. Sometimes the same people, subjects in this story, themselves used different versions of their names in different contexts. For example, the diarist Grigorij Schur (as he was published in German) also went by Zvi Hirsh Shur (in Hebrew) and Grigorij or Grigorijus Šuras (in Lithuanian). I can't begin to describe the complications this all presented to my research, but I have never minded a challenge.

Throughout *Unearthed*, I've done my best to keep spellings as simple as possible for English speakers (Shriftsetzer, not Szryftzecer, for example) and to use the most commonly accepted form of a name or place. In some instances, I've personalized the usage, which is to say I've gone with the form I first heard and adopted. For instance, I refer to the town of Ashmyany, as it is now known, as opposed to its previous incarnations—Oszmiana, Oshmyany, or Ašmena.

In the case of the city where my family lived, for the sake of comprehension, I've used "Vilna" in contexts before 1945 and "Vilnius" when referring to the Lithuanian capital of today. This should be the clearest solution, but I hope you'll join me in seeing any residual confusion as a fascinating reflection of the chaos that reigned during this period of tremendous upheaval.

Prologue

I FIRST LEARNED ABOUT THE FORBIDDEN BOOK IN 1996.

On an overcast Sunday in June, I headed up the New Jersey Turnpike to see my aunt Mollie at her home in Bayonne. That in itself was not unusual. Mollie had invited me over countless times since I was a small child to regale me with stories about our family, before they were lost in the Holocaust. And when Mollie invited you somewhere, you went. But this time, when she'd called to summon me, there was an edge in her voice that suggested an added significance.

Even in her mideighties, Mollie was formidable. My aunt was barely five feet tall, but she might as well have been a giant for how large she loomed. Below auburn hair and arched eyebrows, she had our family's signature high cheekbones, Roman nose, and quick brown eyes—constantly assessing. She was always dressed immaculately, wearing a prominent piece of statement jewelry, either a family heirloom or a more modern treasure discovered in her travels. (Jewelry held special significance in my family, talismans that represented our history and love.) The only thing that belied her sophistication was her thick North Jersey accent.

Now she opened the door and enveloped me in a warm but quick hug.

She led me to the living room, tastefully decorated in midcentury rosewood atop ombre shag rugs in browns and golds. The modernist furniture was accented by more family heirlooms, brought over by my grandmother when she emigrated from Vilna (then a city in a Lithuanian state in the Russian Empire) in 1905, and an astounding modern art collection Mollie had gathered before the artists were lauded as modern masters—Picasso, Matisse, Braque, Chagall.

I was feeling tense. Somehow, I had been designated as the family member to talk to my aunt about giving up driving, which to her felt tantamount to surrendering her independence. I knew she was deeply opposed to the idea, and none of us liked to battle with her. But lately she'd been forgetting things, and operating a vehicle simply wasn't safe anymore. I readied myself to broach the topic with as much diplomacy as possible, but she surprised me by raising another, perhaps even more jarring, subject.

There, without ceremony, beneath a Ben Shahn lithograph of Martin Luther King Jr., Mollie began to talk about the responsibilities she expected me to assume after her death.

Her face took on a serious expression, unfamiliar to me. One essential responsibility I would have to assume after she was gone, she explained leaning in, concerned an *unusual* book.

She walked over to an elegant cabinet and opened its doors. I moved to rise as well, but she waved me back into my seat.

"Wait there," she said, accepting no argument.

Even now, at her advanced age, she was a commanding presence.

Nestled between an illustrated three-volume history of Jewish life in Vilna and a VHS cassette of a PBS documentary, *The Partisans of Vilna*, was a thin book. I recognized these surrounding resources because I had inherited Mollie's preoccupation with the past, all that had happened to our family before, during, and after the Holocaust. As she slid the paperback from the shelf, I thought it didn't look like much, for all the weight the conversation seemed to hold. But she held it with a reverence that fixed my attention.

Twenty-One and One, as the book was titled, was scarcely more than a hundred pages long, with brown lettering on the cover above a wood block–style illustration of arches and alleyways, a representation, I would later learn, of the Vilna ghetto, half concealed by a dark theatrical curtain. Carefully, Mollie leafed through to the only page written in English, a description that explained the book was "about twenty-one Yiddish actors murdered by the Nazis in Vilna 1941–42," my realization beginning to dawn.

She pointed out a black-and-white photograph of my cousin Franya Winter that had been reproduced alongside a Yiddish essay about her. In the image, she was smiling innocently at the camera, no sense of the horror that was to come. Her dark curls peeked out from beneath a kind of veil. Her face was round and youthful, her gaze penetrating. Although this was the first time I had seen this photo, I knew Franya well. As a child, I had spent countless hours poring over old photos of my European relatives from the first part of the twentieth century, and Franya, in particular, had always enchanted me. I knew from Mollie that she had been an actress before World War II, and you could see a spark in her eyes. But like my other family members, I knew nothing about what had become of her, only that she was gone. She didn't make it.

Franya's chapter was very near the front of the book—or rather, since the book was laid out in the customary Hebraic style read from right to left, very near the back. I would later understand that the order of the chapters had their own significance.

Mollie didn't tell me what was written, and since I couldn't read Yiddish, I had no way of deciphering it. But she offered the book to me, and I took it in my hands. As I leafed through the pages, a strange sense of protectiveness came over me.

"When I'm gone," Mollie began, "I want you to take this book."

I understood: I was to be the book's custodian, ensure its safekeeping. Something about this text was important.

"Keep it," she continued, "and pass it on to your children."

I agreed. I thought she was finished and readied to move on to the issue of her driving, when she stopped me, her hand on my arm, and looked me hard in the eyes to confirm that I was listening.

"But don't read it," she said.

My aunt had a singularly forceful personality. My sisters and I considered her opinions on everything from politics to fashion. So at the time, I didn't question why she would issue such a strange order—at least not aloud. I simply accepted her wishes. She was getting older. I knew she cared about family above all else. Maybe she was protecting us from something? If so, my job was to keep this secret buried. That was all there was to it.

Still, I couldn't help wondering what could have driven her to demand such secrecy. As I drove home later that day, the more I thought about it, the more I suspected that Franya's chapter contained some horrifying, shameful episode that Mollie thought the rest of us were better off not knowing. Who knew what my cousin had been forced to endure in the Vilna ghetto under occupation, what awful decisions she'd been compelled to make?

It's easy to say: Who are we to judge? But that's what successive generations do. We sort people of the past into moral categories: brave or weak, heroic or contemptible. Maybe Mollie didn't want to put us in that position with regards to our own family. For all my burning curiosity about Franya and the unspoken history of my family, I wasn't going to second-guess my aunt.

For my entire life, having grown up in a household where the Holocaust was everything and nothing, hugely impactful but rarely discussed, I had my own questions about what had happened to our relatives. In fact, it nearly obsessed me, coloring my entire worldview. In many ways, it had infiltrated my every day because of its absence, a kind of quiet reverberation that is not lost on children. When Mollie would show me the jewelry given to her by a missing relative, I could not help but think of what might have happened. If these people were so important to us, how could we not honor their memories by learning their stories? How could we simply accept their disappearance into thin air?

I could keep the book closed, I resolved, but could I surrender our history? Could I carry that ancestral burden forever, which felt embedded in my being, without ever understanding its source? If I couldn't read the book, what could I do to come to peace with what happened?

The forbidden book sat first on Mollie's shelf and then, after she died shortly thereafter in 1997, unread on mine, amid dozens of Holocaust-related books I'd pored over and collected my whole life. *Twenty-One and One* remained forbidden, its taboo prompting me to eye it occasionally and wonder in frustration why I would be commanded to keep something that I could not know.

1

The Memorial Candle

"How unclouded is your memory!"

I DON'T REMEMBER a time when I was not aware of the Holocaust, a time when I was not consumed by it, a time when it was not lodged in my consciousness or deep in my bone marrow. I also don't remember a time when it was introduced or discussed. From early childhood, I simply understood that Hitler was the most evil of all bad guys, that Nazis killed the Jews, and that we, as Jews, had something amorphous—a movement against us—that we should always fear.

It was not as if I was the child of Holocaust survivors. They, I felt, deserved the right to claim generational trauma from gruesome stories overheard or heavy silences. My grandfather had left his extended family behind and emigrated to the United States in 1904, during the Russian Revolution, and my grandmother followed soon after. Thus, the family that immediately surrounded me—my parents, my larger-than-life aunt Mollie, my cousins—had been forced to watch helplessly from the sidelines while, across an ocean, people they loved, with whom they shared blood, were eviscerated, brutalized, and erased, for simply being Jewish. No one ever sat me down to share the details of their traumatic experiences. They certainly never mentioned the forbidden book, as only Mollie knew about it. Quite the opposite: they stayed silent about everything that unfolded after Hitler marched his armies into Poland in 1939 and then into the Soviet Union two years later. Later, I would learn how common this phenomenon was among that Greatest Generation of American Jews, families like mine whose fathers fought in World War II and whose relatives died in the genocide. The truth about what had happened, or what they knew of it from word of mouth and newspaper reports, was too painful, too brutal, and too close to confront. To discuss it was to expose a gaping wound, and perhaps even to invite in a kind of superstitious danger.

So, I knew nothing about my family's struggle for survival after the city of Vilna, where many of them resided, was invaded in the summer of 1941, and nothing about the circumstances of their deaths. I just knew that their stories lingered in negative space, especially with Mollie.

"They didn't make it," the grown-ups would sigh to shut down my questions. "They're all gone." Vanished. In their wake they left trails I was desperate to follow. I didn't know their stories, yet I carried a deep sense that something terrible happened—and could happen *again*.

I thought about it constantly. As a child in the 1960s, I had nightmares about Hitler marching toward our house from the end of our suburban New Jersey street. In my waking hours, I'd allow myself to imagine what would happen if a new generation of Nazis took over the United States and put the same target on our backs as they had our relatives in Europe, a thought that has likely entered the consciousness of many other American Jews in recent years. Would any of our neighbors, the parents of my friends, take us in and hide us? Or would they buckle under the pressure, point us out to the brutal men in uniforms and bucket helmets, and watch, stone-faced or perhaps weeping crocodile tears, as we were hauled away to gas chambers?

At the time, I didn't think such thoughts were unusual for a kid. I thought they were what it meant to be a Jew.

No one knew about the way my mind spun with worry. I kept my thoughts to myself, following the lead of the adults around me. I restrained myself from raising my anxieties and questions, particularly for my kind and sweet older cousin Lola, a peer of Mollie's whose given name was Israel. He was the only member of my grandmother's family to survive the war. I longed to learn what he heard from the rest of the Vilna diaspora, to hear his story of escape, but I had a sense that it was verboten, even hurtful, to ask. All I knew was that he and his wife, Naomi, were saved by a Christian family in Brussels. Even in the silence I could sense that there was pain, from Lola himself and the other adults who were careful around him. For as long as I can remember, I understood that my role was to lift my family's spirits, to bring them joy and a belief in the future, not mire them in the pain of the past. I was to be the golden child, and I became good at smiling in the face of difficulty and confusion.

It was only years later that I learned from Mollie that an order had gone out for Lola's arrest and deportation, but that he and his wife had somehow escaped the Nazis' clutches, leaping from a train and going into hiding. Mollie would say, "Can you believe that little thing jumped from a train?"

When I was ten years old, another cousin, Cheyna, a survivor on my grandfather's side, came to visit. I remember it vividly because she let her guard down and shared some of her story. It was a hot summer day. I stood with my head resting on our black oval wooden dining table with all its extra leaves in place to accommodate the extended family. The remnants of bagels, lox, and borscht sat uncleared on platters, as I listened to Cheyna describe her childhood in Vasilishok, a shtetl seventy miles southwest of Vilna. There, generations of Boyarskys, my grandfather's family, had owned a water mill, later equipped with a steam-powered electricity-generating plant. It was, as Cheyna would say in her heavily accented English, "It vas a *goot* life, a very fine life."

In June 1941 when Cheyna was fifteen years old, her family learned that the Germans were mere hours away from Vasilishok. Out of options, her mother sent her off with an uncle heading east alongside rows of retreating Soviet soldiers. She wouldn't discuss anything that happened to her while she was in Russia. Even in revealing her history, there was heavy silence. In her telling, the story stopped abruptly when she'd left her family and resumed a couple of years later when she landed in Uzbekistan and worked in an orphanage until the end of the war.

When she returned to Vasilishok after the war in 1945, she learned that everyone she had known, everyone she had loved, was gone. *Everyone.* From the vantage point of a suburban kid in New Jersey, I tried to imagine what that might feel like, to return to the only home you've ever known and find that everyone was gone, disappeared—parents, siblings, friends—with new people living in your home, sitting at your table, wearing your mother's pearls.

The Nazis had massacred almost two thousand of the shtetl's Jews in a single day in May 1942, erasing Cheyna's past. The ones they had spared—barely two hundred people—either were killed later or escaped into the forests, where they took their chances with the partisans who lived hiding in the woods, fighting back against their oppressors. Many of them perished too.

Since there was nothing for Cheyna in Vasilishok, she settled in Grodno, the nearest sizable town. There she lived and then in Poland until she and her husband, Sasha, a disabled Russian army veteran and an orphan like her, were able to emigrate to Israel in 1962, where I would visit her regularly until she passed away in 2018.

Once I heard the stories, they were impossible to forget. Despite being preoccupied with the Holocaust, I was an otherwise happy kid. I'd join in neighborhood games of kickball in the street, bike around with friends, or run over to their homes to play with their Creepy Crawlers and Barbie Dream Houses. I was the youngest of four girls, living out the American Dream in a freshly constructed subdivision of identical three-bedroom ranch houses just outside Asbury Park. The lawns were lush and wide, the traffic slow and infrequent. It was the perfect place for families like ours who weren't overeager to stress their ethnic origins, Jewish or otherwise. Unlike other ethnic minorities, people who experienced bias, we appeared white and were, for the most part, treated as such. We didn't suffer the same kind of day-to-day bigotry. Still, there was no way to separate ourselves from the generational grief that hung overhead like a storm cloud. It may have been largely unspoken, but it was always present, especially for me.

REMEMBRANCE WAS NOT ONLY MY FAMILY TRADITION, BUT IT IS AN ESSEN-tial tenet of Judaism, a theme that emerges in daily prayers, on the Sabbath, in Torah portions, and through the holidays. We are commanded to remember.

On Passover, the most commonly observed Jewish holiday, the importance of memory is reinforced over and over again through recitation, food, symbols, and songs, instructing us to remember the exodus from Egypt as if we, ourselves, were slaves who suffered under the Pharoah and escaped by God's miracle across the Red Sea. As we read in the Haggadah, or "Telling," leads us through the commandment, "And you shall tell your children . . ." This is not just about remembering that we were freed from slavery, but it also reminds us of the difficulties our ancestors encountered. It teaches us not only faith, but empathy for the struggles of others, and to take action to address wrongdoing when we see it, because we have been there ourselves.

In the Hebrew language, there is no word for "history" as we know it. The closest translation is the word *zakhor* (to remember). Its variants appear no fewer than 169 times in the twenty-four books of the Hebrew Bible, almost always in reference to God or the people of Israel and their obligations to each other. This is not about a commitment to historical truth. It is not about precise facts. Rather, it is about establishing a bedrock foundation of Jewish identity based on texts and religious laws brought down from the mountaintop. It is about ritual and recital through storytelling. "To be a Jew," wrote Rabbi Jonathan Sacks, "is to be a link in the chain of the generations, a character in a drama that began long before we were born and will continue long after our death."

My aunt Mollie embodied this ethos wholly.

And her ferocity and loyalty was not reserved only for her family and the Jewish people. In a time when women were not encouraged to speak out, she spoke fearlessly about everything from labor politics to women's rights. Though she was not religious, she had an encyclopedic knowledge of the Bible, about which she would quip, "You want to read about sex? Then read the Bible! Everything is in there."

My aunt was an advocate, as a beloved high school history teacher willing to do anything to help her students, as a modern art dealer, as a tough-as-nails union activist with a sophisticated sense of style. She was either adored or feared (usually adored) by those she drew into her orbit. She was quick-witted, outspoken, thick-skinned, and unabashedly political, all of which made her quite unlike anyone else I knew.

Though she was clearly fiercely independent, I once asked her why she never married. "I never found anyone who enchanted me." She shrugged. "Besides, I never wanted to have to cook for someone 365 days a year." Aunt Mollie was the person we came to for answers, though my mother, Rosalie (or "Ricky," as friends called her), was always present, her sister's diametric opposite with blonde hair, blue eyes, and a mild, unobtrusive manner.

When Mollie spoke passionately, there was electricity in the air. And that was never more the case than when she sat in our living room unspooling tales of our relatives' exploits in early-twentieth-century Europe. While my family avoided discussing the Holocaust, they loved to reminisce about life before the war. When Mollie told these tales, I was her most enthusiastic pupil. From the time I was tiny, I sat at her feet, popping M&Ms like I was at the movies, and begged her to repeat the stories of our family's idyllic prewar existence in Vilna, the creative hub of eastern Poland, stories that took on a kind of magic.

Intrigued, I regularly dug deep into the recesses of my parents' TV cabinet and unearthed a worn manila envelope full of faded family photographs to scrutinize, again and again. I memorized their faces, clothes, jewelry, settings, consumed with knowing them from afar, across time and space. My relatives became so vivid to me that they would appear in my dreams, strolling through the gaslit streets in their wool overcoats and pleated skirts like elegant characters in a costume drama.

Most of the images I pored over while lying on the living room rug with *Bewitched* on in the background showed my mother's side of the family in stiff, formal black-and-white group shots, reflecting the bourgeois proprieties of their prewar life. They looked uncomfortable in their expensive outfits, their faces unsmiling, their emotions in check.

In those formal portraits, some cabinet-style photos mounted on cardboard, my cousin Franya looked as blank-eyed and awkward as everybody else, but in the shots of her alone, she stood apart. Aunt Mollie told me that she had been an actress, part of an avant-garde movement of Yiddish-speaking writers, directors, and performers in the 1920s and 1930s who broke social taboos and pushed theatrical boundaries in ways that shocked and exhilarated their contemporaries. Even in places where people barely spoke Yiddish, the traveling productions packed houses and received rave reviews. This theater encompassed Jewish culture itself, defined by a uniquely Jewish voice—a blend of sarcasm and ominous understanding; they communicated emotions, ideas, and absurdist humor that transcended language. Encompassing Jewish culture itself, defined by constant examination, question marks at the end of statements and interrogation of accepted norms.

Many of the images we had were postcards and publicity stills for Franya's stage shows. She seemed to have stepped right out of a Hollywood movie. She was confident and coy, wearing outrageous hats, fur coats, and palazzo pants. She seemed comfortable in her skin and relatable, playful even in her sexuality as she posed dressed as characters from a sailor or a witch or a little girl. Even in black-and-white, she was in Technicolor. It wasn't difficult for me to imagine her, amber-lit, as she performed onstage or laughed and sang surrounded by friends. I was deeply smitten with her smoky eyes, glamorous 1920s shingle haircut, heart-shaped lips, and cherubic face, full of mischief. In the midst of so much unspeakable death and loss, she seemed vividly, unstoppably alive.

Aunt Mollie once described Franya as a "prima donna," which I imagined was the exaggeration of a proud relative. I wondered: Had she really been so famous? Or was she only a fixture in Vilna, a city celebrated at the time for the breadth and richness of its Jewish cultural life?

Over the years, I've tried to determine which came first, my obsession with the past or my aunt Mollie's unspoken decision to designate me as my generation's keeper of the family memory. This role is known as "the memorial candle," or *yahrzeit*, according to Israeli psychologist Dina Wardi. Certainly, Mollie's influence contributed to a sense of responsibility and fascination that drove me to want to learn more.

———

MOLLIE NEVER FORMALLY SAT ME DOWN AND EXPLAINED THAT I WOULD take on this role of carrying and passing down the family history. She knew so much about Vilna, I wondered if her own mother had designated her before me or if she'd chosen the role herself. She had no children of her own, so it was logical that she should think of one of her sister's four daughters. But she didn't pick the oldest, as one might have expected. Nor was I her favorite. In many ways, I felt less connected to her than my sisters did because I was the only one who hadn't lived with her in their two-family home in Bayonne, across the Hudson River from New York City, before my parents made the move out to the suburbs. Maybe I craved her approval even more for that. Or maybe I was simply the one who listened as she regaled us from an early age with stories about my grandparents and their lively, bright, funny, cultured prewar family, stories that had me rapt. She told these tales in much the same way that other aunts might read their nieces bedtime stories, the most natural thing in the world.

Aunt Mollie told me stories about the dangers my grandparents' generation faced in being conscripted into the czarist army, about the tinsmiths' guild that my great-grandfather headed, about my grandmother's wedding at their grand home, and about the vivid and charming characters that populated their turn-of-the-century lives. In talking about our relatives, Mollie conjured up an entire city. Vilna was the essential backdrop to everything she described. There, the family welcomed her in 1932 with carnations and attention at their lavish home. She washed and pressed her clothing with Franya, the actress, and her *tante* Rivel bathed her and shopped with her at the city's bustling markets. She spoke of beautiful balcony views of the city and hilltops and of magical garden strolls. With her cousins, she attended the theater, meeting the entire cast of Franya's show, all of whom kissed her hand in greeting. The performance ended at eleven and was followed by a concert. Afterward, even the walk home along the cobblestones under gaslit streetlights was fun and raucous, alive with a sense of abandon.

At that time, Vilna was a sparkling place of inspiration and imagination in the midst of a kind of renaissance. Though the city boasted deep history, from remnants of its medieval walls to the oldest church in Lithuania, it was also becoming a beacon of modernity in Eastern Europe. Though automobiles had recently been introduced, mainly horses and buggies populated the roads. In cafés and bars, a young generation traded intellectual and artistic ideas, inspired by shifts like the advent of talkies in Hollywood, the Art Deco movement in Western Europe, and the rise of radio. Perhaps inspired by earlier incarnations like Gertrude Stein's in Paris and beyond, Tante Rivel and others in her sphere held salons, gathering the city's creative class together for cocktails and chatter in elaborate sitting rooms. At the core of this was the Yiddish theater, infusing the bones of the city with energy.

It was the world that had been lost along with the many relatives who did not survive the war—my great-aunt Tante Rivel; my cousins Isaak, Rachmil, and Soma; Soma's wife, Raisel, and their little girl, Basha; and Franya, of course.

My aunt didn't teach me these stories as history, exactly. Rather, she told them as family lore. I suspect they were a way for her to reimmerse herself in the Vilna she had once visited in the summer of 1932, during a glorious trip, and to celebrate the lives our relatives had lived while they still had the freedom to do so.

Mollie was a New Yorker by birth, "a citizen of the world," she would say, "based in Bayonne," but in her soul she was a *Litvak*, a Jew of Lithuanian origin and a Vilna storyteller through and through. I memorized her every turn of phrase, every description of our common ancestors, as though the words themselves were a vital part of their being. In my mind, I could conjure up every one of them as they attended the theater and the symphony or enjoyed long dinners and salon gatherings in the family house where my great-grandfather, the master tinsmith, had established himself at the tail end of the nineteenth century. Even their grand house itself, with its archways and half-moon windows, right off an angled cobblestone street, was like a character.

Over time, I understood that it was my job to take the full measure of this remembrance so that one day I, too, could pass it on to the next generation. And I felt proud to have been chosen.

Mollie was haunted by the family she had loved and cherished and, despite her best efforts, had been unable to save. She clearly carried secrets and pain with her, just as she carried the forbidden book, its existence still unknown to us. My aunt was not one to demonstrate her grief in defeat, so much as in determination. Instead of seeing sadness in her eyes or slumped shoulders, I saw an unbending will to keep their memories alive, shoulders held high.

The characters in her stories were like actors in a movie that never stopped playing inside my head, characters about whom I knew every detail from their personality quirks to their street addresses. I hardly thought of them as dead at all. They felt real as day, like people in my world.

One other factor that contributed both to my interest in the past and to Mollie's faith in me was that I was the only one of my siblings born after the death of my grandmother, whose name I was given in her memory, as is the Ashkenazi Jewish tradition. There was never a time when I didn't know from whom and from where I came. Never a time when I didn't know that I was Meryl, named for my maternal grandmother.

My older sisters all had American names—Carol, Cathy, Charlene—but I was not Mary or Miriam or any assimilated variation starting with the same letter (which was Mollie's doing). I was Meryl, in full Yiddish. And in many ways, that felt meant to be.

From the time I took my first breath, along with my family's traumatic history, I carried within me the other Meryl, the original Meryl. If Franya was the relative who fascinated and fired up my imagination, the grandmother I'd never met was the one with whom I identified most closely. Indeed, her life story was in many ways the story of our family's transition from the Old World to the New. She was born in Vilna, as Meryl Kagan. Upon her marriage to my grandfather, she became Meryl Boyarsky. After she crossed the Atlantic in 1905 and passed through Castle Garden, the precursor to Ellis Island, she became Marie Bayroff. She was the Meryl from whom we all sprang.

I didn't just bear her name. As a child, I was told that I resembled her. When I turned my head a certain way, people who knew her would see her reflected in an intense look in my eyes, if only for an instant. When I misbehaved or showed my willfully daring side, I was told I'd inherited her independent spirit. "She was a *tzatzkeleh*, just like you," Mollie would say. Like me, Meryl Kagan was the youngest in a family of daughters. She, too, was a rule breaker when it suited her, who had skipped school and snuck her way into the Vilna opera house, where her father built metal props for stage sets. I wasn't a troublemaker per se, but I was also not one to hide my opinion or go passively along with a plan that felt wrong. I too followed my passions.

Sometimes, I imagined I *was* her. In my sepia-filtered dreams, inspired by our family's turn-of-the-century photographs, I was dressed, like her, in a long skirt with a white cotton lace blouse and a tight jacket framing a tiny, corseted waist. I, too, had a fox stole wrapped around my collar as I strolled the elegant streets in the chill of early winter.

At other times, I wished my grandmother could be with me. As a small child, I would lie in bed crying, and, when my mother came to comfort me, I would say I missed my grandmother. It made no difference to me that we had never met. I felt I knew her as well as I knew the living members of my family, and I wondered, long before the concept of ancestral or genetic memory reached my consciousness, about whether I could have somehow inherited her being, so that it was in my bones. My love for her was real and deep.

That love, of course, had its origins in mourning, and for more than just my grandmother. The silence my family practiced *was* the mourning, an expression of how much everyone had suffered and lost. And their silence became a reverberation in me. Where they craved quiet and distance, I, like many in my generation, craved information and connection. Little by little, their suffering came through.

⌒

As I grew older, my talks with Mollie became more deliberate. Either we would sit together on my parents' screened-in porch, or she would drive me to her home in Bayonne, an hour north, and have me stay overnight.

Even as we rode up the New Jersey Turnpike, she would encourage me to open my eyes to the world, to see beauty where others saw only the ugliness of oil refineries. "Look," she'd say. "Look, look, look at the composition of the twisted pipes and the wires. Look at the lights . . . look at the color of the sky . . . look at the purples and oranges," colored by the industrial exhaust.

At her house, we would sit on her couch together, surrounded by her collection of modern art, a treasure trove that my sisters and I would later inherit, and she would reel off one story after another. There was nothing didactic or forced about these sessions. She would offer me mint chocolate chip ice cream or a piece of chocolate as I sat at her knee and listened. She was like a sightseeing plane with no fixed destination, circling around all sorts of periods and people before landing on the ones that most took her fancy.

Everything in her house had its story and seemed to spring to life as she shared its background. Two brass kettles that my grandfather Michel Boyarsky had made in the 1890s on his first day as an apprentice to his future father-in-law, my great-grandfather Duvid Kagan, lived in her living room—and now sit on my mantelpiece. As the story went, a woman came into my great-grandfather's shop to order a replacement prosthetic limb. Someone tossed Michel her old brass appendage, challenging, "Here, kid, make something from this." And he did.

Mollie had adapted two tall vases, also brass, also made by my grandfather, into lamps. She'd turned an heirloom geometric tablecloth from Vilna, which looked quite modern, into her bedspread. She had a Russian samovar and a set of silver spoons, which my grandmother had brought over on her crossing to America—traveling second class, not low-level steerage, Mollie never failed to point out. Little did I know then that the forbidden book sat waiting in a cabinet here, just feet away.

She didn't show me the book then. Instead, she pulled out my grandmother's bridal trousseau, her embroidered linens, her white cotton wedding nightgown, copper pots and pans, and a bolt of cobalt-blue silk lace that, many decades later, would be transformed into my wedding dress. Mollie shared the stories behind every piece of precious jewelry, as well, which she kept locked away in a safe built into the wall of her bedroom closet: the gold pocket watch my grandfather gave my grandmother as an engagement present, which would someday be mine; my great-grandmother Basha's gold flower-shaped earrings that were for my sister Carol; Tanta Rivel's rose-diamond chandelier earrings, meant for Cathy; and the garnet pin shaped like a leafed tree branch belonging to Tante Leah, which would go to my sister Charlene. I was entranced by them. Those pieces that the family gave her during her visit to Vilna clearly took on new meaning when, as one of many injustices, Jews had been ordered to surrender their possessions—specifically jewelry—to Nazi soldiers.

Through Mollie, I came to know my grandparents by the objects they had brought to the New World: contemplating these pieces and the rich history associated with them was even better than playing with my Easy-Bake Oven. The way I saw it, I was being initiated into a club established just for me.

During Mollie's lessons, I became almost as familiar with the geography of the old city of Vilna as I was with my own neighborhood. My family, I knew, lived at Ostrobramska No. 11, a house near the rococo Holy Trinity Gate, between the Philharmonic concert hall and the shrine of Our Lady of Ostrobramska—at the center of it all. That gracious home was where my grandmother and her sisters had played as children, grew into women, married, and had children of their own. I learned that the interior stone courtyard it overlooked had served as my great-grandfather's workshop and that, between the wars, the house was a gathering place for actors, writers, painters, and poets. My great-aunt Rivel Lichtenberg, my grandmother Meryl's glamorous sister, who was the widow of a wealthy banker, would play hostess to artists, poets, and authors while dressed in the latest styles from Paris and smoking cigarettes through an ornate quellazaire.

Mollie had a particular way of punctuating her stories with details she was eager for me to remember. She would, for example, make a point of saying that Duvid Kagan, the guild master, was known as *Duvid der geller*, David the Yellow, she said, "on account of the color of his hair." To be sure this and other details were never forgotten, she took the trouble to write them in tiny letters on notes that she left in unexpected places. One of the first I found after her death was on the bottom of one of the kettles my grandfather had made. And I never stopped finding others, attached to objects of all kinds that passed through my aunt's hands: on a band of purple ribbon that Tante Rivel sent my grandmother Meryl in the early 1930s, beneath a pair of Eames chairs, on a State Department envelope sent to Mollie when she was applying for a new passport.

I learned to describe my cousin Rachmil as "very small in stature with very blue eyes . . . but oh so sad." As I repeated that phrase, I could envision him—a man with no clear future path—wandering in the Tiergarten in central Berlin, his blue eyes awash in apprehension. Likewise, I could visualize a young version of my grandmother visiting Vasilishok to meet her in-laws for the first time. She was decked out in fashionable city clothes, a corseted jacket with a fox stole wrapped around her neck. *"And she wore a hat!"* Mollie told me, echoing the wonder my grandfather's shtetl family had expressed when they first laid their eyes on my sophisticated, modern grandmother Meryl. I could not learn enough.

Yet, for all my fascination, I understood there was something odd, even a bit transactional, about my relationship with my aunt. It was in part because of Mollie, her noise and her silence, I realized, that the Holocaust had entered my life with such force and refused to leave.

In high school, when I wrote an essay about my family origins, Mollie went through line by line, making corrections before I could submit it. She changed minute details and even included her parents' exact address in Harlem when they moved to the United States. No detail, it seemed, was too trivial to reinforce.

Except, of course, for the details she didn't want me to know. Except, of course, for the forbidden book.

———

MY RESPONSIBILITY, IN MOLLIE'S EYES, DIDN'T END WITH PRESERVING THE family memory. She had another motivation for making me her protégée. She believed it was our role, as Jews, which is to say my responsibility, to ensure that a genocide like the Holocaust never happened again to anyone. It wasn't enough for me to learn her lessons. It was incumbent upon me to take those lessons out into the world and live them. I was to live by example and call out wrongdoings wherever I saw them. I was to tell the stories, so that history wouldn't repeat itself. I adopted that role wholeheartedly, never considering that this was a heavy weight for a child to bear.

For Mollie, of course, rooting out injustice and taking corrective action were second nature. She was effortlessly, indefatigably political, a campaigner at heart who had organized food and clothing drives for Jewish refugees in Europe at the end of the war and later, as a teachers' union official, had developed a reputation for staring down Bayonne's power brokers and organized-crime bosses over the negotiating table. She prided herself on seeing the world from a slightly different angle and was forever training her students to be conscious of their rights, so they'd know how to advocate for themselves and others. One time, she asked her high school class to read three books about the union movement and produce an essay over a single weekend, only to give Fs to the students who completed the assignment and an A to the one student who didn't turn in anything at all. "You are studying labor history," she told them. "You have the right to refuse unreasonable demands."

It was one thing, though, to apply unorthodox teaching methods to high school history lessons and quite another to give a child the sense that the future of Western civilization rested on her shoulders.

The headlines in the late 1960s and early 1970s were filled with horrors: the My Lai massacre, the Cambodian genocide, race riots, assassinations. I did my best to model myself after Mollie, striving to become an advocate like her.

As a fourteen-year-old freshman in high school, I got involved in my first political campaign, for a Democrat running for a state assembly seat. The next year, as a student council representative and inspired by George Harrison's *Concert for Bangladesh* album, I organized a Freedom from Hunger Day, complete with a performance by the teenage band Ozone, and asked my classmates to donate one day's lunch money to the cause.

My family mourned for the Kennedys along with the rest of the country, and they were broadly sympathetic to the civil rights movement, which erupted across America in response to the killing of Martin Luther King Jr. The unrest reached Asbury Park, just a few miles from our house, and I remember seeing flames rising from buildings. My parents certainly didn't condone the destruction, but they understood what it meant for a whole category of people to have been beaten down and kept in poverty for too long. "We are Jews," my mother would tell us. "We know what it means to be discriminated against."

Yet it was not quite the same. As a child, I felt different but not insecure because I was able to blend in well enough. Yes, I was the only member of our neighborhood group who didn't go to church on Sunday, the only one who had a menorah, but no Christmas tree. During the winter holidays, though, I was invited to sing Christmas carols in the neighborhood, and they even accommodated me by adding "Dreidel, Dreidel, Dreidel" to our repertoire.

It was not lost on anyone that I was Jewish, but I was not taunted or ridiculed for my religion, apart from the time when the word "Jews" was written in chalk on the sidewalk in front of our house. I was the only one in the family who saw it. I erased the chalk with my bare hands and never told my family or anyone else what I'd seen.

My anxiety only grew as I hit adolescence. Each evening I would watch Walter Cronkite or the *Huntley-Brinkley Report* with my parents as a steady stream of attacks on Israel, or those identified as Jews, were broadcast. I followed the murder of eleven Israeli athletes at the Munich Olympics in 1972. I remember the shock and confusion as Mark Spitz, the Jewish American gold medalist, was ushered out of Munich under heavy guard, remarking that the lampshade might have been made of one of his aunts in reference to the rumor that Nazis had done so with human skin. Then there was the Yom Kippur War, and the series of pro-Palestinian hijackings, including Entebbe, where both Israelis and those identified as Jews were held hostage. Perhaps most haunting was the *Achille Lauro* cruise ship, where Leon Klinghoffer, an American Jewish passenger in a wheelchair, was thrown overboard. The attacks felt constant in those days, and my young brain was wired to go to fight-or-flight at the first indication of anti-Jewish hostility. The veneer of our outwardly comfortable lives struck me as frighteningly thin and fragile.

My concerns were almost certainly exacerbated by what I didn't know, as much as what I did. Mollie had shared every detail about prewar life, but that made the holes she'd left concerning wartime even more gaping and ominous. She and my family partially avoided discussing what happened out of protectiveness. They knew, broadly, the horrors that Vilna's Jews had suffered, and they didn't want to burden me, a child, with a cruelty that defied comprehension. Typical of the postwar generation, they preferred to devote their energies to building a brighter future. They didn't believe in dwelling on a past that could never be altered or undone. Yet I was consumed by that same past, this unspoken presence in our home that seemed to permeate everything and nothing at the same time.

Another reason my family might have stayed quiet, though, was that the details about the fates of our relatives were largely unknown. All Aunt Mollie had, for the most part, were the story's bookends. She knew that their European cousins—in Warsaw, Berlin, and Brussels, as well as Vilna—had been alive at the start of the Nazi onslaught. And they knew that, by the time the war ended, almost everyone was dead. The part in the middle remained blurry.

My first serious exposure to the realities of the Holocaust came at age fifteen when I sat down with my father to watch the British documentary series *The World at War*. It was a remarkable piece of television: twenty-six hour-long episodes, starting on October 31, 1973, and running through early May 1974, filled with startling archival footage and frank interviews with wartime political leaders, military commanders, eyewitnesses, survivors, and several former senior Nazis.

It wasn't the kind of program we normally watched. Usually, we sat in front of the TV as a family for the *Million Dollar Movie*. I'm certain that Mollie would not have recommended this show for me, though she was probably watching too. My father, though, was excited to relive elements of his own wartime adventures. He had served in the Civil Air Patrol and then in the US Army Air Force as a soldier stationed in Okinawa during the climactic battles against the Japanese. As we watched, he pointed out the various types of planes and aircraft carriers with a pride that only combat veterans can feel.

Riveted through those fifty-two-minute episodes every week, I began to understand the scope of the war in a more concrete way, in contrast to whatever I'd mustered in my imagination. The series put faces and facts to the amorphous generalized anxiety in my head. And it also felt like a chance for special one-on-one time with my father. We sat down together, my father in our royal-blue armchair with me on the floor beside him.

In the twentieth episode, titled "Genocide," which aired on March 27, 1974, the focus turned to the Nazi program to exterminate the Jews, a subject that had never previously been examined in detail for a mass television audience. It had been less than twenty years since the war ended, and the wounds still felt fresh. Films like *The Sound of Music* and, of course, books like *The Diary of Anne Frank* had referenced the horrors, but only now had the events begun to feel distant enough to look back on with some perspective. Only now was a new generation coming of age who would need to understand the atrocities, because they had not lived them.

Having been sheltered from these grisly realities for my whole childhood, the genocide shocked me to my core. I remember watching in horror and fascination as a woman who had survived a mass shooting in Eastern

Europe described how she'd lain wounded atop a pile of human corpses in a limestone quarry until all went quiet and, only then, crawled out of the earthen pit to safety. Unconsciously or not, a seed was planted in my brain that would later blossom into a search for answers: If this woman had survived that nightmare, left for dead amid lifeless bodies, what had my relatives experienced?

As more awful images flickered across the television screen—hangings, burnings, concentration-camp inmates hobbling naked and emaciated, a bulldozer plowing through piles of dead bodies in mass graves—my father went quiet. I tore my eyes from the screen to look at his face, now slack. He pulled his cotton handkerchief from his pocket to wipe the tears from his cheeks. Without thinking, I climbed into his lap like a little girl and huddled against him. He held me close. Maybe I was seeking comfort in his big, strong arms, or maybe I understood he needed comfort from me.

It was jarring to realize that my father, Alvin Frank, was crying. He was everything you might associate with the Greatest Generation, and then some: strong but tender, an adventurer at heart, a giant, fearless bear of a man who always made me feel safe. As a young man, he'd gone on a date with Betty Grable, played golf with Babe Ruth, and once hoisted a skinny kid named Frank Sinatra onto a piano in Hoboken so he could hear him sing. He was a man who could face down anything. When I dreamed about Hitler invading the Jersey Shore, it was invariably my father who ended up punching the führer in the face or running him over with the green family Oldsmobile. The Holocaust was horrifying enough to break the heart of even the most courageous man. In that moment in front of the TV, as I dared not move to wipe his tears from my face, I understood consciously for the first time how much pain lived in the silence. I understood how much the adults in my life had to bear.

As I look back, I think my father was also crying because of me. I was young and innocent, representing limitless possibilities. In his arms I represented the future, and he was determined to protect that, in a way that had proved impossible during the war, with every fiber of his being.

MOST "MEMORIAL CANDLES" LIKE ME ARE THE DIRECT DESCENDANTS OF survivors, and they struggle with specific repercussions from that. By contrast, my own struggles are a strange sort of trauma, if they can accurately be called a trauma at all. My parents didn't physically live through the Holocaust, and neither did my grandparents. They were an ocean away and were able to make only the most sporadic contact with the relatives who perished in Vilna and Vasilishok, in Berlin and Warsaw. But they certainly lived with a pain that defined them, and what I carry is a symptom of the lasting damage that the Holocaust has caused to the fabric of our modern world.

My sense of responsibility—despite being once or twice removed—is core to my identity. It wasn't only about the Holocaust itself, but about Jewish identity, although my family was more secular than religious. We were "bone-marrow Jews," proud of who we were and culturally literate, but we celebrated only major holidays. On Yom Kippur I fasted with the adults, not necessarily to atone for my sins, but to feel what it was to go without food, as many do each day. On Passover when the Haggadah commanded that we experience the story as if we ourselves were "brought forth from Egypt," I thought seriously about what I would pack to escape slavery across the Red Sea. Even on Chanukah, of course I was excited by the gifts, but I also felt emboldened by the triumph of the Maccabees. So, the pressure—and sense of duty—I felt was as the keeper not just of my family's stories, but of the entire Jewish history.

In a book I once read, a daughter of Holocaust survivors remarked, "It's hard for me to drag their dead around with me all the time." For better or worse, the dead are a constant presence inside my head, too. If I take a walk in Manhattan, I often think about the graves of Native Americans beneath my feet. If I read about Afghans desperate to flee the Taliban, I feel compelled to help them find a way out and offer up my home. My husband tells me I see the Holocaust in everything, and he's not wrong. It's not a peaceful or a comfortable way to live.

That's why, long after Mollie was gone, and my cousin Lola, the survivor, too; long after I took possession of the forbidden book and placed it, unread, on my shelf; long after the photos of my prewar family were tucked away in a drawer; long after I had a family of my own, I realized I had to find some answers—to honor them and myself. No, I would not break my promise to my formidable aunt, whose powerful presence still lingered for me. Nobody says no to Mollie. But I would try to find out what specifically happened to my family in the war, especially Franya, whose images still enchanted and haunted me. I had some questions I needed answered, not just to exorcise the past that had plagued me since childhood, but also to determine how to face the future.

Even now, eighty years later, none of us know quite what to do in response to the Nazis' legacy of hatred and mass murder. Do we steer clear of mentioning it at all, as my parents' generation did in the immediate aftermath of the war, to preserve our children's innocence? Or do we do the opposite? Do we devote time and energy to building genealogical trees and digging through archives for deportation and death records, so we can understand the horror in all its grisly particulars and pass that understanding on to others?

How are we supposed to remember, when remembering is so painful? And how are we supposed to forget, when forgetting is what we have promised ourselves never to do? The forbidden book itself seemed to embody that contradiction—for trying to remember and forget at the same time. Can there be a meaningful balance that dignifies the past while also allowing us to live our lives? Can we tell our children the truth without forcing them to live in fear? Can we keep a family heirloom while promising to remain ignorant of its contents? How much of what Mollie had told me was fact, and how much had she mythologized over time?

At the outset, I was not totally sure what I hoped to achieve, only that plunging into the past was something I *had* to do. I needed to know Franya's fate: From what family secret had Mollie wanted to protect me? Why had she forbidden me, the memorial candle, to read *Twenty-One and One*?

2

The Book

"THEY DID NOT DIE, AND THEIR HOLINESS
DID NOT DECAY WITH ETERNITY"

I COULDN'T READ the forbidden book. But I could learn *about* it. That's what I reasoned, anyway, as I began exploring its history. I began my sideways search by focusing on its author, Shabtai Blecher. As I sat at my laptop on the weekend, one ear on the sound of my kids playing in the other room, I quickly discovered articles about both the writer and *Twenty-One and One* itself on the Yad Vashem website. Realizing I was onto something, I expanded my search to the YIVO Institute for Jewish Research, which had an entire file on Blecher.

Leaning back in my chair, I considered the story was already emerging. The manuscript had a complicated tale of its own, and it began with the avant-garde Yiddish theater.

Just like that, I dove furiously into research. Late at night, after baths and bedtime stories finished, the kids were tucked in bed, I began scouring the Web for any information I could gather. After many nights spent squinting at the glowing screen as my eyes grew tired, I began to piece together a fuller narrative of Vilna's history, specifically with regard to the theater: In Eastern Europe, particularly between World War I and World War II, Yiddish theater companies performed in hundreds of cities and towns, delighting audiences with boisterous productions rife with farce and melodrama.

Since touring was no longer possible after the outbreak of war in 1939, many of the better-known actors set up a revue show in Vilna to keep the community's spirits up, their own form of quiet protest.

One of those actors was my cousin Franya Winter.

Starting in September 1939, Vilna, along with the rest of eastern Poland, was occupied by Soviet forces. When the Soviet Union annexed the city, the new regime organized these same actors into a national Yiddish-language theater company. Many of the performers greeted this development with joy. After all, it meant a regular salary in a time of destitution and an opportunity to revive a theater they loved.

The national theater held its premiere on June 21, 1941. It was the first and last performance. The next day, the Nazis started bombing the city.

Suddenly, amid violence and decimation, and now under Nazi occupation, Franya and the other performers were stripped of their celebrity and reduced to *Untermenschen*, "subhumans," battling to survive from one day to the next. They went from waiting in the wings to waiting for a dreaded knock at the door. The only story left to tell was about the calamity unfolding around them, in hopes that their suffering would not go unnoticed or be forgotten by future generations. They could only hope to record their legacy.

As the situation became precipitously worse, with Jews herded into overcrowded ghetto housing in the city's medieval quarter and many thousands of men, women, and children regularly rounded up and murdered at random, some felt compelled to share their reality.

The Literary and Artistic Union commissioned their secretary and a character actor himself, Shabtai Blecher, to pay homage to his fellow performers and dear friends who had already died or disappeared, absorbed into the daily death tally.

He set to work memorializing twenty-one of his onetime theater friends and peers in individual essays, not only to process grief over the unspeakable loss and to honor their memories, but also to urge the living to remain resolute in the face of appalling suffering. To remind them to find inspiration in these bright lights, now extinguished.

After going on tour with Franya many times, often for months at a stretch, Shabtai Blecher and my cousin had become dear friends. He had sat beside her day after day, performing throughout Europe, laughing and talking, sharing stories and developing a foundation for their deep friendship and understanding. He understood her motivations and, of course, the dynamism that made her magnetic onstage. As I would later learn, he was privy to quite a few of her secrets as well. There was no more ideal person to give the world a sense of her being.

As soon as he finished the manuscript, the Ghetto Union of Artists and Writers made plans to print the book with photographs and artwork. By that point, though, it was the summer of 1943, and, before the manuscript could go to press, the Nazis made rapid plans to liquidate the ghetto—eliminating the remaining Jewish population in Vilna. As anxiety rose to a fever pitch, the printing press was closed and its metal plates melted down to make bullets and other wartime paraphernalia. Blecher and several thousand other able-bodied men, the last Jews of Vilna, together with the remaining women and children, were hunted down and transported to Estonia, where their slave labor was meant to support the faltering German war effort closer to the front. Many thousands of others who were not fortunate enough to receive work assignments were forced out of the ghetto and either slaughtered or sent to concentration camps to await death. Blecher would not make it out alive.

The Jews in Vilna, for whom art of all kinds was like a second religion, took extraordinary measures to preserve as much as they could of their wartime journals, poems, and other writings. They hid them in closets and cellars, smuggled them out to partisan fighters and non-Jewish friends, and even buried them in the dirt beneath the ghetto in front of multiple eyewitnesses in hopes that someone would survive to recover the material. Burying invaluable items felt connected to the deep-held Jewish tradition of disposing of sacred texts and materials by burying them as one would a human being in sanctified ground. But in this case, unearthing them became sacred, as well.

Perhaps, in an act of desperation, Blecher would have tried to bury his book too. As the story goes, though, his manuscript was dropped in haste a few steps from the main ghetto gate. Shortly thereafter, as the dust literally settled, a Polish farmer named Bolesław Boratyński—a hulking man and non-Jew—trespassed into the now-liquidated ghetto, risking serious harm, and found Blecher's collection of trampled loose-leaf pages, yellowed and abandoned amid a pile of discarded clothes outside a haberdashery. The only page missing was the title sheet. Although he could not read its typeset Yiddish text, he could sense its importance. He wrapped the manuscript in a discarded rag, stuffed the pages into his shirt, and managed to steal unnoticed past the German guards. Upon returning to his farm miles away, he walked to his garden and crammed the manuscript into a narrow *L*-shaped tube leading underground.

Not yet bound and printed, the book already had its own story to tell: Across the street from the clothing store where Boratyński found the pages was a courtyard leading to an apartment where the Etingin family—a Jewish mother, father, and two sons—had lived for the previous two years before the ghetto's liquidation. The Polish cab driver and farmer, Boratyński, had first met Albert Etingin, the family's patriarch, before the war, when Albert—a successful businessman known for his generosity—had been kind and helpful to him, loaning him money without strings attached.

The Etingins' home was bombed on the first day of the Nazi invasion in 1941, so a friend offered them a place in a building in the city center, which would house much of the Jewish leadership. (I later learned that Franya was assigned to live in the cellar of the same building, only a few doors away.) There they remained throughout the occupation, through the arrival of Lithuanian fascists, through when the Germans forced the Jews into ghettos (the apartment was within its boundaries), and through when Nazi extermination squads periodically carried out their *Aktionen* and dragged hundreds of innocent people off to their deaths.

The farmer, Boratyński, had never forgotten Albert's kindness. Meanwhile, Albert had managed to obtain a much-desired work permit that allowed him to venture outside the ghetto. One day, as he walked to his designated job producing mattresses near the Vilna railway station, the two men crossed paths. Boratyński told Albert not to hesitate to ask if ever he needed help.

Not long after, the Gestapo summarily executed the head of the Judenrat, the ghetto's internal Jewish government, for providing covert assistance to the armed underground. It was a sign that no one was protected. The Etingins had one last chance to escape: a side gate on the north side of the ghetto on Jatkowa Street.

Later, while interviewing one of the last surviving partisans of the ghetto, Fania Yocheles Brantsovsky, I learned that keys had been surreptitiously duplicated in molds made from bread dough. On the night of September 22, 1943, hours before German and Ukrainian troops moved in for the ghetto's final liquidation, the Etingins bribed one of the key holders to leave the door open. They removed the yellow Stars of David marking their clothing and bundled as much as possible. Though during their first attempt they found the gate heartbreakingly locked, a second attempt won them freedom—from the ghetto at least.

The Etingins, one parent with each son, dashed from courtyard to courtyard along Wilenska Street, one of Vilna's busiest thoroughfares, then across Mickiewicza, the city's main commercial street, just a couple of blocks from the white marble palace where the Gestapo headquartered.

The elements were on their side: a heavy rain began to fall, and patrols were scant. When the Etingins reached the Green Bridge, the main crossing point across the Wilja River, they found the guard post fortuitously abandoned. Still, it took the family the rest of the night and part of the next day to reach the Boratyński house, during which—in order to blend in—they had to remind themselves to use the sidewalks reserved for non-Jews only and break the habit ingrained over the previous two years of walking in the deep roadside gutters.

Once the Etingins arrived, Boratyński greeted them warmly, but his parents and his pregnant wife reacted with alarm. "You're going to get them killed, and us too!" Boratyński's wife, Józefa, admonished him.

It was only several hours later, when Boratyński hit on the idea of digging an underground hideout, that Józefa agreed to let the Etingins stay.

Boratyński made good on his promise: The space where the Etingins were confined was about four feet wide and seven feet long, just big enough for the four of them to sit or lie but not large enough to stand or walk around. There were times when it felt to them less like a shelter than a freshly dug grave. In a starving city, the Boratyńskis had the distinct advantage of growing their own food, which meant they could sustain everyone for as long as the war lasted. The farmer would bring the Etingins food and water and take away the waste once a day through an *L*-shaped opening that also served as an air hole—the same hole through which Boratyński slipped Blecher's manuscript when he returned from the liquidated ghetto.

He passed those precious pages down belowground to the Etingins, native Yiddish speakers who devoured them gratefully, not just once, but over and over.

⌒

THE ETINGINS' STORY FASCINATED ME, NOT JUST BECAUSE IT TIED INTO THE creation of the forbidden book, but also because of this notion of being forced to live belowground as the only means of survival.

I collected more and more information on them, as much as I could, going down late-night rabbit holes, following the trail of minute details. Sometimes I scoured better-known archival websites; at other times, I found snippets of information in languages I needed translated. Often, my husband had to come collect me from the living room and urge me to give up for the night, but I was entranced and would continue working until I heard the morning birds sing.

When the Etingins first arrived at the Boratyńskis' farm, the Red Army was reported to be in Vitebsk, three days' march away. Liberation seemed just around the corner. Months went by, though, and the Russians didn't seem to be drawing any closer. Albert's wife, Sonia, found the anxiety of this interminable wait particularly taxing, and she struggled to stave off despair. By contrast, her husband's spirits never flagged. He told stories or read the newspaper, using a small kerosene lamp to light the pages. But they were still alone with only each other. Now, they had the book, and it was as if each person memorialized in it, including Franya, was a new source of company.

Albert's optimism proved infectious. Their eldest son, Maks, would later say he hadn't minded being crowded in an underground hole for months on end. After the privations and pervasive fear he and his family had experienced in the ghetto, he was content just to be fed and feel relatively safe.

"We had only one weapon, belief," Blecher had written when describing the darkest days of the Vilna ghetto, and the same was true of this extraordinary family subsisting underground in the hopes of better days.

"With belief, we lived." And the book lived on, too.

The Red Army finally reached Vilna in July 1944—ten months later. For three days, the Etingins listened in silent horror as artillery shells detonated above them and Russian tanks rumbled overhead. By the time the Nazis fled and the Russians dug the Etingins out of their hole, the farm had been destroyed and the Boratyńskis had run for their lives.

After so many months lying underground, the Etingin family had lost the ability to walk. It took them days to half-hobble, half-crawl their way back on atrophied muscles to the center of Vilna, tripping past ruin and debris alongside other refugees. It would be weeks before they recovered the full use of their legs. But they had lived.

They made sure to bring Blecher's manuscript with them. It was one of their only remaining possessions and had become a part of them, something to save when so much was lost. Everything else they had known was gone—people, buildings, the very fabric of their city, their faith in humanity—and the desolation around them made the manuscript in their hands feel all the more valuable.

Of the sixty thousand Jews who lived in Vilna before the war, only a few hundred survived. During the Holocaust, Lithuania lost about 95 percent of its Jewish population, more than any other country. Before the war, the population hovered around one hundred thousand. After the war, there were six thousand Jews left in the entire country.

The Soviet authorities quickly set up a Central Jewish Historical Commission, based in the Polish industrial city of Łódź, whose task was to gather documents and testimony for possible future war-crimes trials. But the Etingins had no faith that the Blecher manuscript would be safe in the commission's hands. They were correct, as the Soviets wound up disposing of many valuable relics. Instead, the Etingins held on to it themselves as they fled the Soviet-controlled zone for Sweden first and, eventually, the United States.

Years later, the Etingins' story was covered by a local newspaper. "Escaping death by a narrow margin of hours," the article began, "and living, all but buried alive, for 10 months in a friend's garden, a merry couple, Mr. and Mrs. Albert Etingin, recently retold their thrilling story of imprisonment in Poland while visiting friends." The tone felt upbeat in contrast to the reality of their situation, as if what they'd experienced was an adventure. When I read those words, *buried alive*, they haunted me.

Eventually, the Etingins attended an event at the YIVO Institute for Jewish Research in New York City, an organization originally founded in Vilna in 1925, which relocated to Manhattan in 1940 during the war, to "preserve, study, share, and perpetuate knowledge of the history and culture of East European Jewry worldwide," with a particular interest in conserving manuscripts and books. There, the family met a group of Yiddish-speaking actors and writers whom they felt they could trust with Blecher's essays. These individuals, in turn, arranged to have the book published and distributed to a relatively small group of fellow survivors. By this point, it was clear that one essay was missing, since Blecher himself had died in Estonia in September 1944, just days before the Germans capitulated. And so the book came to include Blecher's original essays, plus an addendum devoted to the author, and was titled *Twenty-One and One*.

In their introduction, the editors of *Twenty-One and One* wrote that the mass killings in Estonia had coincided with Rosh Hashanah, the Jewish New Year and one of the sacred High Holidays in the Jewish religion. But they shied away from including the more gruesome details. Blecher and most of the remaining Jewish prisoners at the Klooga forced labor camp had been killed in an especially horrifying fashion. Not only had they been shot in an "act of last-minute rage and futility," as a *New York Times* reporter on the scene would later describe it, but the retreating Germans had also stacked the bodies of the dead like firewood in large funeral pyres, poured gasoline over them, and set them aflame. The halfhearted attempt to hide the evidence didn't work. When the first Soviet soldiers arrived, days later, they found the charred remains of thousands of bodies, a valley of bones of biblical proportions. Blecher's wife and mother, who were confined to a different Estonian camp, were murdered under similar circumstances. The introduction would read: "Placed between the fingers the pen hardens, and screams, but the fingers cannot write."

MY COUSIN LOLA PICKED UP A COPY OF *TWENTY-ONE AND ONE* SOMETIME IN the early 1960s when he was living in New York, shortly after it was published. He passed it on to my aunt Mollie. Lola's brother Isaak had been married to her, and Mollie had spent time with Franya and had seen her perform onstage during her one trip to Vilna in 1932. And so the book landed—however forbidden—in my hands.

3

The Pilgrimage

"THREE STONES SCREAMED: THREE OLD VILNA PAVING STONES"

M Y TRUE JOURNEY began in earnest in April of 2002.

At that time, I had my hands full. I was raising four children, two boys and two girls, who ranged from seven to fifteen years old, and I was serving as the mayor of Highland Park, a New Jersey town just thirty-five miles from Lower Manhattan. I had decided to run for office in 1999, even writing an open letter in a local newspaper, the *Jewish State*, in which I invoked my aunt Mollie, now gone three years, whose torch I was still carrying. "Why run for political office?" I wrote. "She would say it was my duty as a Jew and as a woman. She would say that if I were given this opportunity, if I had the experience and the talent to make my community a better place, to make it more secure, more economically stable, more comfortable and peaceful for my neighbors, then of course I should run."

I had no idea how essential that belief would become.

On September 11, 2001, I watched the first plane crash into the World Trade Center from my office. My staff was running around, their adrenaline sending them in all directions as they sought to locate our residents who worked in the buildings, process what was happening, and determine what to do in response. But I switched into another mode. I felt a familiar, eerie calm. By the time the Secret Service rushed President George W. Bush out of the Florida elementary school where he'd been reading to a group of second graders, I had our police stationed at all of our houses of worship. I was prepared for disaster.

I remember the municipal attorney saying to me: "For the first time in my life, I'm scared."

"Welcome to my life," I replied. "I'm always scared."

Yet, though I existed in a state of hypervigilance, always poised for disaster, I survived with a kind of numbness to pain too. The more I read, the more I realized that I shared certain traits with the children of survivors. The dissociation I experienced came from a need to shove the pain somewhere else, to bury it too deep to be unearthed. To acknowledge the terror and sadness would be overwhelming, so instead, in moments of crisis, pain, or stress, I simply detached from it. Everything slowed down. There were times when my heart rate dropped so low, I passed out.

I wasn't aware of how unusual this was until, in my thirties, I started seeing doctors for a condition that turned out to be a benign cerebral lesion in my left frontal lobe. I seemed so unperturbed about the initial grim prognosis that multiple doctors asked me if I was the daughter of Holocaust survivors or had been abused as a child. Such detachment, in their minds, had to be the result of significant early-life trauma.

I experienced something similar when I gave birth to each of my four children, eschewing epidurals and medication. The midwife and nurses were amazed by my calm. It wasn't that I was brave or didn't feel pain. As the birth pangs came harder and more intensely, I told myself, *People have been through more than this.* Escaping felt like a luxury that I didn't deserve.

The detachment served me well when managing the fallout from the tragedy of 9/11, but after it was impossible not to be aware of my own disconnect. How would I break free of it? Could I? Did I want to?

The massive loss of that day inspired many people to make changes and pursue passions in their lives that might otherwise have lain dormant a while longer. Whether I was unconsciously triggered by the fragility of life on display, by a desire to break free of my numbness, or simply felt that all my children were finally old enough to not only travel but derive real value from the experience, in the aftermath, I decided to take a family pilgrimage to Vilna—now Vilnius—for the first time.

It was the first time any of us had set foot in the city of our ancestors.

What took us so long? Not geopolitics, certainly. The Cold War had been over for more than a decade, and Lithuania, independent of the Soviet Union since 1990, was a rapidly developing independent country.

Once again it was the echo of Mollie's emphatic voice that gave me pause. For as long as she was alive, she had made it clear she had no intention of ever visiting Vilna again—and she didn't think any of the rest of us should go either. "It's all ghosts," she said, pursing her lips and shaking her head. Everything she had loved there was gone. In her mind, we'd only be poking around in a graveyard, unsettling the dead.

⁓

THE ONE TIME MOLLIE VISITED VILNA WAS IN 1932. HER PARENTS HADN'T wanted her to go, either. After all, Hitler was on the rise. The Jews of Poland and the Baltic states—which is to say, the members of our family—were already facing mounting challenges that threatened the fragile peace of the previous decade. But Mollie, being Mollie, refused to listen and traveled to Paris and Berlin, to Vilna and Vasilishok, to Munich and Salzburg and Innsbruck and the Italian Dolomites. She loved it all.

"My ma's family were all I expected them to be," she wrote home enthusiastically, "and I was treated royally!"

In Berlin, she met our cousin Rachmil, Isaak's younger brother, and his German girlfriend, Friedel. Both struck her as melancholy types, perhaps because Rachmil was struggling to find a job in a gloomy economic climate and was unsure how long the German authorities would allow him to stay.

She wrote that he was "very small in stature with very blue eyes, very nice, but seemed to be oh so sad." That was a phrase that I learned to repeat from her storytelling—"oh so sad." "A man without a country," Mollie called Rachmil in her journal, "one of Germany's lost generation."

Still, they visited cafés, museums, and restaurants and watched a cabaret performance that Mollie described as "pretty filthy." Rachmil took photographs, which was his passion, including one of Mollie and a travel companion flirting with two Prussian policemen in spiked helmets beneath the Brandenburg Gate. While Mollie's blonde friend grinned at someone off camera, Mollie, in a silken blouse with layered bows at the nape, wearing dark lipstick, smiles directly at Rachmil and the camera, amusement in her eyes.

Once she arrived in Vilna, Mollie was welcomed warmly by Tante Rivel, who was widowed by then, and by Isaak and Franya, who all lived under the same roof at the family home on Ostrobramska. She had the good fortune to see Franya perform in Sholem Asch's avant-garde play *Motke the Thief*—a play that has endured into modern times. Afterward, thrilled, she joined the cast for drinks—no doubt local beer, among other offerings—and revelry at a well-known actors' bar to celebrate, the postperformance buzz percolating in the air. She even lent Franya a dress that she'd just bought in Paris, the latest fashion, to wear onstage. The theater's seamstress made the necessary alterations—Franya was a size or two larger than my aunt—and, afterward, miraculously managed to change everything back.

Mollie also traveled to her father's birthplace, Vasilishok, with Tante Rivel, who had never previously set foot in the far-off shtetl, eighty miles away. The journey was not easy: after a long train ride, they climbed into the back of a horse-drawn wagon loaded with straw and hay bales and rode for another three hours across the wooded countryside.

Once there, they met several of my grandfather's relatives, including our cousin Cheyna, whom we would later get to know so well after she visited us in New Jersey, but who was, at that time before the war, still living her "*goot* life." Though happy to meet these distant relatives, both Mollie and Tante Rivel were appalled by the travel experience and the setting, and even more appalled when, at the end of the day, they learned they were out of time to return to the city and had to stay over.

"The small-town life is not for me," Mollie wrote, ever acerbic. She and Tante Rivel were sophisticated, secular, urban people, who felt no connection to the outdoor plumbing and dirt floors of the shtetl. Still, they toured the water mill and electricity works and admired the church dome whose metal covering had been built by my grandfather—and Mollie's father. Mollie in particular relished the stories she heard: how my cousin Yudel from America, now calling himself Julius, had shown up in Vashiloshok with all his finery and his beautiful wife in a sable coat, with the supplies to electrify the family's mill, and lavished his sister Devora, Cheyna's mother, with a long string of pearls the likes of which the shtetl dwellers had never seen. He had been the first of our family to settle in Bayonne and had a successful building business.

Before Mollie left Vilna, Rivel tried to lavish her with valuables too, including a nickel bed frame, to take back to the United States, but Mollie resisted, not yet understanding the precariousness of the lives of her European relatives. Half a century later, filled with regret that the only keepsakes she'd taken were several pairs of earrings, a china trivet, and some needlepoint, Mollie wrote that she had been "too dumb—or naïve" to take more. By the time war broke out seven years later, she understood all too well what was at stake and, afterward, worked at full tilt with the American Jewish Joint Distribution Committee (or "the Joint") to deliver desperately needed aid to the dispossessed of Europe. She would have moved heaven and earth to find a safe passage for everyone in Vilna after the Nazi invasion. But as long as the war was raging, the Joint could do nothing to stop the genocide. Nobody could.

Mollie would have known from news reports reaching the United States as early as February 1942 that tens of thousands of Jews in Vilna had "disappeared without any trace." And the news only grew worse from there. When at the end of the war my grandmother Meryl attended a performance by members of the former Vilna Troupe in New York, she stayed after to ask the actors if they knew what happened to Franya Winter and her family.

"They're all gone," they said, shaking their heads. *All gone.*

My family was devastated by the news that no one had survived. The enormity of the loss was what drove Mollie, I believe, to designate me as the memorial candle with so much vigor.

⌒

BY 2002, MY DESIRE TO PASS A SENSE OF HISTORY DOWN TO MY CHILDREN trumped my aunt's warning. I wanted them to see firsthand where they came from, for them to feel it, to know it, to become part of them. Eli, my second oldest, was preparing for his bar mitzvah, and he chose as his act of service to collect donations of over-the-counter drugs and simple medical supplies for a Jewish community center in Vilnius, which was still suffering from post-Soviet shortages. "*Molodets! Molodets!* Well done!" the doctors and nurses exclaimed in Russian as my young man filled their empty supply room with much-needed items.

My mother, at eighty-five years old, was still in good-enough health to make the long flight and relished the prospect of seeing the city of her parents' birth after a lifetime of curiosity about it. She'd been in her big sister's shadow long enough and could make her own decisions. Given her age, this was a now-or-never trip.

What blew me away about Vilnius was how beautiful it was—the historic Old Town with its cobblestone streets, its tableau of red-tile roofs viewed from either of its two famed hills, its bleached white and muted pastel buildings framing narrow winding streets with late baroque and Renaissance architectural details like sculptured facades and ornate art nouveau metal balconies. Bells rang from the cathedral tower, a landmark once part of the ancient city's walls, and reverberated through our chests. The air smelled of diesel, but also of smoked fish, reminiscent in many ways of the food with which I grew up, food I would have considered Jewish. We breathed it all in.

Somehow, I'd expected to find the old Vilna in black-and-white, frozen in time, as much in ruins as it had been at the end of World War II. Instead, the area where we were staying at the heart of the city was in Technicolor, undergoing a large-scale renovation. Akropolis, the largest shopping and entertainment mall in the Baltics, had just opened its doors, complete with a giant supermarket and shops selling everything from sneakers to books. In some ways, it was difficult to reconcile this decidedly modern place with the old-fashioned, romantic stories Mollie had told.

I knew Vilna had a legacy of openness and enlightenment before the Holocaust. For much of its history, Vilna—or Vilnius, as it was renamed after the war—served as a political football kicked around between Poland, czarist Russia, the French, the Germans, the Lithuanians, and the Soviet Union. Jews were usually the ones kicked the hardest, and also, often, the ones who later gave the most vivid accounts.

In the late eighteenth century, Elijah ben Solomon Zalman, known as the Vilna Gaon (or the "Genius of Vilna"), rose to prominence, not just in that city but throughout the greater Jewish world. A brilliant rabbinical scholar, the Gaon prized not only religious learning, but also secular sciences such as mathematics and astronomy that he believed helped deepen the interpretation of religious texts. As a result, he was opposed to Hasidism, which he felt was not focused enough on serious Torah study and scholarship. With his open mind and appreciation for intellectualism, a spirit that also came to characterize the city, he was considered the guardian of the Lithuanian Jewish tradition. The stage was set for Vilna to become a creative hub, a place where ideas flourished.

In the nineteenth and twentieth centuries, many Jews referred to Vilna as the "Jerusalem of the North," a title supposedly endowed by Napoleon Bonaparte. The French emperor had been stunned by and remarked on the vibrancy of local Jewish life when he passed through on his 1812 campaign. Today, I could still feel the glow.

There was a blend here of old and new. Signs of youthful energy and style abounded, as a younger generation turned their gaze away from Moscow and toward Paris and Milan. So much had changed since the war, and even in the last decade since Lithuania celebrated their independence, yet much of the city still felt unmistakably post-Soviet. Large areas of the center were dilapidated and crumbling, to say nothing of the decrepit postwar housing blocks on the outskirts—boxy, gray, and heavy with history. This city had been under Polish, Soviet, and German rule, and you could feel the presence of all. Many of the older shopkeepers and clerks in public buildings made a point of being as unhelpful and surly as possible. In truth, the residents of Vilnius have a reputation for being a bit blunt and cold (even according to their tourism videos). It definitely felt culturally different from the United States in that sense—perhaps their complicated history had bred a kind of guardedness.

Ultimately, Vilnius was a Lithuanian city with a new population, a new language, new street names, and new monuments and landmarks. They had collected and dismantled all of their Soviet statues and reconstructed them as a social realism museum in Grutas Soviet Sculpture Park, an example of what we might do in the United States with our Confederate monuments. But especially in the Old Town, I could feel the ghosts of the past. The original churches and palaces still rose elegantly, even gothically, above the city. The gaslit streetlamps from my childhood dreams remained, under which I knew my relatives had once strolled, arm in arm, laughing, sighing, living their lives. Original iron signage above many of the shops and restaurants and the beaten metal awnings above gates and entryways made me think of my great-grandfather, the guild master, and his many apprentices. Had my ancestors created some of this craftsmanship, hammering heated iron into elaborate forms?

Before leaving on the trip, I spent late hours online researching everything I could find about my family's probable history in Vilna. The Internet was still in relatively nascent stages, but I scanned whatever relevant records I could find via Google, AOL, and Yahoo! until my eyes burned with fatigue. I searched their names (in many variations), their occupations, anything I could recall from Mollie's stories and from the pictures I'd spent my childhood scrutinizing. Ultimately, I hit gold when I uncovered the name of the street where our family had lived.

Now, toward the end of our first day, as we meandered through the old center, I suddenly spotted a street sign reading Aušros Vartų, which I knew from my research to be the Lithuanian name for Ostrobramska. This was the street where my family had lived! My heart began to pound. I realized that I was energized to an extent beyond what I'd anticipated, being this close to something I'd envisioned my whole life.

We were near the old town hall, a neoclassical palace fronted by six white marble pillars, overlooking a broad, open square. It was starting to drizzle and the kids were getting hungry, but I was not about to quit. I was a woman on a mission. *We can walk a little in the rain*, I said, marching forward. *You can wait a little longer for your pizza*. I followed the street up a gentle hill behind the town hall, my mother—equally enthralled—close behind me. The others trailed behind, half-expecting, or hoping, that I'd give up and make plans to come back another day with a guide who knew the area.

But I didn't feel I needed anyone's help. I'd heard Mollie's descriptions so many times that I knew them by heart. They were a part of me. Though I'd never been here before, it all felt extraordinarily familiar, as if I'd walked these cobblestone streets time and time again. In preparation for the journey, in addition to my other research, I'd studied her letters and journals and the notes she'd left in the margins of books or on yellow legal pads. "It is as if she planned this trip," I wrote home to my father, who wasn't well enough to come with us, "drawing pictures and describing places so that we would be able to identify where we were, where she had been, and why it is all relevant." So often awash in contradiction, Mollie might have tried to dissuade us from visiting Vilnius, but she also gave us the road map.

Now, we followed the path that felt laid out for us. To my right was a large baroque-style palace, all creams and whites, that had once been Vilna's finest Grande Hotel, now a Radisson. I remembered Mollie telling me how her father had been called away from his own wedding in 1901 to handle the metalwork in a plumbing emergency while the building was still under construction. He simply removed his Prince Albert double-breasted frock coat, then the height of male fashion, rolled up his sleeves, and went to work. A little farther along was the extravagant Philharmonic concert hall, where my cousin Isaak, Franya's husband, had once played the violin alongside Vilna's pride and joy, Jascha Heifetz, who went on to become world famous. Then, on the same side of the street, came an ornate triple archway painted in yellow and white with a cross at the peak, that led to the Holy Trinity Church. How many times had I heard Mollie say that the house was "next to the Trinity Gate, between the Philharmonic and Our Lady of Ostrobramska"? I could feel how close we were.

The next building, also on the right-hand side, was Aušros Vartų No. 9. *Almost there*, I thought. *Pace yourself.* The address of the family house had been Ostrobramska No. 11, but this large, elegant, cloudy blue-gray building, with its broad gate, its courtyard thick with climbing plants, and its arched windows set in decorative stucco frames, caught my eye. I chided myself as I fantasized about what life might have once looked like inside, knowing that—when it came to prewar Vilna—I tended to get lost in the magic. The house was so impressive, though, that I took a photo of it, inside the courtyard and out. I wanted to document every element of this discovery.

A few yards farther on was a second building, No. 11, which was a more plausible fit. It, too, had a gate, and the courtyard inside was filled with large, round, uneven cobblestones, consistent with the prewar era. I could not have been more sure of myself as I barged past a young woman selling ice cream in front of the gate. "We've come all the way from America to see this house," I explained with more insistence than was necessary. We were not to be denied.

She let us pass through, and, as we did, I let the moment wash over me. I closed my eyes, inhaling the essence of this place that I had envisioned for so long. I allowed myself to imagine the scene from a hundred years earlier: the tinsmiths in their workshops on the ground floor and my grandmother Meryl and her sisters, all of them dark-haired with a hint of red like me, playing in this courtyard. Evie, my nine-year-old, had the same dancing brown eyes that my grandfather Michel described when talking about his wife, the original Meryl. I imagined Mollie herself arriving here after her long boat journey, exhausted but enlivened by the unusual sights and sounds. When the rest of my family caught up with my mother and me and my children started playing in the courtyard themselves, I meditated on the loops in the passage of time, how time marches on, but the legacies and memories remain.

It would be years before I discovered that this moment of epiphany had been experienced in error. In actuality, the street name had changed following the war, as had the house numbers. Imagine my surprise when I finally got my hands on the official government records and found that I'd been standing in the wrong courtyard, in the shadow of the wrong house! The magnificent home next door that I'd taken the time to photograph, that had seemed too grand and stately, had in fact been my family's onetime home.

Bolstered by our (however incorrect) discovery, over dinner that night I talked excitedly about our plans for the coming days—the places from Mollie's stories that I was intent on searching out. My mother showed a passion for exploring our family's past that I had never seen in her before. It surprised and delighted me, as she and I became partners in my search. All my life I'd known her to be shy, unassuming, and cautious, especially in contrast to her sister. In fact, Mollie had never even told her about the forbidden book, and because of that, I had kept it a secret as well. She learned about it for the first time when I mentioned it to the historians on the trip. Yet here she was at eighty-five years old, following me into strange buildings, unbothered even when we discovered that the back part of No. 11—the place we still firmly believed was our family's house—was abandoned, filthy, and strewn with discarded needles. Like me, she felt the mess had a beauty of its own, representing the inevitable erosion of time. Like me, she was thrilled to immerse herself in a city that had previously lived only in her imagination, now filled with bustling locals and honking horns. She had heard countless stories and songs from her parents, who grew up in Vilna and fell in love here. Those memories took on new life as she gained fresh insights into the lives her mother and father had led before they crossed the ocean to America.

Some of the revelations were about the smallest things: My mother couldn't believe, for instance, that there was an actual neighborhood called Shnipishok because, when she was little, the phrase "Go to Shnipishok!" was the rough equivalent of "Beat it!" When she discovered its true origins, she giggled like a schoolgirl. Seeing her so lit from within filled me up. Delving into the past was giving my mother and me a different kind of future together.

On one particular day when my husband and kids had tired of sightseeing, we ended up at a restaurant, just across from both the real and the mistaken family houses. As we sat in the garden eating delicious local delicacies like bright-pink cold beetroot soup (a kind of borscht) and crusty potato pancakes with sour cream and dill, we marveled at the beauty of our surroundings. The restaurant's facade was a mosaic of black-and-white checkerboard brickwork beneath a wrought-iron sign bearing the imprint of a medieval warrior in full armor. Up the hill was a small square, leading to the Church of St. Theresa, with its spires that reached toward a blue sky. In soothing azure, the Gate of Dawn opened its wide round arches to all who approached. One of the original sixteenth-century entrances to the old city, this structure, a primary Catholic pilgrimage site, held the Carmelite shrine of Our Lady of Ostra Brama (Polish for "pointed arch"), which was said to possess miraculous powers of protection. A golden statue of the Virgin Mary sat in a window overlooking the street and attracted frequent crowds. Asylum seekers had flocked to her for comfort or wisdom many times throughout the centuries, even including several Jews who took refuge there during the war.

"Just look at this place," my mother said, more wistful than I'd ever seen her. "Now I know why my mother was such a snob." We both started to laugh.

Tracing Mollie's steps, my mother and I left to visit Vashiloshok, where her father was born and raised. We left my husband and kids back in Vilna, feeling as if perhaps the children could use a day off from the intense onslaught.

It had been almost one hundred years since my grandparents had returned to visit Vashiloshok after their wedding and my grandmother had astonished everyone by wearing a fancy hat. As the story went, a young man named Lebele whom my grandfather served with in the czar's army had offered to throw a party for the newlyweds upon their arrival, but when my grandparents got to their meeting place, there was no sign of him. As it turned out, his nickname was *Lebele der meshugene*, or Lebele the fool. His misadventures had inspired countless stories, so my grandparents were not entirely surprised to learn near the end of the festivities that poor Lebele had spent several hours waiting with a bag of bagels at the wrong entrance to the shtetl.

Our first stop in Vasilishok was at a convenience store, where we bought shaving cream, which we'd heard could enhance lettering on graves. We figured our relatives' stones—those of my great-grandparents—could likely use sprucing up after many decades of neglect.

"Where is the Jewish cemetery?" we asked the store owner.

She shook her head, and my heart sank. In fact, the Jewish cemetery had been bulldozed in the 1960s, another thoughtless Soviet assault on the memory of a devastated community. Instead, we found ourselves faced with an uneven field, grazing cows pulling at clumps of grass where the headstones once stood. The woman said that the graves were still there, buried beneath the soil. Discouraged, I thought of what it might take to unearth those stones, to fence in the area as a memorial to the many generations of Jews who lived and died in Vashiloshok.

To make matters worse, next to this field was a site where the Nazis had killed an estimated two thousand Jews on May 10, 1942, and it was marked by a pitiful sky-blue memorial with a Soviet-era plaque engraved with the wrong year and describing the victims as "Russians." A second plaque, erected with private funds on the fiftieth anniversary of the killings, was inscribed more accurately in Yiddish, as well as Russian. At that moment, I realized that memory has a language all its own.

We were introduced to a woman in her early seventies with a kerchief wrapped around her head, Teresa Ginel-Gulbatzky, who had witnessed the massacre firsthand at eleven years old. She described approaching in horror and fascination after the shooting had finally stopped to see that many of the victims, whom she recognized as her neighbors and friends, were not yet dead. They lay on the ground moaning and writhing in agony. The Christian residents were too scared to emerge from their homes and help. The images and sounds would haunt her for a lifetime. That day, her father announced that they would not eat, both to mourn the dead and to acknowledge their own grim reality.

"They came for the Jews today," she recalled him saying. "They will come for us tomorrow."

When I told Teresa that my grandfather's last name was Boyarsky, she shocked us by saying that she knew the family. Her brother had been good friends with Schloyme Boyarski. I recognized his name; he was a nephew of my grandfather. We were on the right track.

During her visit in the 1960s when I was ten, Cheyna had told us about a little boy she spotted one day on the street in Vashiloshok soon after the end of the war. He looked to her like family, but she couldn't identify him. She asked the boy his name: it was Miroslav Boyarski. The boy that Cheyna stumbled across was her cousin Schloyme's son. He was the embodiment of a broken world.

Early in the Nazi occupation, Schloyme had fled Vasilishok with his first wife, Tzipele, and infant daughter to join the partisans in the forest. Cheyna didn't say what happened to the wife and child, but she learned that eventually, after the war, Schloyme returned to Vasilishok, alone. He was wounded and nursed back to health by a Polish woman whom he later married, and together they had another child. The new family planned to emigrate to the United States, but before they could leave, Schloyme was murdered by "hooligans" (Cheyna's word), most likely Polish militiamen out to attack any remaining Jews.

The stories I'd heard as a child in New Jersey and the stories Teresa was telling now suddenly converged, only this was the unvarnished, more shocking version. As she peered at me from under her babushka, Teresa told me the tragic story of Schloyme and Tzipele. They escaped the massacre in Vashiloshok as partisans in the forest, but there they found no better luck. While in hiding among the Leninskaya Brigade, they had been so afraid of German soldiers hearing their baby cry that they squeezed her mouth and nose shut and accidentally smothered her. Soon after, Tzipele was killed by a stray bullet.

The way the puzzle pieces began to fit together, the experiences of my extended family, was both validating and horrific, painting a clear picture, even more devastating than I had imagined. Being there in person made it all feel real—and close. I tried to swallow my shock, to compartmentalize and bury my distress as always, but found myself slightly less able. The reality of seeing all of this, of the discoveries, was beginning to loosen the emotions I'd held so tight.

"And there was a son," I said, remembering Cheyna's account of seeing that boy with a family resemblance years later.

"Yes, yes," Teresa nodded. "He still lives in Grodno. Do you want his phone number?"

My mother and I couldn't quite believe what was happening, but in short order we were in a car driving two hours away to meet our cousin. It was dark by the time we approached the meeting point on the highway to Grodno, and the flash of headlights up ahead was so intense that I thought at first we'd come to a border crossing—but no. It was Miroslav, together with his son Vitaly, a trucking-company entrepreneur who drove a big black BMW. He was a giant man with giant hands, and his son, my mother said, looked like a Boyarski—which is to say he had high cheekbones and light hair and eyes. In moments they were showering my mother and me with hugs and kisses, showing us the way back to Miroslav's house for vodka, wine, cake, and many hours of hearty festivities. The pendulum swings from sadness to elation, from mourning to celebration, were as extreme as I'd ever experienced.

Miroslav had been just eleven months old when his father, Schloyme, was murdered by "hooligans," but he'd been told the story many times. In his version, Schloyme emerged from the forest sick and wounded and, with his own relatives gone, was taken in by a local farming family. In time, he fell in love with the daughter, who became his second wife and, eventually, Miroslav's mother. On the day Schloyme was killed, he already had his emigration papers and a sponsor lined up in Freeport, New York. He would have left already but for a delay in obtaining final papers for his wife and son.

Miroslav grew up knowing his father had been with the partisans, but he knew next to nothing about his Jewish roots, not even that his father's birth name was Schloyme. The farmer and his wife had insisted that Schloyme convert to Catholicism and take a Christian name before they would allow him to marry their daughter.

Miroslav grew up believing the version of wartime history he was taught in the Soviet school system: The Nazis and the local militias who worked alongside them in the Grodno region had not targeted the Jews for annihilation. Rather, they had murdered "Soviet citizens." Miroslav was an educated man, a doctor, but he found it extraordinarily difficult to adjust his views about this. He told me that Cheyna—haunted by having spotted him as a boy—had tried to contact him after she emigrated to Israel in the 1960s, but Miroslav's mother was worried he might not be admitted to medical school if anyone found out that his father was Jewish. His mother wouldn't let him read Cheyna's letters.

Later, I would invite him and his daughter, Nella, to my son's bar mitzvah in New Jersey. At the reception, he looked around at the room full of relatives in awe. Then in Russian he said, "For years, I thought I was an orphan."

⁓

I FELT MORE EMBOLDENED THAN EVER TO FIND OUT WHAT HAPPENED TO the rest of my family. After all, the trip to Vasilishok had shown me how possible and rewarding that could be. The more time went on, the more convinced I became that through Franya, I might be able to unearth the entire story of what happened to our family. If what Mollie told me and what I'd learned to be true was correct—that she was indeed a well-known actress—then perhaps there was a record of her somewhere. Of course, I knew that there was a simple answer via the forbidden book, but still under Mollie's sway, I didn't dare look.

~

STILL ENERGIZED, THE NEXT DAY WE WENT TO VISIT THE GREEN HOUSE, a rickety two-story wooden home named for its color, located at the bottom of a hillside park in Vilnius. This would be our first encounter with what remained of Jewish life and culture in the city. Amid the beautiful Old Town buildings and historical landmarks and the romance of Mollie's prewar reveries, it had been easy to forget what had extinguished that flame and thrust our relatives into darkness. This institution—if you could call it that despite its modest appearance—was part of the city's Vilna Gaon Museum of Jewish History, and its mission was to chronicle through photographs, videos, and many other sobering artifacts the story of the annihilations of Vilna's sixty thousand Jews. They were obviously starved for funds.

We had an appointment with the museum's assistant director, Rachel Kostanian, one of the founders. I would soon learn that she was herself a Holocaust survivor who escaped to the Soviet Union, where she was placed in a Russian orphanage and then later reunited with her mother. Her father had returned to Lithuania to try to help others escape. He never returned. All told, she lost forty-eight family members in the genocide. She had devoted her life to the memory of Vilna's Jews, helping to establish this museum at the tail end of the Soviet era, when such commemorations were far from welcome. Rachel, a small seventy-two-year-old woman with an auburn bob, a downturned mouth, and eyes that seemed to hold the weight of the world, welcomed us into the small space warmly. The interior seemed to recall a kind of hiding and felt almost claustrophobic: documents, relics, and photographs were mounted in black frames on cluttered walls. She had also arranged for us to meet Dr. Shimon Alperovich, the chairman of the Lithuanian Jewish Community

Council, an organization that provides support, gatherings, education, and social services to survivors and members of the community. A fellow survivor, he had receding silver hair and a friendly smile and worked for many years as a lawyer in the Soviet government of Lithuania.

At first, as we clustered together and started talking, I spoke in English as Rachel translated. But then my mother stepped in and began speaking to them both in fluent Yiddish. Not for the first time, I wished that I was able to speak the language too. The night before, we had attended *shabbas tish*, or the celebration at the end of the Sabbath, in the basement of a restaurant in the old city with international students from the Vilna Yiddish Institute. It was raucous and fun, and, as they began to belt out Yiddish songs, my mother shocked me by singing along. We had come on this trip at my prodding, motivated by my curiosity about our family history and in hopes of learning anything we could about those we'd lost, but now I saw how much it meant to my mother too. In that moment as I watched her with pride, I couldn't help recalling the story of how, when she was growing up in Depression-era New Jersey, she had complained to her parents about having to learn Yiddish at all. She wanted to speak Hebrew, the language favored by the popular Zionist movement. Many of her friends were studying it. Her mother, the original Meryl, had replied: "Hebrew? Who wants to learn a dead language?"

It was a classic response of a Jew from Vilna, where Yiddish had reigned supreme. So, my mother was sent off to learn to read and write in proper Yiddish at the Labor Lyceum in Bayonne.

Lucky for us that Meryl won the argument, because another giant revelation was about to descend.

I was able to follow their conversation only vaguely, but when I mentioned our cousin Isaak Punski and his wife, Franya Winter, Shimon and Rachel both became visibly excited, eyes widening and hands gesturing.

As it turned out, they had heard of Isaak because of his prominence in the business community and because he'd played occasionally with the Philharmonic. But it was Franya who interested them the most.

Rachel smiled at me and said in English, "She was very, very important, a very well-known actress."

It was as if we had mentioned an actress as famous as Meryl Streep. I could feel that same charge as I had when we'd been close to finding our family home that first day. It was a sensation of puzzle pieces fitting together, as if I was standing exactly where I needed and was meant to be in that moment. Mollie hadn't been exaggerating when she'd used the expression "prima donna": Franya, the same woman whose round face and coquettish expressions had captivated me through photographs growing up, had captivated her audiences as well. She had truly been a famous actress. Her sparkle, her talent, her attraction onstage had been real. This meant that surely I'd be able to get access to information about her, more so perhaps than the other lost relatives, and be able to trace our history. After experiencing this new sense of rightness and catharsis I had during this cursory search through Vilna, I knew that to satisfy my curiosity, my role as the memorial candle for my family, and something else—something less defined, but urgent deep inside of me—I needed more answers.

In my excitement, I almost asked Rachel if she was sure about Franya, but she had just published a book about the cultural life of the Vilna ghetto. Her research focused on the extraordinary profusion of concerts, plays, and lectures that its occupants staged for sixteen months following the first big wave of mass killings, ending in December 1941. If anyone knew, it was Rachel.

I was truly surprised. I'd known, of course, that Vilna had been a center of learning and culture before the war, a relatively small provincial city with an outsize footprint that extended across Eastern Europe and beyond. But Rachel offered the first explanation I'd heard of how intellectual life had sustained the city's Jewish population during the very worst of times and set Vilna apart from other ghettos as a center of "spiritual resistance."

"Education and the life of the mind," she said, gesturing passionately, "were what Vilna's Jews prized above all." Since even the Nazis could not take these things away, no matter how hard they tried, thinking, creating, and performing sustained people and gave them a reason to keep on living.

Through her research, Rachel had become steeped in the world of the Yiddish theater and was as curious as I was to trade information, eager to know everything she could about the players who had built up its reputation. I'd come prepared with the publicity stills I had of Franya in case they helped in our search, so, laying them out on a wooden table, I shared them with her and I told her, too, about the forbidden book, *Twenty-One and One.*

"I've heard of this book," she said to me, her eyes wide, "but I've never seen it." As we left, heading toward the exit, she called after us: "Please send me copies of everything!"

Rachel Kostanian of the Green House had also introduced me to a colleague who had an unrivaled breadth of knowledge about the history of Jewish Vilna, Irina Guzenberg. Upon our return to Vilna on that same trip, my mother and I arranged to meet her. She not only knew all the old stories, but also had an encyclopedic knowledge of the many street-name changes and the precise ways in which the physical appearance of those roads had been altered as buildings were bombed or torn down over the decades. Irina also knew a great deal about the prewar Yiddish theater, and it wasn't long before she confirmed what Rachel already indicated—that my cousin Franya had been a big deal. Again, it sent a jolt of excitement through my body—the chance for more information!

"If you know Yiddish theater, you know Franya Winter," Irina said, as she sat at a table and pored over family photographs I'd brought to show her. "She was a very popular actress."

Irina was unsentimental, no-nonsense, interested only in the facts. She sat behind a desk and in front of a bookshelf, both piled with books, her sensible dark bob and wire-rim glasses underlining her studiousness. I recognized in her a kindred quality; she too was an inheritor of memories.

She was just old enough to have experienced the war—a Jew born in 1940—although she was spared the worst of it because her family lived outside Moscow, beyond the farthest reaches of the Nazis' eastward offensive. She moved to Vilnius when she was seven years old and eventually became a computer engineer, but she also took to working as a tour guide in her spare time to earn extra money to buy books. When in the 1980s Lithuania started to pull away from Soviet control, the computer contracts from Moscow dried up, and Irina found herself spending more time at the Jewish Museum. She did not read Yiddish, but she absorbed everything the museum library had in Russian, including collections of old newspapers. As she explained to me, the theater critics for the Russian-language newspapers in the 1920s and 1930s had almost all been Jewish, which meant that she read a tremendous amount about Yiddish-language productions.

One show that caught her eye was a 1924 production of a comic operetta called *The Romanian Wedding*, the story of a miserly old man who thinks he can buy his way to love by paying off the debts of a beautiful woman's father. I would later realize, in part thanks to the information Irina shared, that the show, staged at the Philharmonic Hall near my family's house on Ostrobramska, was more conventional than some of the productions Franya also appeared in, but it had been a huge hit. Several members of the company earned critical praise. But Franya, in the role of a resourceful relative who finds ever more ingenious ways to keep the young woman out of the arms of the unappealing old creditor, was the unquestioned star of the show. The phrase Irina later dug out of a Russian-language book for me was that Franya was "beloved above all."

It was thrilling to hear: Franya had been a major actress with the ability to move audiences to both laughter and tears. I felt I had understood that even so many decades before, curled up on my parents' living room floor and taken in by her quirky smile—the jaunty tip of her chin in a sailor suit, the unabashed purse of her lips as a train conductor, the free-spirited way she brought her hands to her hips and threw her head back in traditional garb, hair encircled by a flower garland. Even through space and time, I had fallen for her charms.

Irina promised to send me articles and announcements of Franya's performances so I could see for myself just how beloved she had been. In return, she urged me to send her a copy of *Twenty-One and One*. She had heard of the book, but always thought of it as some kind of mythical and unattainable text, the stuff of legends. She was incredulous that I possessed a copy, and even more incredulous that I wouldn't read it. I couldn't blame her. She had devoted her life to learning about Jewish life in Vilna, so eschewing a rare firsthand account of actors who had lived and died there, an account that could only enrich the historical record and deepen our understanding of the Nazi occupation, made no sense to her.

Later, I would return home to my house in New Jersey, and, with a strange sort of reverence—and a mixture of excitement and unease—I would pull that thin book from my shelf and blow the dust from its jacket. I would leaf through the text, meaningless to me in its foreign tongue, and photocopy it, page by page. While still honoring Mollie's request, I put those pages in envelopes and mailed them halfway across the world so that Rachel and Irina, who seemed to have far more information about my cousin than I did, could learn what I was not allowed to know. The packages seemed to vibrate as I dropped them at the post office.

4

In the Claws of the Beast

"LET US NOT EVEN TRY TO PRETTY UP THE TRAGEDY WITH WORDS"

I BROUGHT MY children to Vilnius because I wanted them to see where they came from, to feel the loss and to know what can happen if we are not constantly fighting hate. It is a harsh lesson, but I did not want to be silent.

I did try to temper what I was telling them and showing them, though. As we were hearing some of the more gruesome details of life in the ghetto, the children were playing with a basketball (which they took everywhere they went). Still, when visiting what we believed to be our family home or an abandoned synagogue, they understood the sadness and the loss and the importance of our presence in that place. My youngest, Belle, said to me, "They tried to kill us," and then with her fist in the air as a symbol of victory, "but we are here!"

Although I tried to shield the younger ones from the worst of the experience, they could not escape the revulsion at seeing the Hebrew inscriptions beneath their feet on a sidewalk made of what had once been Jewish gravestones. This they would not soon forget. Toward the end of the trip Eve asked me, "Mommy, is it a mitzvah that we're here?" Indeed it was. These were hard lessons for children, but there were also lessons in bravery and generosity in the people who took action to save lives and those who said, "No!" I hoped that my children would remember those as well.

Fearing what we might see with Rachel as our guide that day, I left my two youngest children at home with a Lithuanian sitter, and together with my two older boys we ventured just eight miles to Ponary, a site where I knew that one hundred thousand (more than seventy thousand of which were Jews) had been murdered over the course of the war. We entered the forest along a narrow, unmarked road that ran alongside the main railway line from Vilnius to Lithuania's second-largest city, Kaunas. The tracks were not quite in the same place as they had been in the 1940s, but it was easy enough to imagine the railway cars grinding to a screeching halt here, armed soldiers ordering their frightened, freezing prisoners out at gunpoint. This spot had been chosen in part for its proximity to the trains.

In the shade of the trees, I shuddered peering around. The forest itself was almost uncannily beautiful, stands of birch, pine, and aspen. Before the war, this had been a popular weekend spot for walks and picnics, for berry and mushroom foraging, but those days were long gone.

At the Green House the day before, Rachel had given us a tour of the museum, educating us about the persecution during the war. In contrast to what I'd previously assumed, and most Americans understand, the vast majority of Vilna's Jews were not sent to death camps and gassed. They were shot dead in this forest and buried in enormous open pits. About two million victims of the Nazi genocide were killed in this horrifyingly personal way, their murderers looking them coldly in the eye as they pulled the trigger at close range. Friends, family, and neighbors looked on.

Lithuania was actually where the Holocaust started, more than six months before Reinhard Heydrich and his SS colleagues articulated the concept of a "final solution" at the Wannsee Conference. This was where the Germans had first put their genocidal theories into practice and where, at sites like Ponary, they worked out how to make an efficient industrial production line of mass death. It was also where they mastered many psychological techniques—manipulation, misdirection, blackmail, outright coercion—that they used to ensure the cooperation of local Lithuanian militias while at the same time maintaining a veneer of deniability, keeping their intended victims off balance. Especially in the first few months, the Germans went to great lengths to make sure Jews were unsure of what was happening to them until it was too late to stage any meaningful resistance.

—

ON THE MORNING OF JUNE 22, 1941, MORE THAN THREE MILLION GERMAN soldiers swarmed across the borders of the Soviet Union from the Baltic to the Black Sea, some in tank battalions, some in trucks, some on horseback, with aircraft screaming overhead and little in the way of armed resistance to hold them back. The scale and ambition of Operation Barbarossa was unprecedented; to this day it remains the largest and most devastating land invasion in history.

In Vilna air-raid sirens began to sound at around ten in the morning, followed two hours later by the first bombardments. Poet Abraham Sutzkever watched in horror as Nazi paratroopers floated down to a wooded hill directly behind the cathedral and the Bernardine Gardens. German voices took over the airwaves—a "hysterical scream," Sutzkever described—and within just two days the streets were filled with German soldiers on motorcycles, German troop transports, German artillery pieces, and German tanks.

A few dozen Lithuanians, for whom the Nazis appeared as liberators after a year of Soviet oppression, stood in the streets cheering. The mood among the city's Jews, alternatively, was panicked. If it wasn't safe to stay, where were they supposed to go? Could they still leave? A large crowd had flocked to the railway station on the first day of the invasion, but Lithuanian officials had locked the gates to the platforms, and, in any case, there were no trains. Others loaded up wagons with suitcases and makeshift bedding and headed out to the countryside, hoping they could make it to Byelorussia (or Belarus) or beyond before the German troops cut them off. Conversely, many Jews in rural areas concluded that they would be safer in the city and hauled possessions and loved ones in the opposite direction.

I have no idea if my family were among those who attempted to flee, but if they were they would not have been alone in failing to find a safe haven. The caravan of wagons heading southeast got as far as the town of Ashmyany before the German advance caught up with them. Many appealed to local farmers to take them in so they wouldn't have to make the dangerous journey back to Vilna at night. With allegiances shifting by the hour, and many of the farmers trying to calculate whether their own safety was better served by appeasing the Bolsheviks or the Nazis, hospitality was not a given.

Those who stayed in line at the train station were eventually able to board two trains heading east, but once they reached the old Soviet border at a town called Radoszkowicze, twenty-five miles north of Minsk, they learned that, without official entry papers, they could travel no farther. A few hundred Communist Party members and former members of the Soviet administration in Lithuania got through. Many thousands more were forced back.

Mendel Balberyszski, a prominent pharmacist and Jewish community leader in Vilna, wrote in his diary: "We have fallen into the claws of the beast."

THE FIRST KILLINGS IN VILNA TOOK PLACE TWO DAYS LATER, ON JUNE 24, AS the Germans were consolidating their grip on the city and the Lithuanians set up a provisional government to work alongside the occupying army. A group of anti-Soviet resistance fighters killed a young woman and about fifteen Red Army soldiers in the garden of a Franciscan cloister and left their bodies out on public display. They also set a synagogue on fire and burned copies of the Torah as members of the Jewish congregation looked on. This would not be the greatest atrocity they witnessed.

The next day, June 25, the top Lithuanian administrator and the German military commander in Vilna issued a joint statement announcing that they had detained sixty Jews and twenty Poles and would hold on to them as hostages to make sure the population carried out all instructions to the letter. Only six of the eighty were ever seen again.

Discrimination and public shaming of Jews ran rampant. Those over the age of ten were forced to wear identifying badges, first a white armband with a yellow Star of David, then a yellow badge to be worn on both the chest and then back, then a white armband again with either a Star of David or a *J* at center. Jews were barred from walking on the main streets of Vilna and could not use the same coffeehouses, barbershops, or public baths as non-Jews. Their theaters and cinemas were shuttered. Radios were banned. They had to buy food in separate lines and, soon, in separate shops, and there was never as much on the shelves as for the rest of the population. Sometimes, Lithuanian hoodlums descended on the line outside Jewish bakeries and beat people at random. Sometimes, German soldiers stood on the other side of the street, cracking jokes about what they were witnessing and taking photographs.

The Jewish community was bewildered by the fact that many of the people they saw enforcing the official orders and committing appalling acts were Lithuanian, not German. They had never previously known Lithuanians to show hostility on anything close to this scale. In Vilna there were almost no Lithuanians before 1939. Even in the rest of the country, the part that had been independent from 1920 until the Soviet annexation, the government had never once passed an anti-Jewish law. The Poles had posed a significant anti-Semitic threat, certainly, but not the Lithuanians.

What the Jews couldn't know at this stage was that the Germans were quite deliberately instigating discrimination and violence from behind the scenes, letting the Lithuanians do their dirty work and paying ten rubles for every Jew snatched. Since most Vilna Jews did not speak Lithuanian, they could not easily grasp, either, just how bitter the Lithuanians were about the Soviet annexation and how much they blamed the Jews, along with the communists, for shattering their dreams of self-determination.

As a result, many Jews, especially older Jews, misread the situation entirely. They clung to memories of the relatively benign German occupation during World War I and hoped the violence they were witnessing would prove to be short-lived. In fact, my own Tante Rivel refused my grandmother's pleading to leave for America, claiming it was just another anti-Semitic convulsion that would soon be over. She was comfortable in her rich life in Vilna. It was a lesson I would never forget. Even those who feared the Nazis could have no idea they were about to fall victim to a genocide.

IT WAS NOT ONLY THE JEWS WHO MISREAD THE SITUATION. JOSEF STALIN also did, with catastrophic consequences. Right up to the moment of the Nazi invasion, and even for a few hours afterward, the Soviet dictator could not believe Hitler would violate the terms of the nonaggression pact their two countries had signed two years earlier, and he rejected every last warning that his advisers and intelligence operatives gave him.

One week before Barbarossa, with the number of credible warnings reaching close to a hundred and his armed forces nowhere near ready to fend off an invasion, Stalin decided that his most pressing problem was political insubordination in the Baltic states. He ordered the roundup of tens of thousands of Lithuanians, Latvians, and Estonians, as well as several thousand Jews and Poles, who were sent in cattle trucks to labor camps deep in the Soviet interior. This purge was a major reason that, a few days later, so many ordinary Baltic citizens greeted the arrival of the Nazis with flowers, tears, and gifts of bread and salt.

As the Luftwaffe started flying into Soviet airspace on the evening of June 21, Stalin put antiaircraft batteries around Moscow on standby, but ordered his commanders not to return fire if attacked. He felt sure the incursions were the work of anticommunist German generals, a rogue attempt to provoke a response from him and destroy the treaty between their two nations. When bombs started falling hours later, the Soviet air force and its pilots were dormant, if not literally asleep. The Germans were able to destroy more than eighteen hundred Soviet planes, many of them still in their hangars or parked on airstrips, in the first twenty-four hours.

The Soviet ground forces were no better prepared, and the country's borders were left almost completely defenseless. With the Germans quickly bearing down on Vilna, the Soviet authorities there made no attempt to fight back, choosing instead to pack up and leave before the Nazis could reach them.

Even as this disaster unfolded, Stalin struggled to believe Hitler had anything to do with it. It was only a week into the invasion, after the Nazis had advanced two hundred miles inside his country, destroyed his air force and killed, wounded, or captured six hundred thousand of his soldiers, that he began to acknowledge the full scope of what he was facing. "Lenin left us a great inheritance," he was overheard saying as he left a defense meeting with his Politburo colleagues on June 29. "And we, his heirs, have fucked it all up."

Mass murder was very much on the Nazis' mind, but in the planning stages and first few weeks following the invasion, this did not yet mean the targeted mass murder of Jews. When Hitler talked about toppling the Soviet Union, what he had in mind was a "decapitation" similar to the tens of thousands of killings that SS death squads had carried out in Poland to crush the local leadership. This involved going after political figures, certainly, but also leaders of nationalist organizations, landowners, teachers, religious leaders, cultural figures, and intellectuals, many of whom were sure to be Jewish but would not necessarily be killed because of their Jewishness.

The Russians endured heavy losses in the initial engagements in southern Lithuania and along the Western Dvina River, but held off the German advance just long enough for their Eighth and Eleventh Armies to beat a retreat and regroup farther north. This certainly looked like a rout by any ordinary military standards, but as the calendar flipped from June to July, it became clear that the all-or-nothing attempt to encircle and crush the Soviet forces all at once had failed.

The Germans faced an occupation quite different from the one they'd envisioned, one in which all the old fears—of hunger, cold, and military overreach—would surely return to haunt them. Military progress was not the only thing they had to worry about. They had captured a vast swath of territory stretching more than two thousand miles and needed to find a way to control it with only a fraction of the necessary security or administrative staff. Somehow, they had to build a durable supply chain to the soldiers at the front without the immediate sources of food and raw materials they had been expecting, while also keeping a lid on insurgent local populations.

How could they avoid a proliferation of resistance movements, sabotage, and anti-German violence? Terror was, of course, the Nazi way, and a time-honored means of control for underresourced occupying forces. Himmler invoked the British in India as a direct source of inspiration. "Like the English," he said, "we shall rule this empire with a handful of men." Since the Nazis were already predisposed to blame the Jews for anything that did not go their way, and since the eastern territories had immeasurably larger Jewish populations than Germany or the other European countries that they had recently conquered, it took very little time for anti-Semitic fear, specifically, to become the cornerstone of their new policy.

Goebbels wrote in his journal that he'd discussed the "Jewish problem" with Hitler. And Hitler, who had built his career on the infamous "stab in the back" theory that held Jews responsible for Germany's defeat in 1918, decided he'd been right all along in predicting that "another world war provoked by the Jews would end with their destruction."

Now, Goebbels wrote, "The Jews in the East must foot the bill."

VILNA HAD ITS OWN PARTICULAR PLACE IN THE NAZIS' PLANS. ALONG with the rest of the Baltic region, the Germans regarded the city as separate from the rest of the Soviet Union and had no intention of starving it out. Rather, they envisioned it as an important hub of a new German colony to be called Ostland, literally "the east country," that would in time be fully integrated into the Reich. Lithuania was considered particularly desirable, a future home, perhaps, for German soldiers after the Soviet campaign was over. As Alfred Rosenberg, the minister in charge of the newly occupied eastern territories, envisioned it: "The Baltic Sea must become an inland German lake."

Many ordinary Lithuanians might have been happy to see their Soviet oppressors replaced by Nazis, believing perhaps that under a German protectorate they could reestablish some of the independence they had lost. But the Germans were not sympathetic to their cause. Not only did the Nazi leadership intend to take Lithuania for themselves, but they also conducted an assessment of the Lithuanian population and determined that only 15 percent of them were *eindeutschungsfähig*, suitable for Germanization, and even then only as menial workers at the very bottom of the social hierarchy. The rest were to be discarded, along with the communists and Jews.

In the short term, however, the Germans found the Lithuanians very useful as enforcers of their authority, and they manipulated them expertly to perform that role. The Germans knew, as most Vilna Jews did not, that a fascist, overtly anti-Semitic movement had taken root in Lithuania in the late 1920s. The group behind this new movement had clashed repeatedly with the country's longtime authoritarian leader, Antanas Smetona, over his refusal to enact anti-Jewish laws. As Smetona's star waned—first with the Nazi seizure of the port of Memel, then with his agreement in late 1939 to station twenty thousand Soviet troops on Lithuanian soil, and finally when the Soviets took over in June 1940, a moment viewed as a national catastrophe—the Far Right's fortunes soared. They accused the Jews of betraying the nationalist cause and of working hand in glove with the communists, accusations that soon became accepted fact across much of the country. The fact that the Jews had endured significant hardships of their own under Soviet rule and fewer than 2 percent of them had ever been party members did not make a difference.

After the Soviet annexation, the Nazis cultivated an elite group of Lithuanian exiles in Berlin, many of them politicians or former members of the security police, and encouraged them to form a new party, the Lithuanian Activist Front, which was pro-Nazi, hotly anti-Semitic, and eager to encourage an anti-Soviet uprising back home. After the Germans launched their invasion in June 1941, the LAF moved quickly to set up a provisional government that stripped Jews of their rights, pushed the idea of herding them into ghettos, and suggested that they did not deserve to live at all.

The Nazis were not thrilled with the Lithuanians' insistence on running their own government—they would handle that problem later—but the LAF's willingness to encourage discrimination and violence against Jews played into their hands perfectly. Not only did this fit in with the emerging Nazi conception of territorial control through terror, but it also meant that someone other than them was willing to take the blame. Even better, once the Lithuanians started committing crimes, it gave the Germans something to hold over them and made them more malleable going forward.

Reinhard Heydrich, the head of security under Himmler, spelled out much of this strategy in a verbal briefing with SS death-squad leaders a few days before the invasion, and again in writing a week after. "The self-cleansing attempts of local anti-communist and anti-Jewish circles within the newly occupied territories should in no way be hindered," he said. "On the contrary, they must be encouraged, without leaving a trace, of course, and even intensified."

When the death squads, or Einsatzgruppen, arrived in Lithuania, their mission was initially that "decapitation" operation like they'd carried out in Poland. The hit list Heydrich gave them on July 2 focused exclusively on the old Soviet power structure: communist functionaries, commissars, "radical elements" of different kinds, and "Jews who are members of the party or of state institutions." Two days later, though, this policy had already started to change. With the military still focused on clearing a path to Leningrad as quickly as possible, a German death squad descended on the strategic town of Daugavpils, just north of the Lithuania-Latvia border, and killed 1,150 Jews whom they later labeled arsonists and saboteurs. The occupation authorities understood that their job was to clear areas behind the front of all potential subversive or disruptive elements. Since, in their minds, Jews were subversive, it was Jews whom they chose to target.

In Vilna the victims selected and seized by Lithuanian militias over the first couple of months were all working-age men because they best fitted the profile of potential anti-Nazi agitators and resistance fighters. Also, they fitted the cover story, designed to lower the guard of the rest of the Jewish community, that they were merely being sent away on work assignments. Around this time, the Germans discovered that the Soviet army had dug pits for fuel storage in the forest at Ponary, and they quickly adapted the site for mass murder. The Einsatzgruppen, mobile killing units, oversaw the transport of prisoners from the Lukiszki Prison to Ponary and developed a system to conduct shootings on an industrial scale: ten people at a time, up to a hundred an hour, up to five hundred a day. The Lithuanians who did the actual shooting were ordered to use rifles only, because single shots aimed at each victim were found to be more efficient than the rapid fire of a submachine gun.

Many of these Lithuanians were radicals and zealots who thought the Jews were getting what they deserved. They looted the dead bodies for jewelry and gold fillings and walked off with fur coats and other valuable pieces of clothing. But it also became clear to at least some of them, over time, that they'd walked into a terrible trap. The Einsatzgruppen had filmed them and threatened to tell the world what they'd done if they didn't continue following orders.

After a few months, the Nazis dropped the pretense that they had any interest in Lithuanian self-determination. They outlawed the country's two main pro-Nazi political parties, including the LAF, the group they'd nurtured from the outset. Far from furthering any cause, the Lithuanians had been turned into the Nazis' slaves, and many of them realized it. "Must we be Europe's executioners?" one anguished pamphlet distributed by Far-Right Lithuanian activists asked. "Will we just stand by as thousands of young fighters go mad? It won't be long before they are spiritually dead . . . and then they will face the risk of being shot themselves as witnesses."

For all their ruthlessness, the Nazis were certainly not infallible. While the security services continued to clamor for the elimination of "subversive elements," the German army had a desperate need for workers to furnish winter clothing and boots to the soldiers at the front, to service tanks and trucks, and to carry out many other tasks essential to the war effort. Since, in Lithuania, the skilled metalworkers, mechanics, leather workers, furriers, and textile workers were almost all Jewish, the mass killings worked directly against the Germans' economic and military interests. By late August, the army was complaining openly that the best workers at a fur factory in Vilna had been arrested and disappeared without a trace. "If the arrests continue in the same vein," the army warned, "the company will not be able to function."

And so a new policy came into being. The Jews of Vilna would be ordered out of their homes and into a ghetto. Those who remained productive for the war economy would be allowed to keep working. Everyone else would be at the mercy of the security services, whose job would be to determine who served a purpose and who was expendable.

THE SCALE OF IT WAS TOO VAST TO GRASP. RACHEL TALKED AT GREAT length about the number of people killed, about the thousands rounded up in *Aktionen* in the Vilna ghetto and transported to Ponary by truck or train, and about the innumerable shtetls in the countryside where every last Jew was hunted down and wiped out.

If I never learned their exact stories, it was safe to assume that perhaps this was how many of our family members had been slaughtered sixty years before—right in this spot.

Aunt Mollie, no doubt deliberately, had never breathed a word of this. She was a student of history and read voraciously. The US and Jewish press didn't cover what was happening enough, but she would have known.

She would have read headlines in the *New York Times* such as "Vilna Massacre of Jews Reported: 60,000 Slain in Two Weeks by Police Under Nazis"—a page 6 article that ran on June 16, 1942. In this story, she would have learned how the victims—men, women, and children—were ordered to strip bare, how they were marched up to the edge of the dirt pit in rows of ten and shot, how their bodies dropped atop other dead bodies, people killed moments or hours or days before.

Mollie would have known, but she never dared breathe a word of it to me. These were the gaps I had sensed, the pain that permeated from the silences.

The longer Rachel talked, though, the harder it was to conceptualize the horror in human terms. The numbers, so large and looming, felt abstract. In my old reliable dissociative state, all I could hear and see were disconnected statistics, that is, until she described the terrible agony of the *Kinder Aktzia*, or children's action, the roundup of children selected, ripped from their parents for death at Ponary.

I was shaken, appalled, and moved in ways I hadn't experienced in years, if ever. All I wanted to do was switch it off. I thought of my own little ones being stolen from my arms. Perhaps three of my four with light hair and blue eyes would be able to pass, maybe hide with a Christian family. But my Evie was dark—with thick auburn hair and deep brown eyes. She looked Semitic. What would have happened to her?

I wanted to reach out and hug my kids, but I was afraid to move. A dam in me was just beginning to crack. My impulse, as ever, was to detach myself from the horror entirely.

Rachel went on to describe the years in the ghetto and the miraculous strength the inmates found to keep living. And how, after years of this push-pull, in the months after the liquidation of the Vilna ghetto in 1943, the Germans had commandeered a slave labor force of about seventy Jews and a dozen Soviet prisoners of war to pull decomposing bodies out of the mass graves at Ponary and burn them so evidence of the genocide would be erased. For nine months, we were told, the stench of burning flesh filled the forest, and the ash and bone left over from the fires was strewn over the ground like fertilizer. It was hard not to think about the smell of ash that had permeated downtown Manhattan only months before. The workers here—known to the Germans as *Figuren*, or ghost figures—were imprisoned in an underground pit next to the grave sites with shackles around their ankles. They carried out their work knowing that, once it was complete, they too would be killed so they could not testify to what they had seen. Just a handful of them managed to escape, through a secret tunnel that they dug night after night with no more than a couple of spoons and their bare hands.

There was nowhere to put the feelings these stories elicited—of revulsion, of terror, of grief. But as painful as the experience was, its importance was clearer than ever as I stood on that precipice, only now truly understanding in my bones the weight of the horror that unfolded here. We must carry the stories along with us, tell them to our children, so that the atrocities are never forgotten, so that history never repeats itself, so that these deaths have meaning. In honor of the dead, I'd brought one of the cobblestones from the courtyard of the house on Ostrobramska, and I placed it now near one of the pits. One hundred thousand was too big a number to wrap my mind around, but, with the stone, I could personalize the experience and imagine just a few of them. Our family, perhaps. Or someone else's.

I looked to my left, and there were my two boys distracted, playing on the ground. I moved to call them to attention, but Rachel stopped me instead. "No, don't," she said. "They can hear everything."

The first monument we came across was covered with crucifixes to honor the fifteen hundred Polish Catholics who had died in this forest. The Poles called this place *Golgotha Wilienska*, the Golgotha of Vilna, which conveyed its sinister nature, but also, unmistakably, Christianized it. And the Poles were not the only ones: next came a monument to the Lithuanian victims, also topped by a large crucifix. All victims deserved to be remembered, but the failure to acknowledge the overall scope of what the Nazis had wrought here, especially against the Jews, was unsettling and deeply disappointing. Ponary offered jarring lessons on the manipulation of memory, because the history of the site since the war was steeped not in mourning, as I might have expected, but in political calculation, bad faith, whitewashing, and wishful thinking.

It was only some distance farther on that we came upon a more comprehensive collection of plaques, written in Russian, Lithuanian, Yiddish, and Hebrew. Even here, there were startling omissions: the inscriptions to the left and right, written in Lithuanian and Russian, made no reference at all to Jewish victims. All they said was that "Hitlerite occupation forces" and their local helpers had "killed 100,000 people and hidden the evidence of their crimes, burning the corpses from 1943 onwards." Only the central inscription, added in the late 1980s and written in all four languages, specified that at least seventy thousand of the one hundred thousand victims had been Jewish.

Much of this mess was the result of official Soviet policy in the late 1940s and early 1950s, directly after World War II. Stalin found it expedient to rail against the "rootless cosmopolitanism" of Jewish members of his party and came to view Israel, whose creation he'd initially welcomed, as a satellite of Western imperialism. A group of Jewish survivors erected a monument at Ponary in 1948 that was pulled down almost immediately in favor of an obelisk commemorating "the victims of fascist terror," without any specifics as to who did the killing or who was killed. Subsequent "official literature" referred to the victims as "Soviet citizens," which was true only to the extent that they had been subjected to a period of Soviet rule before the Nazis took over. For years, the site was so neglected that local farmers dismantled the stone walls around the pits to use as building materials and used the land to graze their animals.

The historical tensions were complex, and they spread in multiple directions. The Soviets had no interest in preserving or reviving Jewish culture. In 1956 they destroyed one of the most significant religious sites in Eastern Europe: the Great Synagogue in Vilna, which was built in the 1630s and had been one of the most significant cultural sites in Eastern European Jewry. Even the Nazis left it intact. The Soviets also ripped up the city's main Jewish cemetery, using the headstones for a variety of construction projects, including a series of staircases in the city's tallest hillside park.

Unfortunately, the Lithuanians, who loathed their Soviet oppressors, were not interested in Jewish memory either. In the wake of the war, so few Jews remained. The Christian Lithuanians saw themselves as the principal victims of the war, having lost their country first to the Soviets and then to the Nazis, and believed with a fervor untroubled by actual evidence that Jews had betrayed the cause of national self-determination by encouraging the Soviet annexation in June 1940. That falsehood, fanned by the likes of Hitler, had helped fuel an anti-Semitic frenzy once the Nazis arrived and spurred Lithuanian fascist militias to participate in the mass killings of the Holocaust—something that, in the postwar period, the Lithuanians were not overeager to advertise. In other words, the deceptively neutral language at Ponary suited them too.

It was largely thanks to activists like Rachel Kostanian that a more accurate memory of the war was at least partially restored, starting during the perestroika era supported by Mikhail Gorbachev, when the state agreed to spend modest amounts of money on reviving Jewish cultural institutions. Still, the problems did not go away—far from it—because the Soviet era gave way to an independent Lithuania premised on the myth that the *real* genocide during the war had been their own suffering at the hands of Stalin's minions. While the Green House Holocaust exhibit struggled to make ends meet on a shoestring budget, in 1992 the Lithuanian government funded a lavish genocide museum on Vilnius's main commercial street as a vehicle for nationalist ideology at the expense of historical truth.

The building had previously housed both the Gestapo and the Soviet KGB, but the museum's content overlooked the Nazi genocide almost entirely, concentrating instead on Soviet purges that targeted Lithuanians in the years following the German occupation, claiming thousands of lives. Some of the people that the museum hailed as heroes of the anti-Soviet resistance had previously been responsible for spreading anti-Semitic propaganda and murdering thousands of Jews. It wasn't until 2011 that the museum offered more than a passing reference to the two hundred thousand Jews killed in Lithuania under the Nazis, and then only on a statistical chart displayed well away from the main exhibit halls, near the toilets. Finally, in 2018, the museum, under considerable international pressure, agreed to drop the word "genocide" from its name and gave itself a more accurate title: the Museum of Occupations and Freedom Fights. On my last trip to Vilnius, in 2021, the building's grand stone facade still bore a plaque, written in Lithuanian and English, that read: "During the occupations of the 20th century, the following repressive bodies operated in this building: the Gestapo and the KGB. The genocide of the population was planned here. Citizens of Lithuania were imprisoned, interrogated, tortured, and killed." No mention of Jews, or the fact that, when the Nazis invaded, Vilna had been Polish for most of the previous twenty years and, at most, 2 percent of its people were ethnic Lithuanians. The vast majority of those tortured and killed by the Gestapo in Vilna, like the vast majority of those killed at Ponary, were "citizens of Lithuania" only through an accident of historical geography.

Though traumatic, the excursion to Ponary had been eye-opening on many levels. With so many unreliable accounts of the horrors that occurred here, under the arch of these towering trees, I felt more responsible than ever to discover and tell our story, both personal and universal—whatever that might be.

5

In the Archives

"EVEN IF ANY DETAILS ARE ALTERED, IT STILL DOES NOT BECOME LIES"

A S THE IMPACT of the trip began to settle, I wrestled with whether I had exposed my children to too much. In his emails to me at the time, my father assured me otherwise. "They're learning," he insisted. It was important.

Like Rachel, I started to question the wisdom of Mollie's edict. The trip to Vilnius had awoken something powerful in me. Now that I was beginning to understand the extent of Franya's reputation, it became much more tempting to learn what had become of her—from a book that sat right in front of me on my bookshelf. Would Mollie *really* mind? Then again, maybe this was exactly the sort of temptation she'd warned me against. Maybe the truth of the book contained shame too deep to confront, horrors too painful to unsee. My mind started to spin, my imagination getting the best of me: Had Franya done something unforgivable in an attempt to save herself, to stay alive?

Ultimately, I dipped my toe in the water, not committing to either choice. I turned to a man named Dr. Moshe Moskowitz. As a retired former chair of the Hebraic Studies Department at Rutgers University, with a particular interest in the Yiddish theater, he was uniquely positioned to translate the forbidden book.

I knew Moshe because I'd attended Rutgers as an undergraduate and taken his Yiddish class. Obviously, I hadn't worked all that hard because I'd forgotten most of it in the intervening twenty years. My classmates and I gave him the nickname "Easy A" because he was far too delighted to find young people with an interest in a near-extinct language to grade us with any rigor. In my case, on the first day of class, he picked up on whatever remnants of an accent I'd acquired by listening to my mother singing old Yiddish lullabies and declared: "We have a Vilna Jew here."

I was smitten.

Moshe was in his early fifties when I was in college, and already he was hunched over like an old man, but that never seemed to impact his winning smile. He'd been born in the United States, but you'd hardly know it from the distinct Old World accent with which he spoke English. He was even more haunted by the past than I, telling people that his most ardent wish was to have his ashes buried at Auschwitz. That, of course, did not happen.

When I met him again, he was every bit as eccentric and dramatic as I'd remembered, and not at all morbid. If anything, he came across as an adorable, consummate flirt with people young and old.

Moshe was a character straight out of an old Jewish folktale, one more factor that made him perfect for the job. He understood the sensibility and the humor of the prewar Jewish world and was keenly attuned to the pain of its destruction.

He was honored to translate Franya's story, and for all his levity, he took the task seriously. As I waited for him to finish over the course of two weeks, I went to the office, made plans for the summer, and completed all the usual tasks as if everything was normal. But inside, I was awash in turmoil. Half the time I felt plagued by guilt; the other half, I felt exhilarated at the thought of finally having answers, of learning the truth. I told myself that, after all this time, Mollie, wherever she was, would understand.

Finally, when I could bear the anticipation no longer, Moshe phoned to let me know that the translation was complete. We made plans to meet the following day. Moshe had written the English translation out in painstaking longhand on a yellow legal pad, and I readied myself for whatever it might contain. Before handing it to me, he reported only a few tidbits of information about what he'd read. He said that Franya had been an important actress who had worked with many of the leading actors and directors of the Yiddish stage. He also revealed that she fell deeply and tragically in love with a fellow actor, a shock because she was married to my cousin Isaak, and he pronounced the name "Rudolf Zaslavsky" as if I should have known it, as if he was saying "Humphrey Bogart" or "Clark Gable." Was this what Mollie had been trying to hide? But then why was Moshe telling me now? He stopped as if he had already revealed too much.

"Meryl," he said, his frame so hunched that I found myself, at five foot one, looking down on his black beret and gray beard, "you should honor your aunt's wishes." And then he added, "Don't read it." He offered no explanation, and I didn't think of asking for one. I simply understood that there was something that I didn't need to know. I was deeply disappointed, but his confirmation of Mollie's directive was enough for the moment.

IN THE THIRTEEN YEARS SINCE I'D PUT *TWENTY-ONE AND ONE* BACK IN ITS place on the bookshelf, I never stopped thinking about Franya and the family. I'd been busy—there was no denying that. In 2010, after more than a decade as mayor, I resigned my post and took a position under the Obama administration as the US ambassador to the United Nations Commission on the Status of Women. By that time, my youngest daughter was fifteen years old and my oldest son was twenty-three. I had much more autonomy, and the notion of traveling the world as an advocate for women's rights and gender equity was both plausible and thrilling.

So, in the moments I could spare, most often late at night, I continued slowly uncovering information about my missing family, especially Franya. In addition to Google searches that led me down historical rabbit holes as the Internet and access to information expanded, I searched through archives at the New York Public Library, the United States Holocaust Memorial Museum in DC, and YIVO in New York.

Then, in 2012, I was invited to observe an election in Tblisi, Georgia. While there, I couldn't help but book a side journey to Vilnius, the first time I'd gone back since the family trip eleven years earlier. I was too close to resist. That's when I first became acquainted with the Lithuanian State Archives, a boxy concrete building with only windows for adornment that sat along a busy highway on the eastern outskirts of Vilnius. It may have looked unwelcoming, almost like a prison, but for me it was a treasure trove. I lost myself in their thorough certificates, digging up my relatives' birth and death records and any other documents I could lay my hands on—proof of their existence. Each item I found held a tiny clue to the mystery of their journeys, from beginning to end. I was so encouraged by the promise of what they housed that when, in 2014, I found myself in the same part of the world to meet women members of parliament in Ukraine, I again made a detour to Lithuania, just an hour's flight away. After that, I continued to make regular trips, traveling from work engagements in Kiev or Yerevan, Armenia.

Vilna had invaded my soul, become even more a part of me than before.

I pored over documents, my tired eyes tearing as I worked to decipher the often faded text, desperate not to miss a detail. My haul would eventually include the record of Franya's marriage to Isaak and a variety of other census and identity documents from which I learned that Franya had spoken multiple languages and had "amber" eyes, rendered, in the official Polish-language designation, as "beer colored." Her profession was listed as "artiste." I was curious about Franya's marriage to Isaak. After all, I'd heard rumors of an affair she'd had with another Yiddish actor. Were she and Isaak still married at that time? What had happened? I could find no records of a divorce.

The archives retained some flavor of the old Soviet bureaucracy. Though they would later become more accessible, I never would have made much headway without the help of an energetic local researcher and guide named Regina Kopilevich. She ran more than she walked, her unruly curly hair—which seemed to match her boisterous personality—flying behind her. When we arrived at the archives, she would jog past tables filled with translators, mostly working on genealogical searches for the Latter-day Saint library, whispering greetings in any one of the seven languages she spoke.

Regina usually had a backpack, if not also a roller bag of belongings clattering along behind her, so she'd be sure to have whatever she needed close at hand. She seemed like both an old soul and a kid, who would have made as much sense in the 1930s as she did now. And her childlike energy was contagious.

Regina worked with a lot of American Jews on the trail of their lost families, but she took a special interest in my family, drawn, like me, to the charisma of Franya Winter. That twinkle in Franya's eye, the layers projected through her variously wide, or demure, smile. "An actor doesn't have just one personality," Regina would say. "They have multifaceted personalities."

Regina had a theatricality all her own. She always did research in advance of my arrival and took particular pleasure in withholding her discoveries until I could see for myself in a grand reveal. Early on, she turned over page after page of an enormous crumbling book marked "1899–1901," then stopped at a particular line of Cyrillic script, inviting me to decipher it. As she watched with a sly smile, her dark eyes challenging, I reached back into the depths of my memory to the Russian I'd learned as a student more than forty years earlier. I sounded out the letters as Regina traced her finger beneath the words. "Merya Davidovna Kaganov," I said with uncertainty. And then it hit me. *Meryl, daughter of David Kagan.* This was a record of my grandmother, the original Meryl! Regina clapped her hands as we beamed at each other. She had wanted me to experience the discovery as my own, and with that came a sense of personal satisfaction. She snapped a picture to capture the moment.

We began photographing documents so we could save the information without access to the materials.

"Ma'am. Ma'am!" barked an ornery staff member. "Photography is prohibited!"

We nodded in understanding, but, as soon as she was gone, turning the corner to reprimand another archivist, Regina winked at me and stood up.

"Take your pictures," she said, positioning herself as my human shield, so the staff member wouldn't see.

Regina found treasures for me all over town. One day, we visited the building that would become the Museum of Tolerance but currently was used as a Jewish museum space for cultural events and exhibitions. With a raise of her eyebrows, she gestured for me to follow her into a back room.

We entered a grand hall, whitewashed and empty but for a lone piano. I looked to her for explanation, as a wave of anticipation came over me.

"Do you know what this is?" she asked. We were playing her guessing game again. I knew that meant something amazing was coming.

My eyes traveled from the high ceilings to the sizable columns, where I spotted Thalia and Melpomene, comedy and tragedy masks, sculpted into the wall above.

"It's a theater," I murmured, mostly to myself.

Regina sat down at the piano. There was a heavy pause. "Not any theater," she smiled. "This was the Yiddish Folk Theater, where Franya performed in 1926." It clicked instantly. I'd read about this theater. My cousin had starred in a play called *The Life of a Woman*. Here she played the role of Naomi. I could hardly find my breath. I was standing on the same floorboards where she had stood. Suddenly, the whole space looked different. Being here with Regina in a space that held the spirit of something—and someone—to which I ached to connect felt unworldly, like one of my childhood dreams.

Regina's fingers found the keys, and she began effortlessly playing a Bach piece, "The Well-Tempered Clavier." The acoustics were magnificent, and the music soared. I eyed the scuffed floorboards, the waiting space. Suddenly, I could imagine the hall full, a crowd of theatergoers applauding thunderously as Franya entered, stage left. I had read a review from a critic who sat in this very audience, and his words echoed in my head now: "[Franya Winter's] game on the stage was very powerful, with passion and delight."

These were moments that brought me closer to the past, the swell of emotion breaking down the barriers of my numbness, bit by bit.

I ASKED REGINA IF SHE WOULD BE ABLE TO ARRANGE FOR ME TO MEET ANY survivors of the ghetto who might have a memory of the theater. Once again, she said, "I have a big surprise for you." She took me to visit Marcus Petuchauskas and his wife, Sofija.

As we walked up the steps to their apartment, she advised me to ask him questions about the theater. "He knows," she said.

"I was at every performance of the ghetto theater," Marcus said, with little prompting.

I was shocked. It didn't seem that this well-preserved man was old enough! I soon learned, however, that he was born in 1931 in the town of Šiauliai, the only son of the deputy mayor. In 1941 his father was executed, and Marcus and his mother and grandmother were sent to the ghetto in Vilna, where he befriended the children of the actors of the Yiddish theater. They never missed a performance. The theater had such a profound impact on him that he built a career around it and eventually became the preeminent theater critic of Lithuania. Although Marcus could not recall if he'd ever seen Franya onstage, he knew the name and recalled a reference to her in a book by poet Schmerke Kaczerzinski, who described Franya as "one of the finest artists of the Jewish theater."

Between visits with Regina in Vilnius, I was excited to continue the search. Using genealogical sites like Ancestry.com and Jewishgen.com, and with the help of archivists at the US Holocaust Memorial Museum, I found detailed deportation and death-camp records. Seeking out helpful contacts wherever I could, I traveled to and searched the archives at Yad Vashem in Jerusalem and the Ghetto Fighters' House Museum near Haifa.

During that time of intense research, I learned so much about my family. I'd known since childhood that my cousin Lola and his wife, Naomi, had survived by hiding out with the help of a Christian family in Brussels, but I was fuzzy on the details. Lola never discussed it. According to my aunt Mollie—who also withheld those details, but shared some of what she knew as I got older—Lola had at one point been arrested and herded onto a cattle train headed to Auschwitz. Somehow, he and Naomi escaped deportation by jumping from the train and made their way back to Brussels. I found some evidence—in France more than in Belgium—that sympathetic railway workers would occasionally loosen floorboards in the tightly sealed cattle wagons, and drivers would slow down or make unauthorized stops to give deportees a chance to lower themselves onto the train tracks and flee. On one well-documented occasion, in April 1943, the Belgian resistance held up a train leaving the Mechelen transit camp for Auschwitz and helped more than two hundred prisoners break free. Roughly half escaped the ensuing gun battle and avoided recapture. Perhaps that had happened to Lola?

My answer came in the form of a letter written by a friend of his, Azaria Dobruszkes, to the Ghetto Fighters' Museum near Haifa, Israel, in the early 1970s, which helpful archivists managed to track down for me. As I read the kind of precious discovery that sent surges of adrenaline coursing through me, I was amazed to discover it not only told the story, but also provided a wealth of supporting documentation, including orders issued to Lola *and* Naomi to report to an army barracks at Mechelen in Antwerp, Belgium, in August 1942. The orders, sent not by the Germans directly but by the Belgian Jewish Association, summoned the couple for work and asked that they bring two weeks' worth of nonperishable foods with them, suggesting, perhaps, a short-term stay.

Lola and Naomi were not fooled. This was life or death. The first transport had left Mechelen for Auschwitz a few weeks earlier, and already word was spreading through the community that the summons was a death sentence. "Instead of presenting themselves to the barracks on August 31, 1942," the letter explained, "they went to hide in a secret house in an attic."

In other words, I realized, since neither of them ever went to the transit camp, thankfully, neither would have needed to jump from a train.

They certainly weren't out of danger after they disregarded the work summons, though. When the Germans realized how ineffective the orders had been since word spread, they and the Belgian police began conducting house-to-house searches instead. Lola and Naomi, the letter from their friend Dobruszkes said, "had to change their hiding place twice, but they did not lose their courage nor their confidence and managed to survive." These discoveries felt like finding pieces of myself, like somehow by reconstructing the narrative, I was putting something back together inside me, as well.

According to Dobruszkes's testimony, Lola and Naomi showed extraordinary bravery during the Nazi occupation. They refused to wear the yellow stars assigned to them in May 1942. Their two stars remained attached to each other (preserved in the Ghetto Fighters' Museum collection), as they were initially distributed, not separated, as they would have been if the couple had obeyed orders and sewn them onto their coats. My cousins could have been arrested or killed on the spot if they had been caught without their stars, marked with a J (for *juif* in French and *jood* in Flemish), but according to Dobruszkes, they went about town without them for several more months. I couldn't help but feel awe at their courage.

Through my research, I also managed to reconstruct much of the story of Rachmil, my sad blue-eyed cousin in Berlin who had left such a melancholy impression on my aunt Mollie during her travels. He left Vilna shortly after finishing high school in 1919, when the city's status was still fiercely contested between the Bolsheviks and the Poles. For four years, he worked toward a technical degree in Mannheim, then as a salesman for a company specializing in distilled petroleum products. In 1930 he moved to Berlin to work for an import-export company, but soon lost his job because of the poor state of the German economy. At the time Mollie visited in 1932, he was battling to stay in Germany, working with the local refugee office of the League of Nations to argue that he couldn't go home because he had no obvious home to go to. Vilna was now in Poland, a country of which he had never been a citizen, and he couldn't go to Russia, the nominal country of his birth, because he was an outspoken anticommunist, and his life would be in danger if he ever went back. I found online a cache of German documents in the archives at the United Nations Office at Geneva, written to and from Rachmil Punski, ordering him to leave Germany as a "stateless Jew." The German authorities said that they would deliver him to the border.

Rachmil's arguments proved effective, enabling him to beat back a number of deportation orders issued by the police in Charlottenburg, his local neighborhood. His residence permit was extended several times until the Nazis' Nuremberg Laws, passed in 1935, kicked off a flurry of restrictions and severely limited the kinds of jobs Jews were allowed to perform. In the wake of Kristallnacht, the infamous "Night of Broken Glass" pogrom in November 1938 when synagogues and Jewish businesses were destroyed and thirty thousand men were taken to concentration camps to die, the Nazis enacted a new bevy of anti-Semitic laws. At that point, Rachmil would have found himself in grave physical danger too.

None of the records I found mentioned Rachmil again for many years. The story I heard from Mollie as a child was that Rachmil left Berlin before the war—he may even have gone to Vilna—but returned to pick up documents to complete an application to emigrate to the United States. Upon his return to Berlin, according to Mollie he was gunned down in the street. I was never able to find evidence of that, though. Sometimes, the realization that Mollie hadn't always known the truth about what happened, that her stories were her best amalgamation rather than concrete facts, was jarring. I had always thought of her as the arbiter of our family history and, really, how to live in general. If she was not quite right about this, could she have been wrong about *Twenty-One and One* too? Should I read the forbidden book? Questions began to poke holes in my wall of resolve.

My best guess about Rachmil is that he never left Berlin, but went into hiding for most of the war, probably with the help of his girlfriend, Friedel Pohl, who was not Jewish. Eventually, his luck must have turned because he was arrested in August 1944 and deported to Auschwitz as prisoner number 193068.

Five months later, with the Red Army sweeping westward through Poland, the Germans ordered every Auschwitz inmate still physically capable of walking, including my cousin, to march hundreds of miles back toward Germany. There were about fifty-six thousand prisoners to start, but almost a quarter of them died along the way from malnutrition, disease, or winter cold. Many of those who struggled to keep up were shot.

Rachmil somehow survived the ordeal. He arrived at Dachau on January 28. But by March 20, he was dead.

Many times I've thought about what might have been and almost was. Rachmil survived in hiding for five of the six years of the war. He survived a concentration camp and torturous journey. If he hadn't been forced to leave Auschwitz, he could have been liberated by the Russians when they overran the camp in a matter of days on January 27, 1945. If he'd only been able to survive five more weeks in Dachau, he could have been liberated by the US Army. If only, if only . . .

As I began to fill in the gaps about my extended family, I still found myself as focused as ever on Franya. Her story continued to intrigue me most of all. Sometimes her image would pop into my head as I searched, winking at me in encouragement or sighing mournfully in frustration. Just as I had felt as a child, longing for the grandmother I never knew, I missed Franya like a long-lost friend.

Digging through all manner of dusty files and reaching out to my growing number of contacts at various archives, I had learned as much as I could gather about her early life, which only intrigued me more. She was born Fraydel Rosenrot in 1896, the daughter of a Hasidic family from the poorest neighborhood in Warsaw. Had she come into the world a generation earlier, there would have been little prospect of her ever performing in public. The expectation would have been that she remain true to her rigorous religious tradition. She would have received little formal education beyond some basic instruction in Jewish ritual and, perhaps, the skills necessary to run a modest storefront. Her main mission in life would have been to marry a man of her parents' choosing and produce as many babies as possible. Even today, it's difficult to imagine a young Hasidic girl with the freedom to don costumes and perform openly. However, her circumstances may have made her parents more accepting of her aspirations.

The world Fraydel (soon to be Franya) came into was changing rapidly. The number of Jews across Europe had almost quadrupled over the course of the nineteenth century, from just over two million in 1800 to close to eight million. Despite rampant poverty and oppression, particularly within the czarist empire, the Jews were developing into a force unto themselves. In 1897, the year after Fraydel was born, the Jewish-Socialist Bund was formed, a political party founded in Vilna and devoted to civil and labor rights that would hold tremendous sway in Eastern Europe over the next two generations. It was also the year of the first World Zionist Congress, an assembly of the World Zionist Organization members to discuss creating Jewish infrastructure in Israel. Yiddish literature, journalism, academic research, music, and theater were all on the rise, especially in Warsaw, signs of a growing secular trend and a harbinger of more rapid change ahead. Even Orthodox and Hasidic girls were finding ways to equip themselves with a full education.

Yiddish newspapers were filled with stories about Orthodox girls in and around Krakow, the part of Poland controlled by Austria-Hungary, running away from home and converting to Catholicism in the hope of securing a better education and a brighter future. That, in turn, prompted the religious authorities in Warsaw and other major cities to negotiate with the civil authorities and create additional opportunities within their jurisdictions.

It's unclear just how much education Fraydel received. I learned from her passport applications that she grew up speaking fluent Polish as well as Yiddish and later learned Russian and German too. That suggests some degree of formal schooling and a household that placed a strong emphasis on culture and literacy. At a young age, she began to earn money by singing songs to non-Jewish audiences, a break with traditional practice so startling I've often wondered how it happened at all. Fraydel's father was blind, which must have increased the economic pressures on the family. But she wasn't just bringing in extra cash. She was singing, in front of men, which according to strict religious tradition was deemed to be *ervah*, the height of immodesty. Women, according to this worldview, were allowed to sing at the lighting of the *shabbos* candles while surrounded by their immediate family. To many, singing in front of a member of the opposite sex would be as shocking as stripping naked.

The cultural leap that Fraydel took was particularly striking to me. In keeping with the fierce and vibrant spirit I sensed she possessed, she would have been among the first of her generation to break with the past, testing new boundaries. Like me, like Mollie, she was clearly not one to take no for an answer. Typically, the teenage daughters of hard-up Hasidic families found work washing clothes or caring for the children of richer households. Sometimes, they would be married off even younger than usual to become someone else's financial burden. Instead, fearless Fraydel was exercising her vocal talents of her own free will in Polish clubs and cabarets.

Fraydel's skill and stage presence must have been undeniable, as well as her ambition. Otherwise, how did she even learn the Polish songs? Clearly, she was a *tzatzkeleh*, a rule breaker with extraordinary determination, like Mollie said that I was, and my grandmother Meryl had been. I felt an even deeper connection with Fraydel.

In 1914 when Fraydel was twenty years old, World War I began, which meant many of the usual rules no longer applied—for men or women, for religious traditionalists or secularists, for Jews or non-Jews. Warsaw endured aerial bombardment and some fighting before the Germans pushed the czarist forces eastward and began an occupation that lasted from 1915 until the Armistice. Many Jews on the Russian side of the front came under suspicion as potential German sympathizers because of the perceived closeness of the Yiddish and German languages and were forced to flee westward, greatly swelling the Jewish populations of cities like Vilna and Warsaw. The overcrowding exacerbated already significant shortages of food and other necessities, but it also brought writers and artists together who took inspiration from each other and expressed appropriately provocative responses to the catastrophe of a continent on fire.

In some ways, creating work in conversation with upheaval came naturally. For centuries, Jews had made art inspired by the precariousness of their standing in the world—and non-Jewish Slavs, having lived through many of the same invasions, occupations, and geopolitical disruptions, had a related frame of reference. As Joseph Buloff, a Vilna-born Yiddish actor who later made a career on Broadway and in Hollywood, observed of his fellow players, "They were drowned so many times, but each time the water rejected them. They were burned again and again and did not go up in smoke."

In Warsaw a new, more politicized form of cabaret, targeted not at the masses but at the intelligentsia, emerged as World War I came to a close and Poland once again became an independent country. *Kabaret literacki*, as it was known, was edgy, satirical, and unabashedly cosmopolitan, featuring Jewish and non-Jewish performers together, who made a point of rejecting and satirizing notions of racial purity promoted by Poland's extreme nationalists. The intelligentsia itself was evenly split between Poles of Jewish and Catholic backgrounds. In fact, despite political rumblings to the contrary, the prevailing cultural impetus in Warsaw was to promote a cultural melting pot, all the better to vie with the cabarets and theaters of Berlin, 350 miles to the west.

Thus, it was a good, if not always comfortable, time to be a talented young performer like young Fraydel. She could draw inspiration from various cultural traditions and pour them into her craft. Even before the war ended, she was invited to spend a summer performing plays at Kalisz in western Poland. And it was during this time that she dropped the name Fraydel Rosenrot in favor of the stage name Franya Winter, to increase her appeal with Polish-language audiences. After Kalisz she was invited to Minsk, the future capital of Belarus, at a time when the city was fighting to assert its independence from both the Poles and the Bolsheviks. As far as I found, she didn't run into any political difficulties there, but she did have to fend off an insistent, older, non-Jewish admirer who wouldn't take no for an answer. Undaunted even by a veritable stalker, Franya hatched a plan with her renowned director, Nahum Lipowski, who told the suitor that she was a minor (she wasn't) and threatened criminal prosecution if he didn't leave her alone.

Next, Franya moved to Vilna when it became part of the newly independent Polish Republic in 1922. (Minsk, meanwhile, had fallen into Soviet hands.) The politics remained tense. Anti-Semitic undercurrents were as strong in Vilna as they had been in Warsaw. Franya experienced this for herself during her first summer season when a group of Polish soldiers jeered at her while she was performing on an open-air stage in the city's lush Bernardine Gardens, which would later be destroyed during World War II and reconstructed in 2013. The soldiers, who objected to her singing in Yiddish, would not stop heckling until she switched to Polish. Far from deterring her, though, the episode only strengthened her resolve. Before long, she was working with Lipowski again at the city's Jewish Folk Theater and performing exclusively in Yiddish.

As it happened, the Yiddish theater of the time was emerging as a cultural force to be reckoned with in Eastern Europe, equivalent to today's Hollywood with movie stars. There was no TV at the time, barely any access to films, so theater was the driving entertainment force. For the overwhelming majority of Eastern European Jews, Yiddish was their native tongue, so the performances spoke directly to them, ranging from burlesque to the highbrow avant-garde.

Forged out of the experience of World War I and its aftermath, this particular theater made the case for a distinctly Jewish cultural identity, in contrast to the Warsaw cabaret scene, while still addressing universal themes and pushing the limits of what acting and stagecraft could be. This new theater blended elements of psychological realism, modernism, German expressionism, and absurdist comedy, and the shows drew rapturous audiences from Moscow to New York and Buenos Aires. The players performed translations of classics like *Hamlet*, reinterpretations like *The Yiddish King Lear*, and shows with lasting impact like *Tevye the Milkman* (which would later be adapted into *Fiddler on the Roof*). Along with Rudolf Zaslavsky, big names like Ester Rachel Kaminska and her daughter Ida as well as Maurice Schwartz (founder of the Yiddish Art Theater) drew crowds of all kinds, inspiring chatter across the Continent. Often, the productions were so vivid and fresh that it didn't matter to audiences whether they understood the Yiddish. As one Dutch critic wrote in 1922: "They have taught us what acting actually is, as opposed to what is usually called acting."

And Franya was part of the revolution.

⁓

I HAD UNEARTHED A GOOD PART OF WHAT FRANYA HAD EXPERIENCED IN her youth, but there was so much more to learn. Who had she become, and what had become of her? As part of my online research efforts, I posted family photos of Franya on a website devoted to prewar Jewish life and sent out an appeal for more information. I also uploaded pages from the Yiddish text of *Twenty-One and One*, safely unintelligible to me but perhaps meaningful to others. In my mind, I was clear that I wanted to dig up Franya's story, all of it, even if I was forbidden from reading the best source. I knew Mollie's request was irrational, knew my adherence was too, but couldn't imagine disobeying my aunt.

Those posts were a shot in the dark, one of many efforts I made to discover new resources, but ultimately that's what enabled Aurore Blaise, the archivist at the Mémorial de la Shoah in Paris, to track me down and link me to Franya, Isaak, and the rest of the Punski family.

6

Un Trésor Familial

"FINGERS TREMBLED ON THE STRINGS OF A JEWISH HARP"

IN 2015 I was working as the executive director of FilmAid, a nonprofit humanitarian organization that used film to support and educate refugees around the globe. I traveled to refugee camps in Kenya, populated with people who had fled Somalia, Sudan, and the Democratic Republic of Congo, where the director there asked me to share my own family's story. I told them about my family's tragic past and my cousin Cheyna, who survived the genocide. She was only fifteen years old when her entire family was murdered, I told them. She was left with nothing, but she escaped and moved to Israel, and there she built a beautiful life, but, I added, "she still cries every night." I wanted to communicate to them that a full life is possible in the shadow of tragedy, but that they, like she, would probably never forget.

I hoped that they would use this opportunity to tell their stories. Afterward, I was surrounded by young men and women who wanted to share their own personal accounts of rape, violence, and grief—stories that would be lost if they weren't documented, and stories that some are beginning to deny ever happened.

For the first time in my life, in the refugee camp, I felt like I was finally in the place I was meant to be. I could not do anything to help my family lost in the Holocaust, but I could help these people now who had experienced their own horror and who wandered through the desert fleeing oppression, searching for a haven, people who lived in their own "diaspora."

It was an unbearably hot and humid summer's day, while sitting at my desk back in our FilmAid New York City office, while looking for a missing email, I checked an old AOL email account. There I found a note that would ignite the memorial candle in me once again. The email was from a woman who addressed me as "Madam" and acknowledged the "liberty" she was taking in contacting me:

> I work as an archivist at the Mémorial de la Shoah in Paris. Very recently, a man gave us pictures he had found nearly 40 years ago in an abandoned house (which was about to be destroyed) near Paris. He had absolutely no idea of whom these pictures were. He only supposed they belonged to a Jewish family because some of them had handwriting in Yiddish on the other side. These pictures date from the 1920s and 1930s.
>
> I managed to identify a woman in those pictures: Franya Winter . . .

My heart caught in my throat.

The archivist's name was Aurore Blaise, and she had spent five months researching Franya and everyone else she could identify from the photo collection. The pictures of Franya, she said, were publicity shots in different stage costumes. And she had a number of family portraits, too, with names of those pictured inscribed on the back. Among those listed were my family members: Uncle Yudel (who was the father of the Punski sons); Tante Rivel (my great-aunt who lived with Isaak and Franya); Isaak's two brothers, Soma and Rachmil (who had no country); and even my cousin Lola Punski, whom I, of course, recognized.

I couldn't begin to imagine how these photographs of prewar Vilna had ended up in an abandoned house outside Paris. It felt like a real-life mystery. In fact, it was a miracle that they had been discovered and saved from destruction at all. Now, after *forty* years, they were being returned to their rightful heirs. It felt like a sign too fortuitous to ignore.

"This is a very special discovery," I replied, begging Aurore for more details. It was hard to contain my excitement.

Aurore was almost apologetic in her response: "I hope these [*sic*] information are not too overwhelming," she worried.

Quite the opposite: I had a million questions. Someone—a stranger—had taken the time to find, keep, and protect this collection of photographs. It was an act of bravery, of kindness, of humanity. And, now, that same someone was taking the time, via Aurore, to find me.

On many levels, I got lucky: a less determined researcher might not have gone to the same trouble of reaching out to me. The Mémorial received batches of family photographs and other memorabilia constantly and did not have the resources to lavish scrupulous attention on each case. But Aurore was young and energetic, having come under the spell of Franya's charm like so many of us, taken by her aura of power and jubilance in the midst of a helpless and dark time.

Aurore was also fascinated by the unusual circumstances that landed the photographs before her: On the first day of April in 2015, a chilly, overcast day, she'd been sitting at the reception desk for the Mémorial's fourth-floor library when two men approached. She looked up at them through her wire-rimmed glasses, her straight light hair framing her youthful face.

"We drove several hours to show someone this," said a tall man in his sixties with a meticulously trimmed white beard, who would turn out to be the more talkative of the two. The man, Serge Mogère, reached into his bag and produced an album of more than fifty photographs.

"It's a *trésor familial*," he explained, or a family treasure, clutching it to his chest not unlike the Etingins had with the forbidden manuscript so many years before.

Aurore initially assumed, based on her experience, that the family in question must be his. So she was surprised to learn that Serge was unsure of the subjects' identities, especially since he had obviously formed a deep attachment to the people in the album. He was a talker and a charmer. As he turned the pages, he rhapsodized over the images with clear affection. Then, he told his story:

Serge was an artist, but in 1975, at the age of twenty-three, he was briefly floundering and took a job working in the state railway's security department, based in Choisy-le-Roi, a suburb on the railway line leading out of

Paris toward the Loire Valley. Every day, he would walk to work alongside the railway line, and, invariably, his eye was drawn to a dilapidated seventeenth-century building, boarded up and long abandoned.

The building, sitting on a corner, had once been a grand home with ornate archways, slatted shutters, and an unusual pepper-box turret supporting a first-floor balcony. One day when he could no longer resist, he stopped to take a closer look and spotted a descriptive metal plaque. The text indicated that the French revolutionary Georges Danton had lived in the house, Maison Danton, for a year before he was guillotined in 1794. Serge was even more intrigued.

Finally, not long afterward, Serge and two of his fellow railway workers talked each other into venturing inside. Who knew what they might find, they speculated, as they crept toward the entrance. Serge's friends hoped to stumble upon a trove of precious antiques.

"The front door was locked," he explained to Aurore, who was rapt as she listened. Serge and his coworkers had little difficulty pushing the boards aside from one of the ground-floor windows and climbed inside. They found themselves in a long hallway, shrouded in darkness apart from sporadic shards of bright light beaming down through holes in the roof. Looking up, they spotted a tangle of spiderwebs, like something out of a horror movie. Serge shuddered, but continued on. The other men followed him up to the second floor, but there they stopped. The wooden steps leading up to an attic were half-rotted and unsafe. Serge, who suffered from a fear of heights, was surprised by his own gall, but felt compelled to keep exploring.

The top floor was even dustier, if possible, rat infested, and strewn with old clothes, papers, and an inexplicable number of broken roof tiles. As he wandered the room, there were spots where he could feel the floor giving way under his weight. He trod softly as the boards creaked. As his eyes adjusted to the low light, he was able to discern that the papers included magazines, newspapers, letters, and official documents. He took a step toward them. On the floor below, dust poured through the rafters, startling his friends. The entire attic seemed on the verge of collapse. "Come down!" they yelped. "You have to come down, now!"

Serge knew they were right. He should make his way down and out to safety. At that moment, he spotted an old black-and-white photograph featuring a woman's face, now illuminated by a rare shard of light. It was as if she was in a spotlight. The photograph was half-submerged in rubble, but he noticed her radiant smile and theatrical pose, her shoulders thrust back and flowers adorning her hair. When he stooped to get a closer look, he was again surprised: beneath the rubble lay many more photographs, some of them on postcards, some sepia tinted, all of them depicting people in pre-war garb.

Even though Serge didn't yet understand what he was looking at, the pictures spoke to him of grief, loss, bygone eras. This was a well-to-do European family, that much was clear. If the photographs had been abandoned in this rotting place, what could have happened to them all? Serge was suddenly filled with conviction: he had to save the photographs. He noticed a language that he didn't understand on the flip side of the images, which he supposed was Yiddish. This, he thought, might be the only evidence left in the world of these people's existence. Feeling the attic floor creak in warning, eliciting more frenzied shouts from his friends, Serge scooped up as many images as he could before darting back down the stairs to safety.

When Serge returned home, he showed the photographs to his mother. "I was relieved that she understood my sense of responsibility for them," he explained. She had lived through the Nazi occupation of Paris and felt sympathetic to his impulse to protect this history. Together they bought a belle epoque–style photograph album with a violet flower motif on the front and carefully arranged the photographs inside. Some of the pictures had writing on the back, in languages Serge and his mother did not know. Some appeared to be theatrical publicity shots, while others were more conventional family portraits. Just a handful did not appear to belong with the others; Serge later speculated that they must have come from a different family who either lived in the house after the war or used it as a storage space for their belongings.

Serge returned and took his own photographs of the area immediately surrounding Maison Danton. He developed them, tucking the six best ones at the end of the album. He knew that SNCF, the French railway company, had bought the land to facilitate construction of a new commuter rail line, and he wanted to memorialize his discovery in case the run-down house did not survive. After all, the building, like the photographs, was a piece of history. But whose?

After that, Serge never returned to the house. He was conscious that he and his friends had been trespassing in a treacherous space, and the risk of going back seemed too great. As the years went by, he came to regret this missed opportunity, especially after Maison Danton was demolished in 1980. The land it stood on was developed into high-rise apartments. The photographs had in some way become his destiny, taking on progressively more meaning as he scrutinized the faces pictured again and again, wondering about their provenance. Taking care of the images was a commitment to himself as much as to the family whose memories he had saved from oblivion.

Serge married, divorced, remarried, and, after moving six times, eventually settled in western Brittany. While he ditched many of his possessions along the way, he kept the photographs, unearthed from the rubble, with him. For long periods they gathered dust on a shelf while his attention turned elsewhere, but he was always conscious of their presence and the tragedies they evoked. Like the forbidden book for me, the album took on a life of its own, a part of him despite being steeped in seemingly unsolvable mystery. Of course, he was especially intrigued by the pictures of Franya, whose energy came through as if she was alive in the room, despite him not even being able to decipher her name. In one image, she wore a valet's uniform, in another a sailor suit. Her hair was wild and changeable, and her expressions—of surprise, coyness, campy theatricality—could occupy him for hours. Though he did not know her identity, Franya sat on his shoulder, as she did mine, an amused smile playing on her face. Like me, he wondered what could have happened to this seemingly unbreakable spirit.

In addition to the theatrical shots, some of which were also in the collection my parents kept in a manila envelope under the TV set in our New Jersey home, Serge had found some extraordinary images of a seaside trip. In one of them, which would eventually become my favorite, Franya was in a swimsuit in the water, her arms raised joyfully above her head as the waves lapped around her waist. This shot was neither a dour family photo nor a staged image. In it, Franya was entirely herself—and she looked free.

Here, Serge thought, was a woman at one with her immediate surroundings, in that moment far removed from the burdens of daily life. He pointed it out to Aurore specially as he leafed through the album.

Periodically, Serge's wife, Christèle, would suggest that he make the photographs more public, so the family's descendants might have a chance of discovering them. For a long time, though, Serge resisted. His sense of ownership was too strong. Still, shortly after the Mémorial de la Shoah opened in 2005 in Paris's old Jewish quarter the Marais, a large Star of David adorning its entrance, he wrote a letter to see if his collection might be of interest. Perhaps he'd be able to judge from the response he received whether this was an avenue he could bring himself to pursue. But the Mémorial never wrote back.

Then in early 2015 Serge was diagnosed with prostate cancer. At first, the prognosis was not good. Forced to confront his own mortality, he thought seriously for the first time about putting his affairs in order. He was traveling to Paris regularly to see a urologist for treatment, and his wife at last persuaded him on one of those trips to walk the photographs through the Mémorial's contemporary doors and into their archives.

"It's time," she told him, "to give the responsibility to someone else."

And so, perhaps against his better judgment, he found himself standing across from Aurore Blaise at her library reception desk. Could he trust her with the photo album he'd cherished for so long?

Later, his wife, Christèle, would tell me that he'd made a conscious choice to bring his friend Jean-Pierre along because he didn't trust himself to part with the photographs. He felt he needed someone standing beside him to press and insist. It turned out that he needed Jean-Pierre's support more literally as well: on the elevator ride up, he was overcome by a sudden attack of vertigo and had to grab his friend's arm to steady himself. Such was the degree of attachment he felt to the images and their subjects, despite never having known them himself. When I heard his story, it resonated deeply for me. I felt seen. Serge's reaction was proof not only that vicarious trauma could be real and intensely impactful, but also that those powerful feelings of connection, responsibility, and even affection could transcend time and space. How could I feel so fused with a cousin I'd never known, driven by a tragedy I wasn't alive to experience? How could Serge have dedicated so much of his life to strangers in black-and-white photographs?

Though he was at the Mémorial to support Serge, Jean-Pierre himself was starting to feel uneasy. He knew very little about the Holocaust and Serge's photographs and found the whole experience confounding. How had his friend become so emotionally entangled in this? Fortunately, with every passing moment, Serge was more confident that this intelligent young researcher was exactly the person to help.

As Serge finished his story, Aurore listened in astonishment, exhaling in awe of what sat before her. She was instantly hooked—by Serge's enthusiasm, by the story's rich history, by Franya's charisma, by the challenge to uncover more. "Her eyes lit up," Serge remembered. "I could see by the way she handled the album that she would do the right thing, that everything would be fine. As police inspectors like to say, *c'est la bonne affaire*—we were in business."

Aurore felt similarly moved. That evening, she went on her first date with the man who would become her life partner. Sitting across the table from him, too excited to feel nerves, she said, "I had the most amazing day at work." It all felt deeply auspicious.

—

THUS BEGAN AURORE'S SEARCH FOR ME, WHICH IN MANY WAYS MIRRORED my search for Franya. She began with the information she could glean from Serge's story, the photographs, and the words scrawled on their backs.

Several of the publicity shots were labeled "F. Winter" and bore the name of a photographic studio in Riga, Latvia. Other individual portrait shots had names handwritten in ink in the Roman alphabet on the front or back, enabling Aurore to identify them right away. Despite some slight variations in spelling due to transliteration from Hebrew or Cyrillic, it quickly became clear that she was looking at three brothers: Isaak Punsky (as his name was written), Mila (Rachmil) Punski, and Lola Punsky. The names, the clothes, and the notes all pointed to the prewar period, somewhere in the old Russian and Soviet empires.

Beyond that, though, many questions remained: How was this actress connected to these brothers? Aurore couldn't read the Yiddish used in most of the inscriptions—she couldn't even identify the language at first. She recognized that some of the other writing was in Polish, which she didn't speak either. A small number of the photographs appeared to have been taken in France, since they had French inscriptions and featured a woman with an identifiably French name, Camille. But Aurore couldn't tell whether Camille was connected to the rest of the subjects and, if so, how.

At that time, Aurore was a junior staff member at the archive, whose duties did not ordinarily involve playing a kind of cross-generational detective. People who walked into the Mémorial unannounced almost always brought mementos and treasures from their own families, with no need to identify their provenance. At most they asked for help locating long-lost relatives or old family addresses for which they had incomplete information. Aurore always loved even these limited investigations and so resolved to talk her boss, the head of the photographic department, into letting her investigate this mystery.

Aurore had sensed Serge's obvious reticence about leaving the photos at all. She had assured him that she herself would take care of them, that she would not allow them to be subsumed by the thousands of images in their possession, which seemed to quell his fears. That's what she explained to her boss as she stood before her desk, pleading for permission to take the project on.

Eventually, her boss nodded. Yes, she could investigate these photos, but she would have to fit the task around her other duties. She also had to be patient. The Mémorial's Yiddish expert was busy on other assignments and would not be free to help her decipher the inscriptions for several weeks. She agreed readily, escaping his office before he could change his mind.

Soon Aurore began filling in some of the gaps. Once she had the Yiddish translations in hand, she learned that the *F* in "F. Winter" stood for "Franya" and that Franya was married to Isaak Punski. The puzzle was fitting together! Two of the group portrait inscriptions indicated that the family lived in Vilna, not Riga, and the photographs themselves suggested that several members of the family, most likely including Isaak and Franya, lived under the same roof.

There were indications, too, of a connection to a family named Rosenrot. One of the inscriptions was written in the form of a dedication to them. Where, though, did these Rosenrots live? If they were in Poland, as seemed logical from the Warsaw address on the back of one of the postcards, how had the photographs ended up in Paris? As in my search, each of Aurore's new adrenaline-fueled revelations, uncovered as she pored over documents at her desk, raised a series of new ones. There were indications of a correspondence between family members who lived apart. One inscription read: "A keepsake for my dear brothers, from Franya and Isaak Punski." Another read: "To remember my family by. For my brothers and their wives. Franya. Vilna, March 13, 1929."

The best chance, Aurore reasoned, of finding out more was if she was able to track down a living relative of the Punskis. Drawing that connection was relatively easy and required just a few Google searches, thanks to the information and queries I'd posted online. Even in our initial correspondence, Aurore and I were able to trade information. I shared that Franya's maiden name was Rosenrot and that she'd been born in Warsaw, which might explain why the family corresponded in Polish as well as Yiddish.

As for why the photographs ended up in Paris, I could only guess that had something to do with Lola. He had studied engineering in Grenoble, in the French Alps, and settled in Brussels, just a few hours' train ride from Paris. "I do not know of any other family members in France," I wrote, but something told me not to close the book on that question.

In addition to the photos, I also posted a copy of *Twenty-One and One*, which was apparently not clear and difficult to read. Aurore asked for a clean copy. "My colleague who reads Yiddish would be very glad to translate the chapter about Franya Winter in English for you," she wrote. I simply could not ignore Mollie's edict. At this point, it was almost like something I had to prove to myself, a bit like a superstition. Once again, I found myself photocopying *Twenty-One and One*, page by page, packing it up, and mailing it across the Atlantic—and explaining to yet another incredulous correspondent why I'd taken a vow not to read it myself.

⁓

SIX MONTHS AFTER I FIRST RECEIVED AURORE'S EMAIL, IN THE FALL OF 2015, I traveled to Paris with my youngest daughter, Belle. When we'd ventured to Vilna together so many years before in search of information and catharsis, she had been a small child—only seven years old. No doubt the search had felt more like an abstract endeavor to her, something her mother and grandmother were invested in that she vaguely understood. Now she was a fully formed adult at twenty-one years old, expressing interest in causes to better the world like environmentalism and able to process what a trip like this meant on a more complex level. Now she could process the way our shared history lived inside her as well.

I was excited to meet Serge, but also nervous. I didn't know what to expect. I was grateful to him for saving the photos and seeing their value instead of throwing them in the garbage, which would have been so easy. On the plane ride over, as I closed my eyes and tried to get some rest, my mind swirled with questions, scenarios, and imagined interactions. What would this person be like, who had pored over the pictures of my family just as I had? Who had adopted the burden of their journey as a North Star in his life's work? Who had, like so many before him, been enchanted by Franya's magnetism?

Now, in the Marais neighborhood of Paris, Belle and I approached the Mémorial de la Shoah on the Allée des Justes, or Walk of the Righteous, a pedestrian street bordering the institution that was renamed in 2006 to honor almost four thousand French people who risked their own safety to help the Jews during the Holocaust. Their names were etched in gold on shiny black plaques running along the length of the sleek stone wall surrounding the Mémorial building.

I felt a sense of hope rise in my chest, only to have it plummet just as quickly as we reached the entrance. Two Parisian police officers stood guard outside, machine guns in hand. The last year in France had been rife with anti-Semitic crimes, including, in the wake of the shooting of twelve people at the satirical weekly *Charlie Hebdo* after they published a cartoon of Islamic prophet Muhammad, the murder of four Jewish people at a kosher supermarket. Although Belle and I had seen sporadic police throughout the city, it was impossible not to notice that they were stationed at every Jewish site by necessity. On this day as we readied to meet Serge, the reality of our history—and the continued bigotry against us as Jews—felt suddenly like too much to bear. I looked at my daughter, with her hair newly bleached platinum blonde. She was the embodiment of possibility. How could anyone hate her? I thought of the schoolchildren taken away from their families. I thought of my cousin Cheyna's constant refrain whenever she would tell fragments of her past, "Why, why, no *shalom*?" I took a shuddering breath—and I broke down in tears.

I surprised myself in that moment. If the swell of emotion was any indicator, my carefully constructed veneer of stoicism was cracking. I knew this was ultimately a good thing—that somehow through this search, I was beginning to break down the barriers that had long protected me from feeling all the pain, but also kept it locked inside of me. I wanted to be able to be fully present for my children when it came to this, to break free from the constraints of my dissociation and numbness, so that they might also break free. I wanted them to remember like me, but not to carry that history like a burden. I wanted to be able to understand and connect to what happened to my family without it coloring every experience of my life. This seemed like the path to that catharsis, but the flood of emotion was deeply uncomfortable along the way.

Arm in arm, Belle and I walked past the Mémorial to the end of the street so that I could regain my composure, as I pulled my scarf closer around me.

"It never ends," I told Belle, wiping tears from my cheeks with the back of my hand, suddenly reminded of my father as we sat watching the World War II documentary series so many years before. "To be a Jew is to be in danger."

We turned around to double-back, and that's when I saw them: Serge and his wife and daughter in the distance, waiting at the entrance to the Mémorial like a sign. Serge's humanity stood in stark contrast to the devastation I felt at seeing the men with guns. Here, directly in front of me, was evidence of goodness for goodness' sake, underlined by the names that ran along the wall. There were still decent people in the world. Moved beyond understanding, I ran into his arms like we were long-lost family. He embraced me, as I thanked him over and over again, tears streaming down both of our faces.

I finally pulled back to get a good look at him. He was tall and elegant, with an artist's long, delicate fingers and a facial expression as animated as his manner of speaking and telling stories. He wore wire-rimmed glasses that only magnified the charming crinkle of his eyes. His wife, Christèle, had wavy hair and wore red glasses, dangling earrings, and a warm smile. She was quiet, empathetic. Her grandparents had taken her to visit concentration camps as a child, and the experience had stayed with her. But perhaps their eighteen-year-old daughter, Maïwenn, captivated me the most, as her round face and dark-brown eyes—framed by long dark-brown hair—reminded me of Franya. Again, I couldn't help but think about how our history lives on in future generations, even without the blood connection.

Serge and I had been communicating over email and phone for many months, so I knew all about his discovery at the broken-down house in Choisy-le-Roi and his realization as a very young man that taking care of the photographs was inexplicably his spiritual destiny. Meeting him in person was something else, though. I couldn't get over the fact that this engaging and charismatic man had somehow forged an unbreakable bond with the lost members of my family. What had compelled him to do such a thing? He was not Jewish himself, though he was half-Black and thus had his own unique understanding of prejudice and loss. But I wondered what in his background or worldview had given him such sensitivity to the lives and memories that had been ravaged in the war?

"There must be *some* connection," I had repeated to him, not once but several times, always hungry for the underlying motivation, the whole story.

The only answer he could come up with was that, as French citizens, he and his family were keenly aware of the history of the Nazi occupation and the way it had split the country, in part because, shamefully, many French officials and ordinary citizens had participated in the roundups, arrests, and deportations of their Jewish neighbors. When Serge saw the photographs and, later, the Yiddish writing on the flip side, he realized that this entire Eastern European family had almost certainly perished, and that moved him. He didn't need any personal association with Judaism to feel responsible. I wanted to understand more about what had formed that sense of justice.

Beyond the initial entrance to the Mémorial was a courtyard surrounded by bars, another reminder of the need for protection—for me, evoking a sense of imprisonment. On one side was the Wall of Names, etched with the identities of seventy-six thousand Jews, including eleven thousand children, who were deported during the Holocaust, many with the support of the Vichy government, of which only about twenty-five hundred survived. At center stood a giant cylindrical sculpture featuring the name of the Jewish ghetto as well as the concentration camps where so many people were tortured and slaughtered. I was struck by the way it had oxidized over time, as if tears ran down the length of it.

Inside, the building was modern, but a bit dark. Together we boarded an elevator to the library and archives on the upper floors and, when the doors slid open, were bathed in light from floor-to-ceiling windows. It felt as if we had risen from the depths to a kind of heaven. Their Documentation Center housed more than thirty million items, so, for me, that was like some kind of nirvana. There was so much information to be had.

Aurore met us there. In person she looked smart and studious as expected, but over dinners throughout the trip, I'd learn there was so much more to her, a lover of graphic novels, video games, and of my Jersey hometown hero, Bruce Springsteen. Aurore was not Jewish, but her parents had educated her about the importance of personal histories and about the Jews who had been part of the community during the war. Her perspective underlined again for me how important it is to educate our children about the past, to create not a sense of fear, but rather understanding. I was fueled in large part by the question, *What do we tell our children?* Aurore's parents seemed to have done a great job.

In some ways, the fact that Aurore wasn't Jewish helped her as an archivist here, as she didn't bring preconceptions to the table—just a deep curiosity. The archivists brought boxed albums out to show me, with white gloves on. The photos were preserved in plastic, but to see them, Franya in all her glory, was a miracle. I knew these people intimately, and thanks to aunt

Mollie, I was able to identify each of them for Serge, Belle, Aurore, and everyone who stood observing the occasion in the library. Congregated around a wooden table, we went through the photographs, and I told stories about the characters.

"This is my uncle Yudel!" I exclaimed. "He married two of my grandmother's sisters." (This was a norm of sorts—a widower marrying the sister of his deceased wife.)

"This is my Tante Rivel. She was very sophisticated."

"This is my cousin Lola," I said, searching the face of a man I had known, captured on film. "He survived the war in Belgium. I adored him!" In fact, Belle's middle name is Lola, in honor of him. He called me "Carrotle" because apparently "Meryl" means "little carrot" in Yiddish. When I was an adult, we would write regularly. Once, he picked me up at the train station in Brussels with a dozen roses and with carrots tied to the bottom. I tried desperately to find the descendants of the Christian family who had saved them so many years before, but had no luck.

"This is my cousin Soma. He was a journalist," I continued.

"Here," I said excitedly, "are the family's horse and carriage. Here are individual portrait shots of Lola and Rachmil, and a family dinner with friends around the end of World War I." On and on we went, and, in some ways, in talking about them with such a captive audience, I felt as if we were breathing life into them again. As I held the photographs, I couldn't help but think about how my family members had once held them too. The thought sent shivers down my spine.

I'd seen only a half-dozen of the pictures before, and each new one was a revelation. Franya seemed even *more* joyful and full of fun in the theatrical shots, and even *more* awkward, and sapped of sparkle, when posing with her husband and the rest of the Punski family. Interestingly, the image of Franya in the water with her arms raised above her head came across as more ambivalent to me than it had to Serge. Yes, it conveyed a sense of freedom, but this was also a pose of surrender. Maybe I was looking through my Holocaust-tinted glasses (honestly, I always was), but it reminded me of a well-known image from the Warsaw ghetto of a ten-year-old boy in short trousers, an overcoat, and a cap being forced to raise his arms at gunpoint.

As we leafed through the collection, I wracked my brain for any story that might plausibly explain how the photos ended up in France. Tante Rivel, I now recalled, had traveled to Paris regularly to buy ornaments and silk flowers for her hat-making business, and in 1901, she bought a gold pocket watch there for my grandfather to present to my grandmother Meryl as an engagement gift. Did Tante Rivel have a friend or business associate in Paris to whom she had given the photos for safekeeping?

Aurore shared some new information as well: she had learned more about a younger brother of Franya's named Nisen, who at the start of the war was living in Paris with a wife and young son. Aurore had "the strong hunch," as she put it, that it was Nisen who brought the photographs to Choisy-le-Roi. Her theory was certainly compelling, not least because it put a family member in the right place at the right time, but I wasn't as sure. It made sense that Nisen's sisters, Franya and Raisel, would have given him pictures of themselves and their husbands. Why, though, would they have sent individual portrait shots of Lola and Rachmil Punski, Isaak's brothers and Franya's brothers-in-law? Nisen would only have known them through his sister, and, as they lived in different places, the connection was distant, surely. It was also unclear how the house in Choisy-le-Roi fitted into Aurore's theory, since official records showed Nisen living more than thirty minutes' drive away in the Marais, the old Jewish quarter, the same part of central Paris where the Mémorial de la Shoah now stood. Was there a record we hadn't yet found that would show Nisen and his family relocating to Choisy-le-Roi? Had he hidden out there to avoid arrest and worse?

The only information available at this juncture came from French roundup and deportation records. Aurore had looked up the name Rosenrot, under different spellings, and came across a Nysen Rozenrot, born in the same Warsaw neighborhood as Franya to parents with the same names as hers, who had been sent to Pithiviers, a Jewish internment camp fifty miles south of Paris, and from there, in June 1942, to Auschwitz.

According to information that I received from the archivists at auschwitz .org, he died less than a month later, of what camp doctors diagnosed as gastroenteritis aggravated by overall bodily weakness. He was just thirty-one years old.

⌒

Before we left the Mémorial building, I called Serge's daughter, Maïwenn, to my side. All morning I had been regaling her with tales about Tante Rivel, who always loomed as a glamorous figure in my mind—her tastes in fashion, the salons she'd hosted for artists and writers, and the way she'd smoked cigarettes through a long, dramatic holder. She seemed to reflect a kind of grandeur of bygone eras.

Ever since I'd begun corresponding with Serge, I'd been thinking about what I could give the Mogères that would equal in value what Serge's rescue of the photographs, and the memories they unlocked, had given to me and the rest of my family. I explained that to Maïwenn as I handed her a small red-velvet box.

"These belonged to my aunt Mollie," I explained, as Belle and I shared a knowing smile. These were part of the jewelry collection I had inherited upon Mollie's death. "Tante Rivel gave them to her at the end of her trip to Vilna in 1932. I want you to have them."

Maïwenn opened the box to reveal garnet earrings, sparkling in deep magenta, and faceted into the shape of flowers. She gasped. Tante Rivel had been determined to hand them down to the next generation, and I wanted my gift to convey that same sense of continuity of memory—a continuity that Serge safeguarded so carefully for forty years.

All three Mogères, Serge, Christèle, and Maïwenn, were astonished by the gesture. Several years later, Serge told me he remembered thinking, "Why give these earrings to people who are not family?" Then it hit him: "We were now members of the family."

It was true: we had built a bond that could not be broken. And I was now fully committed not just to the Mogère family, but to my own journey into the past. If Serge, who had known nothing about the Punskis and Rosenrots, was able to take such extraordinary care to rescue them from obscurity, how could I not follow his lead and work to recover every trace of their lives that I could find? To me, the gift of the photographs was an unmistakable sign: my job was to finish what Serge had started. I was no-where close to done.

We went to lunch at a nearby Jewish deli, where Maïwenn ordered a bagel with lox, her first ever. It was perhaps her way of acknowledging that she wasn't just a girl from Brittany anymore; she was part of a Jewish family too. Once again, I found it hard to believe that the Mogères would react and behave this way if they didn't have a meaningful connection of some kind to the war and its legacy.

As it turned out, they did. But I wouldn't learn the details until the following summer on Bastille Day, when my husband, Steven, and I returned to France to stay with Serge in Brittany. We rented a car and drove five hours to the coast, just across from the Isle of Jersey. (We were right at home—it was the Jersey Shore!) We drove past medieval relics and lush countryside, then finally arrived at a lovely country house, which was exactly as I might have pictured for an artist. It was warm and welcoming, with Serge's work on every wall.

When Serge showed us to our bedroom, I was struck by his art on the wall. There were two watercolor paintings of nude women whose likeness to Franya was uncanny. There she was, with the posture and expressions I recognized from two of the publicity stills he had rescued. The women had the same coloring as Franya, her expressive eyes, and even the same heart-shaped lips. I ran out to the living room to ask Serge if she was the inspiration for the nudes, but he had no idea what I was talking about. Any resemblance was unconscious. As I pointed out the details to him, for the first time he realized that she had penetrated his psyche. Franya was his muse.

Over a steak dinner (what they imagined Americans liked to eat) and traditional gâteau Breton dessert, he began to share some extraordinary family stories, particularly about his mother's experiences during and after the war. Long before he was born, Serge's mother, Madeleine Formentin, had been married to a member of the Resistance who fought and died in the Berry region, on the border between the German-occupied North of France and the nominally "free zone" that persisted for two years after the Nazi invasion. After she was widowed, Madeleine raised two sons in a tiny two-room apartment in a working-class area of Paris, where she had to put up with persistent, false rumors that her strikingly blond younger son was the result of a relationship with a Nazi officer—a phenomenon the French like to call *la collaboration horizontale*. But Madeleine was no collaborator. Quite the opposite.

One day, after her husband had been killed but while she was still pregnant with their second child, word went out that the French police and the Gestapo were in the area rounding up Jews and were about to raid her building. The warning wasn't enough time for Madeleine's Jewish neighbors. The building was on a cul-de-sac, and there was no way to escape without running directly into the police line. The apartment next to Madeleine's was occupied by a Jewish woman with an infant son, and soon she was knocking frantically at Madeleine's door. The police had already come once, she said, but she hadn't answered, and they'd gone away without forcing their way in. She did not think she would be so lucky this second time. Without hesitation Madeleine ushered the woman and her baby into the kitchen, which was partitioned off from the rest of the apartment and thus not visible from the entranceway.

As Madeleine described it, she never feared for her own safety. Her only concern was that the baby would cry and give them away because the walls were thin, and it was not always easy to tell whose door the police were banging on. Mercifully, the baby stayed quiet. To make room for her new houseguests, Madeleine made other arrangements for herself: she moved in with her late husband's mother in the countryside and had her second baby there. By the time she returned almost two years later, the war was over and the Jewish woman and her son were able to safely move back into their own home. Madeleine's generosity had saved their lives.

Serge was matter-of-fact about this story, which seemed extraordinary to me. "My mother was no hero," he told me. "She just hated the Germans, and she wasn't going to leave a woman she knew at their mercy." Madeleine, he explained, was from the North of France, which meant that her family had suffered deeply during the Franco-Prussian War of 1870, and again during World War I. Resisting *les boches*, a derogatory term that the French had used for the Germans for generations, was a deeply ingrained response.

Serge was equally matter-of-fact about another revelation: his own back-story. After the war, his mother went to work as a seamstress for a Jewish clothing manufacturer and became romantically involved with him. Ulti-mately, he cheated on her, and she responded by striking up an affair with an art student from Guadeloupe, Dédé Mogère, whom she met in an under-ground jazz club. Soon after, Madeleine realized she was pregnant—with Serge. The clothing manufacturer offered to raise the coming child as his own. Though she may have accepted that plan at first, in the end his mother married his biological father—that art student from the jazz club—when Serge was five years old.

I was floored by this story. Serge may not have been raised Jewish, but he certainly understood from an early age that his mother had connections to Jews in their neighborhood. He even had memories of meeting the clothing manufacturer when he was little. He also knew what it meant to have a cloudy history, wrapped up in complicated identity. In my mind, this had to be part of the reason he'd felt such an affinity for Franya and the Punskis.

Serge, though, did not see it this way. He never thought of himself as having a Jewish side and resisted the idea that he needed one to feel a con-nection in the rubble of the Maison Danton. Growing up, he'd been much more connected to being half-Black, awash in the fraught complexities of French colonial history. Even this, though, was not something he saw as a defining characteristic, especially as his ethnicity was ambiguous to an out-side eye. Rather, he thought of himself as having forged his own path, sepa-rate from either of his parents. He liked to view the world as if from above, as an observer, a student of history, and an artist.

As soon as I heard the story about Madeleine saving her Jewish neighbors during the war, I asked to meet Serge's mother. But Serge hadn't been able to see or speak to his mother for ten years—not because of animosity between them, but for reasons to do with his relationship with his younger sister, who was Madeleine's caretaker. Families are always complicated.

I traveled to Paris again in May of the following year. At that point, my interest in talking about the war helped Serge break the impasse. Describing my story, he had pressed for a family meeting at which all of us—Serge, Maïwenn, his mother, his sister, and I—would be present. I loved the idea that perhaps Serge could reconnect with his family as a result of this strange journey. Maïwenn had not seen her grandmother in ten years! We gathered at a "neutral location," an empty North African café in Choisy-le-Roi decorated in bright colors, not far from where Serge's mother and sister lived. I didn't know, going in, what kind of family fireworks to expect, but from the moment we sat down at a booth, everyone was completely cordial.

Madeleine was ninety-seven years old by then but in remarkably good shape, animated (like her son), quick-witted, and happy to answer any queries I threw at her. She wore a pageboy hat, her white hair tucked beneath, a crisp collared shirt, and oval wire glasses. As she talked about the Gestapo raid on her building and her decision to shelter the Jewish mother and her baby, she was no more inclined than Serge to see her actions as out of the ordinary. "When the opportunity comes to save someone, you take a moment, but you don't really think about it," she said. "You either do it or you don't."

She said this as if it was the most natural thing in the world, no big deal for a young single mother to risk everything for a neighbor she barely knew. I thought about the importance of human connection, of the relationships that had been lost and now gained. My eyes welling, I said, "If my cousin Franya had had someone like you, she might have lived."

Afterward, Serge pulled me aside. "I brought you together with your family," he said, "and you've brought me back together with mine."

7

The Vilna Ghetto

"THE PEN IS FROZEN BETWEEN THE FINGERS AND
SCREAMS—BUT THE FINGERS CANNOT WRITE"

MY OBSESSION WITH learning about Franya was becoming more con-suming by the day. Sometimes, I felt I could almost sense my actress cousin beside me, urging me on. There had to be more information available. Still, as my research broadened, I kept bumping into uncomfortable evidence that the stories I'd heard from Mollie as a child—especially ones involving my relatives' experience with the Nazis—did not always match the records. From the documents we'd unearthed, I now knew that Lola most likely did not jump off a train heading to Auschwitz. Rachmil was not gunned down on the streets of Berlin.

In some cases, Mollie had offered more than one version of the same story. When I was in high school, she told me that Franya was in fact killed *outside* a concentration camp because she had been identified as a notable person capable of causing trouble among the inmates. I wondered: If this was the great mystery contained in *Twenty-One and One*, why bother insisting that the book was off-limits? While some of the false narratives were surely a result of missing information, the fact was that Molly had read the forbidden book at some point. In the end, she knew at least some of what had happened to Franya. Again, in my most anxious moments, my mind wandered to untenable places: What if Franya had been an informant? Was that why I wasn't meant to read the book?

I had dug up her personal testimonials about Franya and Isaak that Mollie sent to Yad Vashem toward the end of her life, and these, too, contained a number of errors. Mollie wrote that she'd seen Franya perform in *The Dybbuk*, a famous production by the most prominent of all the traveling Yiddish theater ensembles of the prewar era, the Vilna Troupe. But I knew from Mollie's journals and letters that the play she'd seen in 1932 was *Motke the Thief*, not *The Dybbuk*. And while Franya had been part of several ensembles that performed in the city of Vilna and toured extensively, she was never, to my knowledge, a member of the Vilna Troupe.

Some of these errors were more understandable than others. Mollie did not have access to the online resources I did and could not easily check her memory against official records. When she wrote, for example, that Franya was born in "Białystok, I think, or thereabouts" instead of Warsaw, it was almost certainly an honest mistake. Her belief that Franya had been in the Vilna Troupe was based, as she wrote on the form, on a group photograph she'd seen in her three-volume history, *Jerusalem of Lithuania*, in which Franya was seated near Ida Kaminska, a celebrated performer who *had* been in the Vilna Troupe.

That said, the forms Mollie completed were designed to give Yad Vashem information for the record, and it was clearly more important to estimate than to leave no history. All my life, Mollie had drilled me on the importance of memory. She corrected every little thing I got wrong and warned me that the price of failing to remember the past could be another Holocaust. Yet she clearly had to estimate some of what she shared in 1991.

Though I was surprised by some of Mollie's mistakes, I considered them *zakhor*. They represented a kind of remembrance, Mollie's best understanding of the truth. In many ways, a deep connection to our history seemed more important than the minutia. It was also a matter of expectations. I thought of Mollie more as a storyteller in the *Litvak* tradition than as a scrupulous historian. What mattered to her was telling the *stories*, not nitpicking every factual detail. With that mindset, it wouldn't have been too much of a stretch for her to tell Yad Vashem that Franya was "next to" Ida Kaminska in the group portrait she'd seen in her three-volume history when, in reality, someone else was sitting between them. That was a minor detail.

Mollie wasn't just imparting information about Franya and Isaak; she was *making a case* for them, as families do. If that meant a little exaggeration here and there, I wasn't necessarily opposed to it. After all, who, if not she, should control the narrative? If anything, I was impressed by how accurate many of Mollie's stories turned out to be. I wondered, in researching the practice, how likely it was that my grandfather Michel would have made those two brass kettles sitting on my mantel from a discarded prosthetic limb. I learned that brass was in fact commonly used to make replacement arms and legs in nineteenth-century Europe. Separately, I looked into some of the stories about Lebele *der meshugene*, my grandfather's simpleminded friend, during his service in the czar's army. One such story had him and Lebele on a ship on the Caspian Sea as they made their way from Russia to the Middle East. While most of the men were sleeping, so the story went, Lebele lifted the wooden spoons they kept in their boots and threw them all overboard, greatly angering the soldiers when they woke up. As I grew older, I doubted that soldiers would really keep spoons in their boots, but my reading taught me that this was indeed a phenomenon in the Russian army and persisted well after the czarist era.

The persuasiveness of these details outweighed any misgivings I had about Mollie's reliability. I did notice one typical Mollie touch in her submissions to Yad Vashem, however. Asked to provide information about the circumstances of Franya's death, she wrote simply: "See *21 and 1*." Seemingly, she didn't want even casual browsers flipping through Yad Vashem's files to find out the truth without adequate forewarning. Or maybe she'd had a hunch that one day, I or other family members would seek out her testimonial documents. Maybe *we* were the ones she wanted to continue protecting from the ugly truth.

⁓

MY FIRST REAL CLUE ABOUT FRANYA'S FINAL DAYS CAME FROM MY VISIT TO the Mémorial de La Shoah. Aurore knew I didn't want her to give me a full rundown, but she agreed to feed me small crumbs of information that quenched my hunger and satiated me for the time being. I figured that I could use those bits as a foundation for more research while still honoring my pledge not to read the book. As it turned out, Aurore explained, Franya had not died in Vilna or in the pits at Ponary, as I had suspected. Instead, she had perished in Ashmyany, a town thirty-five miles to the southeast that had been Polish Oszmiana when Vilna was part of Poland, but was incorporated into Lithuania as part of the Vilna district after the Soviet annexation of 1940. Now, it was in Belarus. Naturally, I looked up Ashmyany in the many books about World War II I'd been amassing and realized, with horror, that the area was associated with a notorious act of Jewish cooperation with the Nazi genocide. Was this the reason my aunt had wanted to shield me from the truth? Was Franya involved in killing her fellow Jews? I felt sick to my stomach.

According to their records, in October 1942, the Nazis ordered the Jewish ghetto authorities in Vilna to send police officers to Ashmyany and select 1,500 Jews there for liquidation. The policemen were given special dark-blue uniforms and peaked caps with Star of David emblems and were initially greeted with joy when their cars pulled up. The locals thought perhaps they were being placed under more sympathetic Jewish authority after sixteen months of hell at the hands of the Germans and their Lithuanian helpers. Soon, though, dozens of Jewish officers were engaged in the grim task of assessing who among the 4,000 people remaining in the Ashmyany ghetto was contributing meaningfully to the German war effort—and who was expendable. Widowed women and children were the Nazis' prime targets.

Of course, the police officers didn't tell the Jews of Ashmyany any of this. Rather, they claimed they were choosing women for a new work assignment in another town, and their children would be allowed to go with them. People were unsure whether to believe this. After all, they'd been misled again and again. Also, the Jewish policemen showed little empathy in their selection interviews and insisted that they, not the townsfolk, would have the final word on who went. According to one report, the senior policeman in Ashmyany, Felix Dessler, brandished a revolver and turned it over in his hands as he peppered his interviewees with assessments and questions about their contribution. That would hardly be comforting.

Over the next two days, the officers sent their recommendations to the ghetto leadership in Vilna, and the ghetto leaders did what they could to reduce the number of people marked for death. They told the Nazis that most of the women whose husbands had been killed earlier in the war were now gainfully employed and, therefore, not as expendable as first thought. The Gestapo agreed to bring the number down from 1,500 to 800, then finally to 600.

On October 23, the entire Ashmyany ghetto was summoned to the town's main square. Almost everyone showed up. Whatever their misgivings, they chose to put their faith in the fact that Jews, not Nazis, now appeared to be in charge. Indeed, when a resistance fighter working undercover with the ghetto police tried to warn them that they were being earmarked for liquidation, they refused to believe her. Only when the Jewish police started going house to house to look for stragglers and began the chillingly familiar process of ordering people to the left or right to determine who would live and who would die did the Jews of Ashmyany realize how wrong they had been.

The atmosphere in the square quickly turned from cautiously optimistic to panic filled. Someone in the crowd began to chant *El male Rahamim*, the funeral prayer for the dead, and others, including some of the Jewish policemen, burst into tears. In the end, 406 people, most of them old or sick, were driven to a freshly dug pit a few miles out of town and shot by Lithuanian militia men under Nazi supervision.

As I read about the history, it didn't take long to understand that Franya was more likely to have been a victim of this horror than a perpetrator—if she was involved at all. Still, the tragic story introduced the very real possibility that she, like the Jewish police officers sent to Ashmyany, could have been forced to commit terrible acts over which she had limited or no control. Such were the appalling moral choices that life under Nazi occupation presented.

For many Jews, in Vilna and in Ashmyany, the killings of October 1942 pointed to an irredeemable corruption and depravity in the Judenrat (the Jewish-run administrative bodies that governed all Jewish ghettos). It was proof that they would stop at nothing, not even the murder of their fellow

Jews, to save their own skins. Many took to calling the Judenrat the *Juden-verrat*, a play on words that, with one extra syllable, turned "Jewish council" into "betrayal of the Jews."

There were other points of view, however. Jakob Gens, the controversial head of the Vilna Judenrat, felt he'd done what he could to save as many people from death as possible. In a public meeting a few days after the killings, Gens freely acknowledged the anguish that the episode had caused, calling it "one of the most terrible tragedies of Jewish life, when Jews lead Jews to death." But, he argued, he'd had no better choice. "At a moment when five million are no more," he said, "it is incumbent upon us to save the strong and the young, not only in age but in spirit, and not play with sentiments."

Gens had sympathizers as well as detractors, people who understood the extraordinary pressures he was under and refused to rush to judgment. Since he was married to a Lithuanian Catholic, he could have been exempted from living in the ghetto at all. Indeed, his wife often begged him to leave for the sake of their fifteen-year-old daughter, but he told her, "My place is in the ghetto." That earned him considerable respect. Where many saw the ghetto police collecting onerous fines day in and day out and raged that they were shamelessly lining their pockets at the expense of their fellow Jews, others saw evidence of a more subtle strategy because Gens would frequently use these funds to bribe the Nazis into sparing people's lives. "On several occasions," one ghetto diarist reported, "[Gens] successfully intervened to free prisoners on the eve of their execution."

The way Gens saw it, saving the lives of even a few justified his cooperation with the Nazi death machine. Shortly before he was himself killed by the Nazis in September 1943, Gens said that if anyone was to be left in the Vilna ghetto by the time the Germans were defeated, he would have "a quiet heart and a pure conscience" in the knowledge that he'd done his duty to his people.

I had every faith that Franya was a good person and ardently wished she'd been able to die with her own quiet heart and pure conscience. Still, I continued to worry about the price the Nazis might have forced her to pay before she reached the end. Certainly, Mollie would have wanted to protect us from knowing that.

———

VILNA UNDER THE NAZIS WAS NOT SOLELY A PLACE OF HORROR AND MORAL compromise. It was also a place of spiritual resistance, where artists, actors, and writers worked to perpetuate some semblance of the life and culture they had known before the war. In their own way, they used their creative prowess as a weapon against the Nazis' efforts to erase their humanity. They wrote journals and poems and songs, they preserved valuable documents and collected Jewish folklore, they set up a lending library, and they organized a variety of performances, exhibitions, and lectures. Despite the constant, oppressive presence of hunger, misery, and death, they set out to imbue the ghetto experience with as much nobility as they could.

When I wasn't harboring fears about Franya's terrible truth, I allowed myself to imagine the opposite—that she had been part of this vibrant movement of artists who so valiantly rebelled against oppression.

I decided that, for the sake of my sanity, I should explore the history of this theatrical movement too. Not only did it carry more lightness, inspiration to balance desperation, but it also seemed core to understanding Franya. Maybe there would be clues here to her trajectory.

I learned that the Yiddish avant-garde that persevered during this impossible period had been a long time coming. Even before the turn of the twentieth century, Jewish writers and artists with "serious" literary tastes had complained about a theater culture they found creaky, sentimental, and hollow. The turn-of-the-century Yiddish stage was dominated by operetta, which too often recycled the same tired plotlines about love triangles and young people disobeying their parents, as well as formulaic musical numbers and arrangements. Intellectuals, including Yitskhok Leybush Peretz, one of the leading writers and playwrights of the period, made several attempts to interest Yiddish audiences in something more high-minded, but the operettas proved wildly popular and nothing else could compete. An exasperated Peretz said the popular theater was as noisy and chaotic as "Noah's ark with all of the animals," an insult seemingly directed at the audience's lack of sophistication as much as the contrivances and crocodile tears spilling from the stage.

With the arrival of World War I came an idea actually spawned by the Germans occupying Vilna for the first but not the last time: Perhaps a Yiddish theater might be a persuasive way to win the hearts and minds of the city's Jewish population? Much of Vilna's intellectual elite had fled the German advance in the summer of 1915, but the idea of founding a Union of Yiddish Dramatic Arts was taken up enthusiastically by a group of young refugees from the Russian front, almost all of them amateurs with little or no stage experience. The fact that this group had no precedent to draw on proved more of an advantage than a disadvantage. They ended up devouring everything they could read about Stanislavski and the Moscow Art Theater and set their own artistic goals from scratch. Unlike traditional Yiddish performers, they fostered ensemble playing instead of promoting stars. They strove to integrate every detail—set design, lighting, costumes, makeup—into the overall artistic vision of the piece. And they believed, above all, in the integrity of performance. That meant learning their parts inside and out and delivering them with passion and nuance. They didn't want to muddle their way through productions, the way many theater companies had done before the war because of the pressure of putting on a new show every few weeks. And they certainly weren't interested in parading in front of the audience at intermission, as Yiddish headliners often liked to, because it would break the theatrical illusion they were striving to create.

As the war progressed, food shortages intensified to the point where members of the troupe were subsisting on just one potato a day and would faint from hunger during rehearsals. Typhoid and dysentery were rife. Yet the show went on and became a sensation. War and adversity helped strip away the frivolity of theatrical performance (as it would again in the ghetto under even grimmer circumstances a quarter century later) and intensified the emotional truths the actors were able to communicate to their audiences. The troupe's first production was ostensibly a light comedy, Sholem Asch's *The Compatriot*. But its plot, about a European Jew in New York refusing to assimilate into the city's German American culture, served as

Family home to the left of the Trinity Gate, Vilna 1930s postcard.

Cousin Basha Punski, Franya's niece, Vilna, approx. 1937, presumed murdered.

grandmother, Meryl Kagan Boyarski Bayroff.

From left to right: Soma Punski, Uncle Yudel Punski, Tante Rivel Kagan Lichtenberg, Israel (Lola) Punski, Isaac Punski, Franya Rosenrot Punski (Franya Winter) Vilna, approx. 1925.

פֿראַניע ווינטער

די פֿרוי פֿון אָנגעדענקעם מוחר יצחק פּונסקי. א כאװנס ייִדיש וײיבל. א מוסטער־ייִדלעך. אין פֿריִער צײט א זאַק און שפּאָנדל אין האַנט — אַזוי איז זי געווען אין פֿריװאַטן לעבן.

סימפּאַטישע קינדער ניט געזאָנט. אָן די דאָזיקע פֿאַרליבע פֿרוי, שוין מיט א ביסל אַשטריקלעכ אין די האָר, איז זי באַליובטע און שאָלאָמנודעטע סוישפּילערין פֿראַניע ווינטער'ם.

פֿראַנידל ראַמענראַט. געבוירען אין דער וואָרשעוונער פֿאָרשטאָט סיאָנע. אין 1896. די פֿאָקטער פֿון אַם־פֿאַרשעליבעכ חסידישע עלטערן. דער פֿאָטער איז לאַנגע יאָרן בלינד געווען. שטענדיק געטשטעט געזונגען. א שיין פֿנימל מיט א זום שטיּ מעדלע האָט זי געהאַט. שוין די פֿרעכיש לירדלע געווונען. און כדי צו העלפֿן איז זי אויסגעטראָטן אַן אומפֿאַרטאָנט אין קאַבאַרעטאָן און רעװויטעאטאַסקלעדער. 1917

זינגען. אין קאַלרישער מונטער סטאַנפּער. זעך פֿאַלשער מאַרט אַ אַלרעם מונטס. וואָ עם פֿאַרליבט זיך אין אַ קרוים. זי טענדט ווי דאַן צום ייִדישן סטאַמ־דירקטער בוים ליפּאַוונסקי. ער זאַנ ווי אויר העלפֿן זיך באַ פֿרײען און איר פֿאַרשפּילעג. ליפּאַווסקי דראַם דעם קרוים. און ער טענ אים אָנקלאַן אין פֿאַרפֿירד מינדעראיעריקען. און דאָרן קריסט לאַמט אי צדה.

ווען וײילנע װערטע אָנגעשלאָסן צו פּוילן. גײט ער פֿון פּוילן מעציאַסור סטאַאסער ראַדין. (דער פֿאָטער פֿון דער שוי־שפּילערין נאַדיע ראַדינע). קײן וײילנע. זי טרעט אויף אויף זיך טעאַ

Franya Winter in *Twenty-One and One.*

Franya, publicist shots, mid-1920s.

Franya at the Seaside, location and date unknown. *(From the collection of Serge Mogère at Memorial de la Shoah, Paris, France.)*

Franya's Internal Passport, 1922. *(Lithuanian State Archives.)*

Rudolf Zaslavsky in *Tevye the Milkman*,
unknown date. *(YIVO.)*

Rudolf Zaslavsky, date unknown. *(YIVO.)*

Rudolf Zaslavsky (left) theater program for performance of *Tevye the Milkman* starring Rudolf
Zaslavsky as Tevye, F. Winter as Tzitle (Cajtl) and Sz. Blecher as Fedja, from 1931 tour. *(YIVO Archives.)*

Mollie and cousin Rachmil Punski, who perished in Dachau only weeks before liberation (Berlin, 1932).

Mollie Bayroff, 1960s.

Mollie and her friend Rose Cole in Berlin, 1932.

Abraham Joseph Rosenrot, brother of Franya. *(From the collection of Serge Mogère at Memorial de la Shoah, Paris, France.)*

When I die, when I pass away, when I won't be here anymore, this postcard will remind you of a brother who loved you.
Abramek Rozenrot
To beloved sister Frania

The Rosenrot Family: (left top) Nisen Rosenrot and Mizda Grinfas Rosenrot (left bottom) Susie Otakovsky Rosenrot, Jacques Rosenrot, and Abraham Rosenrot, approx. 1929, Paris. *(From the collection of Léa Rosenrot Guinet.)*

Victims of massacre at Ponary. *(Unite States Holocaust Memorial Museum.)*

Examining photos at Memorial de la Shoah, Paris, with Serge Mogère and Aurore Blaise.

Fania Yocheles Brantsovsky, last surviving partisan of the Vilna Ghetto, translating Ghetto Yiddish Theater poster starring Shabai Blecher, 2017.

Irina Guzenberg, translating an article, "Franya was beloved above all," 2017.

From left to right: Meryl Frank, Carol Frank, Rosalie (Ricky) Bayroff Frank, Alvin Frank, Cathy Frank, Charlene Frank, 1965.

Meryl Frank with Franya's nephew, Marcel Rozenrot, at Hopital Rothschild, Paris, November 2021.

Meryl Frank in Ashmyany, Belarus.

a manifesto to assert the troupe's Jewish identity, and as a politically bold declaration of independence from the German forces occupying the city.

Soon the Vilna Troupe, as it became known, was putting on a new play every two weeks and experimenting more and more. The ragtag group of amateurs quickly matured into consummate professionals who rehearsed all day, performed every evening, and often stayed up late into the night to critique and improve their work. In less than a year, the Vilna Troupe left the city to go on a near-permanent tour, first to Kovno (now Kaunas, in Lithuania) and Warsaw and, eventually, to the capitals of Western Europe and the Americas. In the United States, they traveled to major cities like New York, Philadelphia, and Baltimore. Later, when Franya joined the scene, touring was still the norm, though more within Europe.

The constant travel represented another unique element to the company's theatrical style, an encapsulation of the nomadic experience of European Jews. This was reflected in the fluid lives the actors lived, in the need for portable sets that could be transported and rebuilt on a nightly basis, and in the variety of locations they visited and creative ideas they absorbed. The actors also helped make the case—along with a new generation of Jewish novelists, poets, and playwrights—that the Yiddish language was not some inferior dialectal cousin of German, as the guardians of high Germanic culture liked to think. It was a linguistic force in its own right, with the power to span oceans and universalize centuries of Jewish soulfulness and suffering.

Franya would have known all about the Vilna Troupe, I imagined, especially in the wake of their landmark production of *The Dybbuk*, the story of a young woman possessed by a demonic spirit, which opened in Warsaw in 1920 and became their biggest international hit. She was never part of the troupe herself, but was soon appearing in similarly audacious Yiddish-language productions and building her own formidable reputation. Among her first shows in Vilna was *Yankele*, a musical about a yeshiva student who makes fun of his teachers for their religious orthodoxy. This was unusual not only because it featured a thirteen-year-old protagonist, but also because all the boy parts were played, provocatively, by women. Soon after, in 1922, Franya appeared for the first time in *Motke the Thief*, the play Aunt Mollie would see a decade later. Sholem Asch's epic coming-of-age story about a career criminal finding material success, only to confront his own moral degradation, would later become an important model for Hollywood gangster movies like *Scarface* and *Little Caesar*. Franya played a circus tight-rope walker who uses her acrobatic skills to defraud a crooked pawnbroker and helps Motke wriggle his way out of trouble.

As long as she was with Lipowski's company in Vilna, Franya appeared at the Philharmonic Hall, only steps away from my family's house. I loved to envision her waving good-bye to her castmates after a rehearsal or a performance, sighing as she emerged outside and began walking along the cobblestones, which glimmered below illuminated streetlamps.

I figured that this close proximity might be connected to how she met my cousin Isaak. He had performed at the Philharmonic himself as an amateur violinist. Perhaps they met backstage after a show, or maybe Tante Rivel invited Franya to the house for one of her regular artistic salons, where vodka and hoppy beer flowed. Either way, I pictured them meeting in a crowded room, a moment of calm amid the chaos. Isaak would no doubt have worn a straw hat and bow tie, Franya perhaps a drop-waist dress or pleated skirt. How exciting she must have seemed to him, an actress with undeniable charisma and unabashed humor. How safe he must have seemed to her—a sensible man, a successful businessman with an interest in music, from a good family. His aunt Rivel was a patron of the arts, liberal, glamorous, and educated in a way Franya's parents could never understand. The couple married in 1923. Suddenly, the Hasidic girl from Warsaw's impoverished Praga neighborhood had financial security, something she had never known before.

Soon Franya was also performing for bigger names, including Ida Kaminska and Zygmund Turkow, the founders of the Warsaw Jewish Art Theater, who invited her into their traveling company in 1925. Among the shows they performed was *Green Fields*, a comedy about a Jewish family living in an isolated rural area and the romantic misadventures that ensue when a young Jewish scholar comes calling.

A spirit of heady, youthful rebellion inspired many of these productions, not unlike the spirit that propelled Franya into the theater in the first place.

Thematically, the plays she appeared in were about breaking down barriers, rejecting tradition, courting controversy, and, ultimately, creating a space in which European Jews could be unabashedly modern, a legitimate part of the cultural conversation. At the crossroads of myriad languages and cultures, Vilna was the ideal city in which to experiment with these notions. The vibrant Jewish population was nothing if not a receptive audience, the city at that time a center of Yiddish literature, political organizing, and cultural leadership.

From her publicity shots alone, it's obvious that Franya threw herself headlong into each of her projects. I lost hours examining the images I knew from my childhood and those that Serge saved, wondering how she managed to transform herself, always projecting a brilliant light. She could be innocent or playful, sensual or outrageous, as the material demanded. Nothing about her stage persona offered even a hint of the modesty of her religious roots.

Even as the avant-garde gained steam, operettas continued to be wildly popular, and Franya performed in those too. She had all the necessary skills: she could sing, she could dance, she was funny, and she had the acting chops to breathe life into even these tired stereotypes. I loved reading the reviews I found of her various performances, both because of the insight they offered and because they transported me to a different time and place. I could just envision the anticipation of the audience, the packed theaters, the laughter and gasps ringing out to punctuate the plot.

Observing one of Franya's many performances with the Palais Theater troupe, the editor of the Yiddish-language daily *Vilner Tag* was struck by her versatility and temperament, even with such light material, and declared her to be a "fine actress . . . very powerful, passionate and delightful." The Russian-language daily *Vilenskoye Utro* (Vilna Morning) was so enamored that it took the unusual step of publishing a poem on its front page to praise her selfless devotion to her craft and to her fellow actors. "Sincere tender feelings are born in you," it raved, "from a true artistic soul." Avant-garde or broad operettas—I would have given anything to watch either, seeing it all just once for myself. I owed my early theatergoing experiences to Mollie, who took me to see shows from *Pippin* to *The Threepenny Opera*. But, not surprisingly, I developed a special interest in Yiddish theater history above all else.

Not everything Franya did was Yiddish in origin, a sign of the changing times. One big hit from 1924 was a musical bedroom farce, *The Virtuous Susanna*, which involved the collaboration of a French composer, a German lyricist, and a plot derived loosely from the story of Susanna and the Elders in the book of Daniel. Franya, in the title role, won what one critic in Vilna called "the explosive endorsement of the audience." It was also an opportunity to work with Leib Shriftsetzer, a beloved comedy veteran whose direction was praised for its inventiveness and deft management of multiple characters, all trying to hide their sexual exploits from each other.

Franya's ability to switch modes—from dark, edgy drama to comedy, and from high art to vaudeville and musicals—made her unusual and highly sought after. From 1927 to 1929, she had a two-year contract with the New Jewish Theater in Riga, where several of the beloved publicity shots were taken. By the time she returned, she was hailed almost universally as a "prima donna," which meant, in this context, a leading lady or star, garnering her the best roles and the adoration of audiences. Once again, as I read reviews by critics from all across Poland and the Baltic states that invoked that term for Franya, I smiled at how I'd assumed Mollie was exaggerating when she'd described our cousin that way. Certainly, Franya had been well known.

After her contract ran out, she was on the road again, traveling abroad with her fellow actors to Poland, France, and Romania on journeys that were both exhausting and exhilarating. Packed houses roared with laughter and fervor. Then, in 1930 and 1931, she took the role of the female lead in a company run by Rudolf Zaslavsky, one of the leading male actors of the day. It was, as their friend Blecher would describe it, a "fateful encounter."

⁓

ZASLAVSKY WAS A LARGER-THAN-LIFE FIGURE, ALMOST PREPOSTEROUSLY SO. He'd found fame as a young man performing as the first Yiddish-language Hamlet, and then again as the original Tevye the Milkman, the character who would find worldwide fame after World War II as the protagonist of *Fiddler on the Roof.* When Zaslavsky came to America in 1924, the *New York Times* called him "the Edwin Booth of Soviet Russia," referring to the preeminent actor of classical American theater, and his peers on the Yiddish stage did not disagree. "As a dramatic actor he had no equal," a former member of his company, Abram Nuger, wrote years after his death. Not only did Zaslavsky have a rich, beautiful voice capable of expressing the subtlest feelings, but he was also dramatic as a personality. "He knew how to wear a tailcoat with royal chic," Nuger remembered, "and fenced like a Spanish hidalgo." I hired researchers to scout Yiddish, Russian, Polish, Lithuanian, and Latvian newspapers for any mentions of Franya and Rudolf Zaslavsky and found a treasure trove of articles, announcements, posters, and reviews.

When Rudolf and Franya met, he had dark hair that he combed back and parted to the side. His classic boyish looks—piercing close-set eyes, a straight nose, narrow lips—were like the perfect blank canvas for his various roles. Carrying a kind of grace, he reserved a debonair half smile for the ladies.

Zaslavsky's wife, Bertha, was an actress who often went on tour with him herself. Indeed, during the 1927–1928 season, the Zaslavskys had performed together in Vilna, and it's quite likely that they, Franya, and Isaak had all met and socialized together. The theater scene was a tight one.

Franya and Rudolf were, in many ways, polar opposites. By all accounts she was unpretentious and unspoiled, a team player who kept her ego in check and worked with her fellow actors to bring out their best. According to her friend Blecher, whom I knew only as the author of the forbidden book, she not only studied her lines rigorously but would also stand for hours in front of the mirror to practice facial expressions. She was always first to the theater to do her makeup and change, and she made a point of being kind and considerate to everyone around her.

Zaslavsky, on the other hand, was opinionated and arrogant and didn't care who knew it. He believed fervently in theater as high art, but more fervently still in the cult of Rudolf Zaslavsky. When he arrived at the theater, he expected to be treated as the legend he believed himself to be. Forget the ethos of the ensemble; in every production he had to be the sun, moon, and stars around whom everyone else revolved. As the lore goes, once when on tour in Kiev as Tevye, one of his fellow actors dared complain that the poster for the show mentioned no other performers. (This was apparently in a time before agents made such contractual arrangements.) Zaslavsky wasn't pleased. He marched the other man out into the street to look at the sign and recited the poster's multiple mentions of him as director, star, and "leading figure of the Jewish stage." Then, he told his costar to "go hang" himself.

Tales circulated about Zaslavsky browbeating actors as well, which came up repeatedly in my research. "Your elbows are sewn to your sides and your hands are dangling like helpless wings!" Nuger remembered him yelling at one fellow performer. In a production of Ibsen's *Ghosts*, Zaslavsky took particular pleasure in tormenting his costar, Katina Plavina, who had a habit of blanking on her lines and was playing his mother. At the climax in the third act, Zaslavsky, playing the tortured Oswald, cried out to Plavina, "What kind of life was it that you gave me?" When he received no response, he ad-libbed several rounds of "Mama, Mama!" and, leaning over so the audience couldn't see his hands, pinched Plavina hard several times on the butt. This behavior would not have gone over so well today.

Plavina was so shocked that she burst into tears, prompting the audience, who assumed she was in character, to applaud loudly. "Oh, Plavele-mamele!" Zaslavsky said afterward. "Forgive me! I was so immersed in the role, I don't know how it happened. How about that applause, though?"

From fellow actor Shabtai Blecher, I would later learn that Franya and Zaslavsky had a passionate affair. She fell hard for the actor. And Blecher was in a position to know. I found not only that he had appeared in many other productions with her, but also that he was with both Franya and Zaslavsky every step of the way as a fellow member of the touring company in 1931. Blecher was clearly her confidant, the close proximity in which they lived leaving little room for secrets.

At first when I learned of the affair, I wondered why she would jeopardize the stability of her relationship with my cousin Isaak. But one need only look at the family portraits to see how she shrank and dulled in that environment. For someone for whom drama and human experience was so fundamental, the quiet hum of normal home life might have felt suffocating. It also might just have been that, as many costars do today, she and Zaslavsky got caught up in the romance of their onstage relationship. The adrenaline that comes with performance is intoxicating by comparison to humdrum daily stresses, especially when a dashing leading man is showing interest in you.

From Serge's photographs I sensed that Isaak and Franya's marriage might have lacked chemistry. One could explain away how stiff she and Isaak looked in the group portraits. But even when posing alone as a couple, Franya's natural liveliness appeared muted. Isaak looked awkward at her side as well. Or maybe things went sour because Franya was constantly touring. I could only speculate. Still, I could imagine that Franya found Zaslavsky to be a force of nature, commanding and volcanic, and he found her to be a match for him—a talented, playful, quick-witted partner. He and Franya were both versatile, strong-willed artists who had broken away from traditional backgrounds and found their calling in the theater. Despite their different personalities, they had a lot in common.

It is difficult to imagine Zaslavsky seducing Franya before he'd sought to rattle her, the way he liked to rattle all the actors he worked with. He would have found it difficult to resist skewering her popularity as a musical comedy star. It was his avant-garde art, he insisted, that was truly "for the masses," while the operetta companies served only to dazzle and mislead. Franya might have called him out on this, the way she had pushed back against other bullying men in the past, like the stalker in Minsk. And, if so, that may have caused him to look at her as an ideal sparring partner—a challenge. Had that, in classic romantic-comedy tradition stretching back to *The Taming of the Shrew*, caused sparks to fly?

Despite my research, I couldn't find answers to that question—or about what came next. For now, I would have to be satisfied with understanding more about this chapter of Franya's life without knowing the rest.

⌣

UNFORTUNATELY, THERE WERE DARKER FORCES AT WORK AND BIGGER OBstacles to overcome. The success of the Yiddish theater struck many people as a sign of great cultural strength, proof that Jews could integrate into the societies where they lived. Their identity was defined, first of all, by Yiddish and all that it invoked, including the idea of a Jewish homeland that transcended national boundaries and brought all speakers of the language together as one.

As the darkness of the 1930s began to descend on Europe, however, this assertion of a separate Yiddish culture began to look a whole lot more precarious. Jewish institutions of all types scrambled to respond to a mounting wave of anti-Semitism, and any celebration of Yiddish culture, in the theater or elsewhere, came to feel like a call to arms. This became a way of emboldening Jews to face down the growing threats of violence and refute the stereotypes poisoning political discourse and the opinions of ordinary people.

The storm clouds gathered slowly at first, then with mounting speed. For a number of years, Franya's career continued to soar, with more accolades for her work in both comic operettas and in more high-minded fare. When Maurice Schwartz, New York's leading Yiddish-theater impresario, brought his hit show *Yoshe Kalb* to Europe in 1935–1936, Franya was hired to join the touring company. The play, about a young mystic's fall from grace, was based on a popular novel by Israel Joshua Singer, the older and, at the time, better-known brother of Isaac Bashevis Singer. Franya played Tzivya, a simpleminded woman whom the mystic is accused of impregnating. The part gave her an opportunity to display her full dramatic and comic range and, under other circumstances, could have instigated a bright new phase of her career. Working with an internationally acclaimed theater director opened all sorts of possibilities, and indeed, when Paul Burstein, another big name on the New York Yiddish stage and a prolific recording artist, toured Poland in 1938, he too called on Franya to join him.

By then, though, the future was anything but bright. Despite knowing better, I found myself wishing that Franya had somehow joined Burstein in New York and left the coming carnage behind, enjoying a future in the American theater. I could so clearly imagine that alternate reality. But it was not to be. I didn't know what had happened to Franya yet, but I knew she hadn't made it out. Like for so many people, it simply became too late to leave. Any hope she might have had of one day appearing on the New York stage was soon eclipsed by the march toward all-out war.

The threat was twofold. The Nazis, in power in Germany since 1933, were on the move and openly touting their desire for *Lebensraum*, or needed territory, to the east—an idea that directly threatened Jews since Hitler, inspired by the American idea of Manifest Destiny, had talked frankly about the necessary annihilation of native peoples to make room for settlers from a "superior race." In quick succession, Germany annexed Austria, pressured its European neighbors into ceding Sudetenland, sought to Nazify Danzig (a nominally free city surrounded by Polish territory on the Baltic coast), and in March 1939 took over the Lithuanian port of Memel (today Klaipeda). Jewish communities took in each of these developments with their hearts in their throats. Nobody could yet conceive of a program of mass extermination and still assumed that "no one would let that happen," but people were certainly afraid of all the old czarist evils—discrimination, pogroms, mass displacement—and had already seen the Germans attempt to push Polish-born Jews in their territory over the Polish border.

The political climate in Poland, meanwhile, was becoming a problem all its own. The relatively tolerant, assimilationist policies of the country's first leader after independence, Marshal Józef Piłsudski, unraveled quickly after Piłsudski's death in 1935. Random attacks on Jewish men became disturbingly common, and politicians looking for scapegoats to blame for a weak economy and rampant poverty talked ever more openly about throwing Jews out of the country. A coalition of ultranationalists ran for office in November 1938 with slogans like "Poles, awake to action!"—an echo of the Nazis' "Deutschland, erwache!"—and "Not a single grosz in Jewish hands!" (*grosz* being Polish money) and won a decisive parliamentary majority.

The theater was not immune to such developments. In Warsaw gangs began ripping down Yiddish theater posters and harassing actors and theatergoers. Zygmund Turkow, the famed Yiddish actor, director, and playwright, sounded the alarm with his fellow performers in Warsaw, saying that "in a time of general depression and despondency," it was their duty to provide "the spiritual food which the Yiddish masses need so badly in their battle for existence."

Things were hardly better in Vilna. The university cut its admission of Jews to 8 percent of the total student body—in a city that was 40 percent Jewish—and introduced "ghetto bench seating" to segregate Jewish students from the rest. (Many of those students protested by refusing to sit at all during classes.) The city, meanwhile, eliminated its long-standing subsidies of Jewish schools and sent bailiffs to grab tables and chairs out from under children studying in classrooms. There was even an attempt to outlaw *she-hitah*, the ritual Jewish slaughter of animals, prompting a meat boycott that successfully postponed a final decision on the question—until the Nazis marched into Warsaw in 1939 and it no longer mattered what the Polish authorities had to say.

I wish I knew more about my family's experience during these earth-shaking events, especially Franya's movements. But communication, like much else, came to a halt at the very moment when Mollie and my other American relatives were most anxious to hear news. I don't know whether family members like Raisel, Soma, and Basha were able to outrun the Nazi onslaught and get out of Warsaw. Unlike Franya, they were not well known, and so the records were harder to find. But all indications sadly suggest they did not. What I do know is that the Yiddish theater in Poland as it had existed for the previous twenty years was over in an instant. Touring was now out of the question, and the dream of a nation called Yiddishland that bonded Jewish people from all over the world, and which the theater had done so much to sustain, was broken. Now, basic subsistence and survival were top priorities.

Vilna was not yet under Nazi occupation because, under the terms of the Molotov-Ribbentrop pact, the secret nonaggression agreement between Germany and the Soviet Union, it was far enough to the east to remain a free city. Still, it went through drastic changes, swelling with more than ten thousand mostly Jewish refugees from Nazi-occupied western Poland with no way to house and feed them. Soviet troops marched in on September 19, 1939, four days after the Nazis began their siege of Warsaw, and while they didn't stay in Vilna long, they did arrange for the city to be given to Lithuania and become its new capital.

Vilna's Polish majority found this move particularly infuriating, since they outnumbered ethnic Lithuanians by about fifty to one. They unleashed a wave of anti-Soviet, anti-Lithuanian, and, for good measure, anti-Semitic violence so severe that the Soviet military felt compelled to march back in again to restore order. Franya, Isaak, and Tante Rivel were at the mercy of these enormous changes, hoping to stay safe.

A period of relative calm followed, but few believed it could last. Lithuania's independence, like Poland's, dated back less than twenty years. It seemed only a matter of time before the country was annexed either by Stalin or by Hitler. Though some escaped, the vast majority of Jews in Vilna found themselves trapped between two belligerent superpowers they had every reason to mistrust and fear.

The one trace of Franya I've found in this period comes from the diary of a refugee actress, Shoshana Kahan, who fled to Vilna from Warsaw and was subsequently able to cross the Soviet Union to China. In December 1939, she reported attending a dinner at Franya's home, which is to say my family's home, at which a group of actors discussed the possibility of using Kahan's name and reputation to resume professional theatrical activity in Vilna. She also gave the group an account of the situation in Warsaw, and they observed a moment of silence for fallen fellow actors. Finding this diary entry confirmed everything I had heard about the family home being a gathering place.

Kahan did not end up staying long enough to participate in the venture. But Franya and many of the other performers did indeed put something together. It was a cabaret show in a tradition known as *kleynkunst*, not dissimilar to the Little Theater movement in the United States, which strove for high theatrical standards in a stripped-down format featuring set-piece scenes, satirical sketches, and musical numbers.

The initiative lasted only a few months. In June 1940 the Soviet Union responded to the devastatingly rapid Nazi invasions of France, Belgium, and the Netherlands by annexing the Baltic states, including Lithuania. They seized private property and denied the residents much of the autonomy they had previously taken for granted. My heart sank as I read that Isaak lost his lumber business, and he, Franya, and Rivel, the only remaining members of my family, were forced out of that grand house on Ostrobramska. No more evenings around the corner at the Philharmonic. No more carefree dinners or evenings together.

A Soviet census from April 1941 shows Isaak and Franya sharing an apartment across the street, at Ostrobramska No. 8, with four other people. A precisely drawn map included in the census documents shows that the apartment was split into five rooms, along with a kitchen and a corridor, to accommodate two married couples and two single men. The largest bedroom measured 23 square meters, or about 250 square feet, the smallest about a quarter of that size.

The Soviet takeover brought some limited benefits to Vilna's Jewish community, not least the fact that for all their many faults, the Russians were not Nazis and could perhaps be counted on to offer some protection against a German takeover. This was only marginally consoling to the many Jewish landowners and business entrepreneurs who had lost their wealth and livelihood, Isaak among them, and who knew that Stalin could initiate oppressive policies of his own. But it did mean an increase in public-sector jobs because Jews were invited to replace politically suspect Lithuanians in many lower- and midlevel positions. All limits on Jewish admission to the university were lifted.

To the delight of many actors who had not had steady work in a couple of years, the Soviet authorities also made the unexpected decision to establish a Yiddish national theater. That meant a return to the stage and a salary not just for Franya and her friends, but also for Isaak, who was hired as a "supplier," according to the census.

Franya was cast as Etty-Menny, the wife of a humble tailor who suddenly strikes it rich and struggles to hold on to his newfound wealth, in Sholem Aleichem's fable *Dos Groyse Gevins* (variously translated as *The Big Prize*, *The Lottery*, *The Raffle Ticket*, or *200,000*). The premiere of the play was a major event in Vilna, attended by the cream of the city's intellectual elite, including Abraham Sutzkever, Shmerke Kaczerginski, and other members of the literary avant-garde. The timing, however, was ominous. *Dos Groyse Gevins* opened on June 21, 1941. The Nazis started raining bombs on Vilna about sixteen hours later. This would be the last performance of the famed Yiddish Theater of Vilna.

There was no second night.

⁓

AT THE END OF 1941, NEARLY SIX MONTHS LATER, THOSE WHO REMAINED began discussions about forming a ghetto theater in Vilna. "We must be true to ourselves, and resist the enemy with this weapon," director Max Wiskind, formerly of the Jewish theater in Białystok, urged his fellow artists. The idea was controversial. Sixty percent of Vilna's Jewish population had already been killed and most of the rest pressed into slave labor. The idea of music and dancing and cabaret jokes under such circumstances struck many people as frivolous, not to mention a disruption of traditional Jewish religious practice that says mourners should avoid live music and other entertainment for up to a year after the death of a close family member.

Herman Kruk, the foremost diarist of the ghetto, who also ran the lending library, wasted little time in denouncing the invitation he received to the opening performance as a disgrace, and he was soon joined by organized labor groups who distributed leaflets that argued: "You don't make theater in a graveyard."

Still, the performers began a cycle of shows, revues, and concerts in January 1942 and continued for more than a year in an old high school auditorium that was now part of the Judenrat's administrative complex. It turned out to be far more respectful and serious-minded than detractors had feared. A big part of the program was dedicated to the memory of the dead at Ponary. A pianist played Chopin's famous funeral march, and a strong lineup of singers offered a "Prison Lament" and many other Yiddish songs ("Night," "O Lord Why Has Thou Abandoned Me?") that moved the audience deeply.

The evening was followed by many others like it, and the theater was packed each time because audiences found the experience cathartic in exactly the way that Judenrat leader Gens had hoped. Franya's friend Shabtai Blecher was a regular performer, as was another actress who had known Franya, Dora Rubina. I didn't see Franya's name listed as a performer.

Yiddish poet Abraham Sutzkever was one of the first to argue that the theatrical performances were essential acts of defiance and survival. The medieval ghettos had their theaters, too, he would say, only now an entire language and culture were on the line. In one of his most powerful poems, he addressed the theatrical performers directly on this point:

> Perform, Jewish actors, in tatters and in walls,
> Where life shrivels like hair that's caught fire
> When the red drops of your loved ones are flowing hot on the stones,
> And the alleys convulse like half-slaughtered hens . . .

The Germans broadly tolerated these cultural activities, as they did in ghettos in Warsaw, Łódź, and elsewhere. The internal affairs of the ghetto were the responsibility of the Judenrat, and as long as the Judenrat approved, the Germans raised no objection. In Vilna, though, that changed abruptly in January 1943, when the most treasured singer of the ghetto, a soprano with a heartbreakingly beautiful voice, curly brown hair, and a wide smile, named Liuba Lewicka, was arrested just ahead of the opening night of a sold-out operatic performance she'd been promising for weeks.

On the afternoon of the new show, Lewicka was intercepted at the entrance to the ghetto by the local SS commander, Franz Murer, who was known for taking pleasure in searching Jews returning from work and handing out harsh punishments to any he found smuggling in food. Murer struck such terror in the hearts of ghetto residents that word would go out whenever he approached to clear the streets as fast as possible. Unfortunately, Lewicka received no such warning and was carrying a bag of cornmeal grits and some butter for her mother, who was dangerously weak from hunger. When Murer found the bag tucked into Lewicka's coat, he drove her to Vilna's Lukiszki Prison and ordered her to be stripped naked and given twenty-five lashes.

For a month, Lewicka was kept in solitary confinement in one of the towers of the immense yellow-brick prison. Every day she sang, either as a form of payment to the guards in exchange for bread or to lift the spirits of her fellow prisoners. There was no song she sang more than "Two Doves," an old folk song about two birds in love forced apart by a malevolent force. "A curse on the person, so evil, so cruel," went the concluding lines, "who destroyed our love so soon." There was no doubt whom she had in mind when she uttered the concluding curse.

The Judenrat pleaded for her release. According to one account, Gens urged Murer to take a sick old man in her place, to no avail. The Nazis understood how much Lewicka's singing had meant—she was widely known as "the nightingale of the ghetto"—and by singling her out for torture and death, they saw a prize opportunity to break the many spirits she had done so much to buoy. The Nazi officer in charge of the murder squads at Ponary, Martin Weiss, drove her to the forest himself, bringing his girlfriend, Ellen Degner, along for the ride. According to Abraham Sutzkever, who told the story at length after the war, Ellen Degner took the lead in humiliating and threatening Lewicka, ordering her to undress and threatening to gouge out her eyes and bash in her head with a spade if she didn't hurry. It was Degner who then picked up a gun on the edge of the pit and, as Lewicka sang, riddled her with bullets.

⁓

THERE WERE, I REALIZED, NO EASY DEATHS IN THE GHETTO. PEOPLE IN Vilna took to telling each other with grim humor, "May you live to be buried in a Jewish grave." Poet Abraham Sutzkever, who had an adventurer's heart and more connections than most, was one of the very few blessed to join the partisans in the forest, survive, and live to a ripe old age. A handful of others, including Sutzkever's wife, Freydke, and his friend and fellow writer Shmerke Kaczerginski, got out the same way. Vilna diarists Kalmanovich and Kruk survived the ghetto only to be burned on the funeral pyres of Estonia. "A day will come," Kruk wrote a few days before his death, "when someone will find the leaves of horror I write and record. People will tear their hair in anguish, eyes will plunge into the sky, unwilling to believe the horror of our times."

Was it this anguish that Mollie wished to spare me by keeping silent about Franya's fate? Is that why she offered me sanitized versions, knowing them to be incorrect? How terrifying or disappointing was Franya's end,

considering how awful the rest of the stories had been? It felt like the answer
to all things. In some ways, it felt like once I found Franya, I would be able
to settle internally and find my place. I would no longer be wandering.

But, as my research deepened, I realized I might need some serious inner
fortitude to absorb whatever I eventually found out. Even without reading
Twenty-One and One, the emotional stakes were rising. I was growing ever
more attached to Franya, as if I'd known her. Serge's photograph collection
had just been the start of it. I was now delving into every aspect of her upbringing, her theatrical career, her personal passions, and the many kind-
nesses she was said to have lavished on others. All of it seemed to dissolve the
decades of distance between us and bring us closer.

One breakthrough came when I started researching at YIVO, the Institute for Jewish Research founded in Vilna before the war, now based
in New York, and obtained copies of a significant number of documents
relating to Franya—playbills, photographs, and so on. Most of these had
been smuggled out of Vilna in an astonishing operation spearheaded by
Vilna intellectuals like Sutzkever, Kaczergynski, and Herman Kruk. They
led a team of Jewish workers recruited by the Nazis to go through the cultural treasures of Vilna—including books, manuscripts, and ritual ornaments from the Great Synagogue, from the fabled Straszun Library, from
dozens of prayer houses, and from YIVO's vast collections—and send the
most valuable artifacts to Germany. The Nazis were intent on building an
unprecedented collection of Judaica as a perverse symbol of triumph over
people they were in the process of annihilating. They had sent their top
expert, Johannes Pohl of the Frankfurt Museum for the Study of Orien-
tal Peoples, to Vilna in January 1942 to coordinate the effort. This was a
twisted type of memorializing.

Everything came through the YIVO building before being sorted and
shipped, and the materials piled up so fast that the number of Jewish workers expanded over a few months from twelve to almost fifty. Sutzkever and
his friends concluded, reluctantly, that the books the Nazis had their eye on
were probably as safe in Germany as they would be anywhere else as long as
the war was raging. But Pohl wanted only about twenty thousand volumes,

one-fifth of the total. The rest was to be sold to paper mills for recycling. So the Jewish workers started smuggling as much material as they could into the ghetto, stashing it in cellars, behind walls, even in holes in the ground, "with the hope," as Sutzkever later wrote, "that the day would soon come when free people would be able to discover them for the benefit of our people and for all humanity."

The members of "the Paper Brigade," as they called themselves, proceeded to hide all sorts of precious documents under their clothing—letters written by the likes of Leo Tolstoy, Maxim Gorky, and Romain Rolland, as well as Theodor Herzl's diary, the only surviving manuscript written by the important rabbi, the Gaon of Vilna, and so on. Their paper cuts were badges of honor as they stuffed crumpled relics like so much buried treasure beneath their shirts.

To skirt the limitations on how much they could bring out by this method, the brigade also built a secret repository beneath the YIVO building and hid five thousand books and manuscripts there. Other valuables ended up in the basement of a Carmelite monastery around the corner from the cathedral.

One of the Paper Brigade members, Uma Olkenicka, had been the director of YIVO's Theater Museum before the war. It was likely under her influence that many of the theatrical artifacts, including the records relating to Franya, were scooped out of the trash. Olkenicka was also a talented graphic artist who designed YIVO's logo and did the artwork for the forbidden book *Twenty-One and One.*

Heartbreakingly, like so many, she did not survive. When the ghetto was liquidated in September 1943, she refused to abandon her mother, and both were sent to their deaths at Treblinka.

The brigade received significant help from another remarkable woman too—Vilna University librarian Ona Šimaitė. She told the Germans she had overdue library books to collect from Jewish students and not only talked her way into the ghetto, but also set up a one-woman smuggling operation that continued for years. Šimaitė brought in food and sometimes weapons, and she brought out books and documents that she hid in her house, her office, and a variety of other locations. In 1944, a few months after she smuggled a sixteen-year-old girl out under her overcoat, Šimaitė was arrested and tortured by the Gestapo and subsequently sent to Dachau. But she survived and, in 1946, gave a detailed description of where she had hidden the precious papers.

Retrieving all the rare books and documents after the war, including the ones she stashed, was far from a simple matter. Even after the materials were tracked down and identified, it was difficult to determine where they should go. Veterans of the Paper Brigade were determined to get them to YIVO in New York, where they knew they would be cataloged and protected properly, but they ran into considerable resistance from the US government. The US State Department argued that since Lithuania was once again part of the Soviet Union, any treasures from Vilna should be regarded as Soviet property. That position shifted once the Cold War started, and it became clear that the Soviets had little interest in preserving Jewish cultural artifacts. But the bureaucratic tug-of-war dragged on. It was not until 1949 that most of the Nazi collections, sitting in warehouses in and around Frankfurt, made their way across the Atlantic.

The materials hidden in Vilna proved an even greater challenge. Poet Abraham Sutzkever, one of the original Paper Brigade members, smuggled some out when he traveled to Nuremberg to testify at the war-crimes trials in 1946. By that time, he understood that the Soviets were not likely to value the documents and books. Others he gave in dribs and drabs to a variety of couriers, including members of the American Joint Distribution Committee, the organization for which my aunt Mollie had worked. In one spectacular case, Sutzkever delivered two large bags of valuables to veterans of the Warsaw Ghetto Uprising (an act of rebellion that many said rose in direct opposition to the more passive and metaphorical response of the Jews in Vilna). The veterans sneaked them across an unguarded section of the Polish-Czech border, carried them to Prague just a step or two ahead of the Czech secret police, and then handed the material back to Sutzkever through the open window of a train as it pulled out of the station headed for Paris. Some, including the collection at the Carmelite monastery, were not recovered and sent to the United States until the 1990s—fifty years later!—when Lithuania was once again free of the Soviet yoke.

By the time I consulted the YIVO archives in New York, I was awed by the stories and by the many acts of bravery that had allowed the documents I was handling to survive. To me, it spoke volumes about the endurance of culture that what was deemed most important to save, despite risking life and limb, was the written word. Even after all the decimation and destruction, the core of Vilna's Jewish culture shone through—the belief that art and ideas were the greatest treasures. *Of course the Etingins saved the forbidden book*, I mused. The real religion of this place was creativity and deep thought.

The YIVO Institute for Jewish Research in Manhattan, where the Etingins had found publishers for the forbidden book so many years before, proved to be one of the most essential stops on my research journey. Inside that grand brick building adorned with "Center for Jewish History" plaques was the only prewar Jewish archive and library to survive the Holocaust in Eastern Europe.

Though the facade was classic, the interior was modern and welcoming, with desks for researchers to use. The air had that comforting smell, a mix of fresh paint and old books. As soon as I walked in, I knew I was in the right place.

~

By January 2017 I had decided to take a sabbatical from my consulting work to research and write a book on what I was learning about Franya and my family.

My children were excited by the idea, but my husband, Steven, whose family knew nothing of their Holocaust-related tragedy, was always a bit weary of my obsession with the past. Through my research, which sometimes veered off into his family, I found the deportation records for his own grandfather's brother and family and subsequently their death records at Auschwitz. On his mother's side, fortunately, there was a memorial candle, his great-aunt Lillian Silberling Weiss, who like Mollie visited the European relatives in Krakow and Bielsko, Poland, in 1937 and kept her correspondence with them. The photographs and letters, some pleading for help from the ghetto, are now in the possession of her daughter, Susan, who shared them with me.

Not a single one of my husband's six siblings knew about the losses in their family. "I don't look back," his father would say. "I focus on the future," and so, his children followed his lead.

I was determined that my children would know their history and that the family would not be erased. Steven said that he didn't understand my need to tell the story, but he was fully supportive of my journey and hoped that in it I would find some peace.

So, I signed up for classes on the destruction of Jewish Lithuania and on the Yiddish theater, and I began requesting materials. Everywhere I went, the archivists were thrilled with what I had found and happy to assist in my search. Here was no exception, and they happened to be featuring a current exhibit about the Yiddish theater, so my timing couldn't have been better. Just outside the library, I was confronted with an oversize poster from the Krakow Yiddish Theater with an illustration of a bearded man and a horse and cart. Blazed across the top was "Rudolf Zaslawski Towje Mleczarz," Polish for "Rudolf Zaslavsky in Tevye the Milkman."

The staff there led me upstairs to their back offices and to an empty desk. They emerged with stacks of materials. Pulling protective white cotton gloves over my hands, I began sorting through files dedicated to my cousin and many other actors with whom she had performed. I found Franya's actors' union cards and took off my glove for only a second, to hold the paper that she had held. It was a physical connection to Franya that I had not previously known. It sent a charge through my body.

The archivists gave me existing files on Rudolf, and then on Blecher too, and I devoured them all. I found playbills starring Rudolf Zaslavsky and scoured the fragile papers for names that I would recognize. The names F. Vinter and S. Blecher appeared regularly. Proof that they had all performed together.

These documents before me were saved by the Paper Brigade of Vilna and later by the Monuments Men and Women, a group of American and British museum curators, art historians, librarians, architects, and artists responsible for finding and preserving artistic and cultural treasures that were plundered by the Nazis. They were a part of history that the Nazis had meant to destroy in order to erase my family's existence. But for the determination and ingenuity of an extraordinary group of individuals, many of whom did not survive themselves, they would have been gone.

8

Revelation in Iowa

"But from thinking about writing to actual writing is a distance"

IT WAS BECOMING impossible to deny my huge, self-inflicted handicap. Was part of me resistant to reading the forbidden book because I needed to prove that I could get there on my own, work hard to piece together Franya's journey from scraps, so that I earned the answers?

Was it crazy—and in direct opposition to my goal of honoring my family by finding out the truth and carrying on their stories like a true memorial candle—to ignore the one source that was sure to provide me with solid answers to my questions about Franya's fate? Admittedly, yes. A little bit. For me, though, this had evolved into a profoundly emotional journey, more than an exercise in historical research. As I fleshed out more of Franya's story, I found myself opening up and becoming more whole too. I had slowly felt the numbness lifting, my protective layers cracking and falling away. I was beginning to wonder if getting to the bottom of these mysteries might free me from the Holocaust lens that colored my entire life experience. I envisioned a kind of catharsis. Could the history that lived inside of me become nourishing rather than heavy? I wasn't just trying to find Franya; I was also on a journey to enrich my own identity. I wanted to make my peace with a past that had been eating away at me all my life. I couldn't do that by trampling over my aunt's dying wishes. I had to trust my instincts; they had gotten me this far. It had to feel right, and I wasn't there yet.

More and more, I did start nibbling around the edges of *Twenty-One and One*, though, if only to learn what I could about the book *aside* from its actual contents. That much I felt comfortable doing. Yad Vashem, the World Holocaust Center in Jerusalem, had a page on its website from which I learned some of the bare-bones facts about Shabtai Blecher (the book's author and Franya's friend), Bolesław Boratyński (who rescued the manuscript from the ghetto gutter), and the Etingins (who held it close all the way to New York). Blecher, I knew, had not survived. But what about the others? Could I still trace them? Interview them, maybe? This was a new angle from which to approach the lingering unknowns. That's when discovering more about them as a means to get to Franya became a sort of obsession.

I figured I'd begin with the most obvious source. I searched the phone book for an Etingin or, failing that since I had hit the snag of varied spellings countless times before, an Etingen, Edington, or Attington. It also occurred to me: If Yad Vashem had documented that Boratyński had rescued the manuscript and sheltered the Etingins, wouldn't that have qualified him for induction into the museum's hall of heroes, the Righteous Among Nations? To my frustration, my initial searches turned up nothing at all.

Refusing to admit defeat, I jumped on a plane to Vilnius (formerly Vilna) and recruited Regina Kopilevich once again, to help me scour the Lithuanian State Archives. We met at my hotel for breakfast where she declined to order but proceeded to take lox and other delicacies from my plate and wrap it up for later. As always, she was a ball of energy, full of the same magic that she displayed when she led me to the former Yiddish Folk Theater and revealed that Franya had performed there, then sat down at the piano to play Bach herself. But here too we had little luck. The archives were not as forthcoming in 2016 as they would later become, and we could find no trace of the Boratyńskis. All we found on the Etingins was their ghetto address. The trail went cold.

At this point, I had archival contacts all over the world who had helped me and who periodically sent me information as it came across their desks or when they found a moment to search. No one seemed able to find anything relevant. Discouraged, I boarded a plane back to New Jersey empty-handed. Just when I had given up hope and began to eye *Twenty-One and One* in desperation, bargaining with myself in my head as I fought to ignore its siren's call, an amazing new lead dropped into my lap.

Over the course of my work for the United Nations and during my now myriad trips to Vilnius, I had made many good friends in Lithuania. One, the local director of the National Democratic Institute, Michael Murphy, had been out of town during my visit but had invited me to stay in his apartment in his absence, so we had exchanged a number of messages. He reached out now to tell me that, on a recent visit to Montreal, he had wandered into an upscale poster store, Galerie l'Affichiste. Upon discovering his Lithuanian roots, the shopkeeper had mentioned that her father had survived the Holocaust in Vilna and might be an invaluable source as one of the few remaining living links to the war.

"My guess is he'd have been fairly young, perhaps a boy," Michael wrote, "but old enough to remember and not to want to go back to Vilnius."

By now I was spent and frankly reluctant to track down another dead-end lead. I thought that perhaps I would email this man first to see if there was anything worth traveling to Montreal to speak with him about.

Michael apologized for not knowing more, but he'd left the store before it occurred to him that this might be of interest to me. He needn't have apologized. "I don't really have a relationship with the owner," he cautioned, "so this will be a bit of a cold call for you."

Then, almost as an afterthought, he mentioned the shopkeeper's name: Karen Etingin.

My jaw dropped. I sat in front of my computer in utter shock for what could have been minutes or hours. My heart pounded in my chest. What were the chances of our stories intersecting this way, of me literally stumbling upon exactly what—or who—I'd been searching for without success? I'd traveled to Vilnius, France, Israel, and scoured archives in New York and Washington, DC. Who could have predicted that the answer lay in a poster shop in Canada? The synchronicity was so pronounced that I was tempted to look to the heavens and thank Mollie or Franya for the help.

Unable to contain myself, a few weeks later, filled with excitement, I flew to Montreal. Karen's father was Henry Etingin, the younger of the two brothers who had survived alongside their parents. Henry had been eleven when the Nazis invaded and thirteen when he and the rest of the family hid in the hole that Boratyński dug for them in his garden. Karen and her mother, Kiki, agreed to join me for lunch and tell me what they could. The Etingins had taken on a kind of larger-than-life status in my mind, like favorite beloved characters in a novel. The idea of meeting them and hearing what felt like their epilogue firsthand was overwhelming.

Filled with nervous energy, I arrived at the restaurant, a casual local café on a quaint shopping street. Right away, Henry's wife, Kiki, exuded a kind of elegance, with shoulder-length blonde hair and a crisp top. Karen looked a bit like her mother—the same arched eyebrows, but with dark-brown hair swept back from her face. After everything our relatives had been through, how strange to be able to sit here freely together and order a niçoise salad.

The Etingins had done well after coming to North America, they told me. Albert, the patriarch, founded a successful real-estate company, which he ran until his death in 1970. His two sons followed him into the same business, Henry in Montreal and Maks in New York.

In a familiar turn of events, Karen and Kiki had little to tell me about the war because Henry didn't like to talk about it.

"I asked Henry about his experience in the Vilna ghetto only once," recalled Kiki, a sadness washing over her face. "He told me he'd had to step over dead bodies." She never asked him again.

I thanked Henry through his wife and daughter. I understood that he was reluctant to talk. I'd known so many people like that throughout the years. Of course, it would have been amazing if he would have spoken with me. What I did learn was that he didn't remember the book, but then, he was just a child.

"Maks is the one who knows," both Karen and Kiki kept repeating. Maks didn't mind talking about the past. After reading through old newspaper archives and a segment of an interview with him that had been published in a book, I later learned that Maks had indeed told his story a number of times. But he was in his late eighties now and in poor health, and his daughter Orli told me he was not well enough to speak. (He died in 2019 at the age of ninety-two.)

This was not exactly the outcome I'd hoped for. Still, I'd pried open the door. Among other things, I learned that Yad Vashem *had* in fact honored the Boratyńskis after receiving testimony from both Etingin brothers as well as Boratyński's widow, Józefa, in the early 1990s. Soon enough, I had my own copy of Yad Vashem's file.

Henry Etingin's account—the only evidence I could find that he'd ever told his story from beginning to end—was handwritten in block letters over four pages of a Hyatt Regency hotel notepad, apparently while he was away from home over the New Year in 1992. He stuck rigorously to the facts as he knew them, his own memory of the events, and expressed enormous gratitude toward the Boratyńskis as he recommended them for the recognition. "Bolesław," he wrote, "never asked for or took any money from us, and he saved our lives by risking his own. He had nothing to gain and everything to lose."

⌒

ONCE BACK AT HOME, I CONTINUED MY RESEARCH.

I was constantly checking and rechecking sources, which changed rapidly as more documents were shared online. Each day I sat down in front of my computer, hoping for that next piece of the puzzle to fall into place.

Then finally in early 2017, my repeated Google searches for Franya, under every conceivable spelling of her first and last names, yielded a promising new hit: the testimonial narrative of one of her fellow actresses, Dora Rubina. She had participated in the Yiddish ghetto theater, and survived the ghetto in Vilna and many other misfortunes, before being liberated by the Soviet army at a Nazi transit camp in northern Poland in March 1945.

Bracing myself for new revelations, I clicked through to the link titled "The Path of Suffering of Jewish Actors." Chills ran through me. Rubina's experience was the closest I had come to one that mirrored Franya's, as she'd been both a peer and a fellow performer in Vilna. They'd existed in the same sphere with the same general set of circumstances. The testimony had originally been taken for the Białystok Ghetto Underground Archives, most

likely because Rubina was born in Białystok and was only now cataloged in
Yad Vashem's collections, making it accessible to me. Six pages were available for download, but in Yiddish only, so I couldn't read them right away
and had to send them to a translator. What I could read, though, was a detailed accompanying English summary of Rubina's account, which included
a reference—in list form—that stopped me in my tracks:

> . . . resistance to the Germans by Franja Winter, the actress; murder of the
> actress by the Germans.

My heart raced as I absorbed what I'd read: resistance, murder. Here, apparently, was another source, beyond *Twenty-One and One*, that might tell
me what had happened. Here was the confirmation that I had been seeking.
Was this my opportunity to learn the truth and still stay true to my aunt's
wishes? Had I gotten there myself? I reread the abbreviated text, finding
the word "resistance" reassuring. It seemed to confirm what I'd wanted to
believe about Franya all along—she was strong, a fighter, loyal to our side.

I was able to make arrangements to have the testimony translated right
away, though I knew it would not be immediate. I reexamined the summary countless times, noting that Rubina must have met up with Franya
in late 1939 or early 1940, after she fled Nazi-occupied Warsaw. Vilna was
still free of German control then. I found that the two of them had been
in a revue ensemble together, then in the Yiddish state theater established
after the Soviet Union annexed Lithuania in June 1940. Clearly, they had
known each other well. Maybe they had even been friends.

It was clear from the summary that Rubina's experience even after Vilna
had been harrowing. The text referenced escape, recapture, the arrest of her
husband by the Gestapo, deportation, forced labor, a "death march" marked
by terrible hunger and disease, and, finally, liberation. Eventually, she made
her way to California, where she passed away in 1983. Only a hair's breadth
separated the experience of those who died at the hands of the Nazis from
those who survived.

In the meantime, I had decided to take on another endeavor as well.
Years of research, plus countless stories about the sanctity of books and the

written word in Jewish culture, had made me want to try writing about my heritage. This felt like the ultimate fulfillment of my role as the memorial candle for my family—creating one place for all of the information and realization I had amassed over the years. At this point I was working as a consultant, enacting women's leadership training, and could make my own hours. So I surprised my husband at dinner one night by announcing that I had signed up for a two-week intensive course at the University of Iowa's Summer Writers' Festival, "The Novelist's Tools: Fiction and Narrative Nonfiction."

I was sitting alone on the college quad, surrounded by students hanging out on the grass, when I received an email with the full translation of Rubina's testimony. At first I was afraid to open the email. If I'm honest, though I had been anticipating reading it for weeks, arguably for years, a kind of emotional paralysis came over me. I was confronted with a dilemma: I was far from home and the people I loved. The years of hard work and discovery had rendered me less emotionally protected than when I started. I was open to whatever might come. In my gut, I knew I would feel this pain to my core, no matter how strong I wanted to be. Reading Dora Rubina's account was going to be taxing, and now I had to face it alone.

Again I remembered Mollie's admonition and worried that there might be something truly frightening about the story I might be better off not knowing. Then I had an unorthodox idea: I would ask my professor if I could read the testimony aloud in class. All but one of my classmates were white Americans from the Midwest, the sole exception being a doctor who now lived in New Jersey but was born and raised in the Midwest. As we each read aloud our writing assignments, it became clear to me that as a Jew, I was an anomaly, exotic, quite different from my classmates. One was writing about her experience as a rancher, and another was writing about his childhood in rural Iowa, and yet another about a long-lost love affair, far removed from the story I was seeking to tell. I knew from our shared writing exercises that they knew almost nothing about Judaism and even less about the tragedy of the Holocaust. Suddenly, I saw it as a challenge, even an obligation, to bring them into the experience with me. The professor was more than amenable to the idea.

I found myself reading Rubina's testimony to a room of people I barely knew at the very next class meeting. She recounted the "horrifying days" that followed the Nazis' arrival in Vilna; about the men snatched from their houses, never to be seen again; about the establishment of the ghetto; about a "purge" of people without work permits; about the devastation in the acting community as news reached them that one performer after another was dead.

Then she turned her focus to Franya. I looked up from my laptop at my classmates, who sat around the rectangular wooden table in the windowed room, eyes glued to me. My teacher nodded to me in patient encouragement. Inhaling, I gathered my strength and continued reading.

Franya Winter, Dora explained, did not receive a yellow work permit. Knowing that this was tantamount to a death sentence, she hatched a plan and escaped the ghetto with a group of workers. According to Rubina, Franya then sought help from a Christian acquaintance with whom she spent a few days, until the woman forced her to surrender payment in the form of "*her worthwhile things, such as jewelry and gold . . . and chased Franja into the street.*" Pausing, I tried to imagine such a betrayal, and there was anger, but also a kind of pride. Franya had refused to give up her treasured jewelry, after months of proclamations demanding that Jews turn in all their valuables. It was a small act of rebellion, but it showed her strength in the face of the most repugnant human behavior. And of course our family had always seen our pieces of jewelry as talismans, more meaningful than just a pretty bauble.

As the story progressed, Franya was captured in Ashmyany, just as I had come to suspect, in 1941. Dread welled up inside me as I forced my eyes back to the screen.

"*Franja Winter, just like the rest of us, did not want to die,*" I read, voice shaky. "*She struggled with her last abilities . . .*"

My brain registered what my eyes were reading before my lips could form the words, and, in that split second, I stopped and slammed my laptop shut. Words eluded me. I sat upright, jaw clenched, unable to move, breathing deeply in an attempt to keep my composure. The room seemed to morph around me, suddenly unstable. And in that classroom with near strangers, I broke down. I could not stop my tears from flowing.

My classmates said nothing.

"You don't have to share any more than feels comfortable," the teacher said gently.

But I was determined to continue. I owed it to Franya. Her story, no matter how gruesome, needed to be told. Wasn't that why I had started this whole quest? Wasn't that the ultimate goal?

I reopened my laptop, exhaled a stuttered breath, and searched for the strength to form the final words.

As I reached the conclusion, the classroom fell into a hush again.

"And that is how the actress, Franja Winter, who all the years helped spin the thread of culture and artistry, ended life."

People were quietly sobbing.

After a long silence an older man, a church deacon from rural Iowa, said, "The terrible thing is that, in thirty years, no one will know that this happened."

My response was swift and unforgiving.

"It is *still* happening," I said. "Every day."

9

Twenty-One and One

"THE FINGERS TREMBLE AS SOON AS THEY TOUCH THE CREASED PAGES"

THERE ARE MANY reasons I can point to for why I finally felt ready to read the forbidden book: for one thing, I already knew the worst. Dora Rubina's testimony had outlined what had happened to Franya, and, while it hadn't been pretty, it had been clear. I understood why Mollie had tried to protect me. The truth did hurt. But now the harsh reality had been dragged into the daylight. I thought of Dora Rubina's conclusion to her testimony, "May this remain as a memory for generations and generations."

I felt like I was nearing the end of my quest, but I was having trouble attaching to a sense of closure. *Twenty-One and One* was the logical last stop on my journey.

It was April 2017, and the world was in flux. Donald Trump had taken office in January with a decidedly undemocratic bent, followed by a rash of hate crimes he did not condemn. According to the Anti-Defamation League's Audit of Incidents, which had just been released on the heels of swastikas being spray-painted on a Virginia Jewish community center, anti-Semitic incidents were up 86 percent in the first few months of the calendar year alone. Tensions were mounting. For the first time in a long while, perhaps since I was a child having nightmares about Hitler and his Nazis marching in New Jersey, the anger and hatred against Jews felt fervent enough to inspire something larger, the second Holocaust that Aunt Mollie had been so adamant about my preventing. This all lent a sense of urgency to the story I wanted to tell in hopes of making people understand.

But I couldn't tell the story without reading the book.

It was early afternoon on a gloomy day when I walked into my living room, resolved. I settled onto the couch, my laptop resting on my knees, and opened the translation of Franya's chapter in the forbidden book.

Even having made a firm decision, I felt guilty as I selected the document and watched it open on my screen. This moment had been so long coming.

I was no longer afraid of what I might learn. But I *was* a bit afraid of what Mollie would think, even from beyond the grave. Over the years, whenever people found this hard to understand—she had, after all, been gone for two decades—I would tell them, "If you knew my aunt Mollie, you'd be afraid too."

The truth is that my yearning to know more about Franya finally outgrew my reluctance to go against my aunt's wishes. Plus, I had a strong sense that Mollie might even approve at this point, now that I'd gone through the journey. Either way, I felt that I had earned the truth. I knew that an introduction and short chapter weren't going to tell me everything. I had no illusions about that. But I hoped that *Twenty-One and One* would transform Franya in my mind, once and for all, into a fully dimensional being.

With an exhale, I began to read.

———

Three stones screamed: three old Vilna paving stones.

The Vilna "waker" Leizer Ran, awakens people, crying: "Avrohom Morewski, go eulogize the holy martyrs!"

The Ponar wind rushes through the bloodied pages of the death chronicles.

And the pen shouts to the pen write!

But from thinking about writing to actual writing is a distance. The pen is frozen between the fingers and screams—but the fingers cannot write.

Because—what, what can they write?

Again and again, pouring out words about the horrors? To repeat and repeat the accursed names of the Nazi executioners?

But living people and living Jews must live in the merit and glory of the courage that grew at the peak of the destruction and horror.

About the dark times, so much has been told and described and some in conflict with one detail or another, that with this one can truly only scream. But it is not possible to compose such measured, rhythmic sentences.

And what's the point of writing? To sigh! To write! To paint!

Because motives obstruct the facts and, even if any details are altered, it still does not become lies.

But with words, one letter can set the truth on its head.

THE LANGUAGE OF THE INTRODUCTION—WRITTEN BY ABRAHAM MOREWski, a onetime member of the Vilna Troupe who survived the war—felt more like poetry than biographical prose. I sat back against the couch, shaking my head. Every step of this journey had surprised me. Nothing went quite as expected. Never, when I imagined reading the book, had I imagined being quite so moved by the use of language itself, the beauty of the imagery and expression. The forbidden book was even more amazing than I could have dreamed.

I realized right away that whatever Aunt Mollie's intentions, knowing the truth about what happened to Franya before reading this manuscript had been a gift because it allowed me to take in the entirety of the creation without being absorbed in the singular pursuit of knowing.

The introduction referenced Shabtai Blecher, who, of course, had been the original author of the manuscript, heralding him as one of the incredible actors of his time, as well as a "holy martyr."

Actors—holy martyrs!

Bright names from a dark memorial chronicle.

How unclouded is your memory! Your names are blossomed and filled with rays! And how deep is the foundation into which your executioners have sunk—the hands that murdered master singers while their fingers trembled on the strings of a Jewish harp.

Actors—holy martyrs!

The ghetto chronicles about their creative lives and bloody death, which are exposed here, will without a doubt tell the reader a lot, a lot more than the most beautiful figures of speech. And let us not even try to pretty up the tragedy with words. Let us guard the words of abuse with them, so as not to weaken the thresholds between the miserable life and the eternal rest.

Actors—holy martyrs!

They did not die, and their holiness does not decay with eternity.

Only as I turned to Franya's section did I realize that the chapters were organized chronologically by date of death. Franya's was Chapter 3. She had been among the first to die. Had I realized, I could have discerned that early on.

The information that Blecher shared about my cousin was more direct than the introduction had been, and it filled in many gaps, not just about her last days. As a true friend and confidant, he drew a picture of Franya as a generous and immensely talented woman who loved deeply and cared for her impoverished family and friends throughout her life. He also did not shy away from her affair with Rudolf Zaslavsky, fleshing out my hazy speculations.

Both she and Zaslavsky were adored for their roles in comedy as well as tragedy, so they both loved to laugh and emote. Based on his description, I imagine them wrestling with ideas together, challenging each other, and loving passionately.

But the best clue *Twenty-One and One* offered about the relationship is that, according to Blecher, the roles Rudolf and Franya played in an adaptation of Sholem Aleichem's charming romantic novel *Stempenyu* echoed their own adulterous affair.

Stempenyu tells the story of an illicit romance between a brilliant wandering klezmer musician who can play music so sweetly on his violin that it melts even the most stubborn hearts, and Rokhele, the beautiful and unfulfilled wife of an uninterested man, who falls helplessly under his spell. "His words seemed not only to draw her closer to him but to surround her on all sides," Aleichem writes in his novel, "as by a network of invisible silken cords." Rokhele, he observes, "was entirely filled with one desire—to see Stempenyu and to be near him. She thought only of him."

The theatrical version of the story provides more clues about the real-life romance. If Blecher was right that life was imitating art, then Zaslavsky must have sensed Franya's discontent in her marriage with Isaak and gradually broken down her defenses by suggesting that she could find some greater satisfaction with him, just as Stempenyu did with Rokhele.

"I know that you are not alone here. You have a husband, and I know him," Stempenyu says in the second of the play's four acts. "But you are still alone, alone and sad, tied up and tormented, just like me."

Rokhele replies, defiantly, "How do you know that? You don't even know me."

"I know you well," Stempenyu counters. "I even know what you are thinking now. One heart knows another."

When the novel was first published in 1888, it caused a sensation, but by the early 1930s, the story no longer had the same shock value. Jewish readers and theatergoers were far more sophisticated, urban, and secular. Sexuality was a common theme on the Yiddish stage, and tales of adultery and affairs between actors were regular fodder for gossip in the newspapers.

Still, that reality did nothing to quell the drama around Franya's own affair. On one leg of their tour, in Krakow, Isaak showed up to confront the lovers and told Franya he was throwing her out of the house. Blecher was silent on what happened next, but this was plainly a breaking point, the moment when the bubble burst and cold reality overtook the headiness of the love affair. Just like Rokhele, Franya ended up returning home to her husband, who, like Rokhel's husband, was "a fine and worthy specimen of a man." Zaslavsky eventually emigrated to Argentina, where his wife had moved years earlier.

Though it was short-lived, the affair was clearly intense and life-changing because its scars stayed with Franya for the rest of her life. As Blecher put it, this was "one of her greatest tragedies"—quite a statement, given that he was writing from the ghetto in 1942.

Looking up from Blecher's chapter, I thought about Franya's perspective. For all her difficulties with Isaak, he was a good companion, and she must have decided that what mattered most to her was family. She'd been attached enough to her life in Vilna to encourage her younger sister, Raisel, to marry Isaak's younger brother, Soma.

This was another realization *Twenty-One and One* offered: when Raisel and Soma had a daughter, Basha, Franya formed a special bond with the girl—closer, Blecher writes, than the bond Basha had with her own mother. When Franya wasn't able to be with her niece, she would spend many hours sewing dresses or knitting stockings for her. After Raisel and her family moved back to Warsaw in the mid-1930s, Franya regularly sent them money, food, and clothing. She would, Blecher says, "give them from her last bits."

Zaslavsky, meanwhile, carried on being Rudolf Zaslavsky. He lived, at least nominally, in Buenos Aires, but kept up a relentless touring schedule all over Europe and the Americas. His egomania did not always serve him well—one critic accused him of surrounding himself with lesser talents to make his own star shine brighter—but it did continue to provide a stream of extraordinary stories.

In 1936 he pulled a truly outrageous publicity stunt: while on tour in Danzig (modern-day Gdansk, in Poland) and apparently not receiving enough press attention, he faked his own death. Newspapers all over Europe and from Glasgow to Philadelphia covered the fake news.

Perhaps Zaslavsky was tempting fate. A year later, back in Argentina, he suffered an asthma attack during a rehearsal with the People's Theater company. His doctors had been urging him for months to take time off and revive his health in "mountain air." But Zaslavsky had refused to listen. This time, he died for real.

Zaslavsky had left Europe before the worst began in Vilna, but Franya was not so fortunate. Still, even as her fortunes turned and she was forced to live with multiple families in relative squalor, according to *Twenty-One and One*, Franya was unfailingly hospitable and generous to anyone who called on her for help. "Her house," Blecher wrote, "was an open house to all. On free evenings, actors would gather there to talk and play the lotto. . . . The table was always set and no one ever left her house hungry." Just as I had suspected, even in the worst times, Franya tried to create joy.

By then, she had mostly lost the chance to perform, and, even when she could, she was no longer being offered the roles she wanted. There was evidence of some vanity and insecurity. She kept being overlooked for young female leads and blamed the management for failing to recognize her talents. Blecher saw other reasons for this shift: Franya was forty-five years old now and looked older still (with "already a little ash color in her hair"), hardly a surprise given the level of stress and upheaval she was experiencing.

⁓

THERE IS NO RECORD OF FRANYA'S, ISAAK'S, AND TANTE RIVEL'S EXACT thoughts and movements during the terrible summer of 1941 when the Nazis invaded. I don't know what they made of the rapidly evolving situation, when reliable information was almost impossible to come by, or how quickly they understood the terrible danger they were in. As I read *Twenty-One and One* and thought back to my own in-depth research, German ghetto records, and detailed accounts of neighbors and friends, which I assumed must have been similar to their own experiences, I began to connect the dots that led to Franya's end. I began to understand—and almost envision—her experience.

I imagine that Isaak, like many other men of working age, spent July and August confined to the house to avoid the *khapunes* (or Lithuanian Hitler Youth, who rounded up Jewish men). Perhaps he found himself a hole to hide in, like Albert and Maks Etingin. Perhaps, like many others, he dug deep into his pockets to contribute to a five-million ruble payment that the German civil administration levied against the Jewish community within days of taking charge, hoping to placate the authorities and bring an end to kidnappings.

Isaak and Franya most likely heard the rumors about mass shootings in the forest. Perhaps they found it difficult, as others did, to give the reports credence at first. Perhaps they too couldn't believe the Germans would kill off their best workers. Or perhaps they simply clung to any shred of hope. "It is impossible now to understand," wrote survivor and Vilna biographer

Mendel Balberyszski after the war, "but the truth was we didn't want to believe the most tragic and dreadful information." Herman Kruk, the most prolific of the Vilna diarists and one of the first to foresee the looming catastrophe, observed how willing most people were to believe that the Soviets were on the counterattack and might reach Vilna any day. "We console ourselves with bubbles in the air," he lamented.

The first hint of the atrocities at Ponary, the forest enclave near Vilna where so many Jews had been executed starting in summer 1941 right after the Nazi invasion, reached the city within a few days. A Polish journalist living within earshot recorded in his diary how, starting on July 11, he heard gunfire in the forest hour after hour and day after day and understood that Jews were being slaughtered there in large numbers. But Vilna's newly formed Judenrat immediately quashed the idea as an impossibility. Later, when the Germans started shooting women and children, one woman who made it back to Vilna wounded but alive left her doctors so incredulous that they circled fingers near their heads to indicate they thought she was crazy.

By the time more reports emerged and the full horror became clear to all, the Jews had lost what little freedom they had left. The Germans had herded them into a few streets in the medieval quarter in the center of Vilna, close to forty thousand people crammed into a maze of buildings and courtyards previously occupied by six thousand and cordoned them in with barbed wire and armed guards.

For Franya, Isaak, and Tante Rivel, it would have been a short walk from their apartment to the Philharmonic Hall, followed by a left turn toward All Saint's Church, then right onto Rudnicki Street. As the registration lines grew, they would have been left waiting for hours, conscious that they were entering a place from which they might never leave. "People say that going into the ghetto is like entering a darkness," Herman Kruk wrote later that day. "Thousands stand in line and are driven into a cage. People are driven, people fall down with their sacks, and the screams reach the sky."

The three remaining members of my immediate family were assigned to a cellar on Dzisnienski Street, also known by its Yiddish name, *Dysnos*. I had read the diary of Yitskhok Rudashevski, a teenager whose family I found in an original German register moved into the building next door, who was immediately struck by how dirty, stuffy, and crowded his quarters felt. I have no doubt the same was true for Franya, Isaak, and Tante Rivel. Rudashevski wrote that there were fifteen people in his tiny apartment. With no bed available, he and two others lay down on a pair of doors taken off their hinges. Sleep was impossible. "I hear the restless breathing of people with whom I have been suddenly thrown together," Rudashevski wrote in his diary. "In my ears resounds the lamentation of this day."

I wondered about the way my family's daily lives changed, the easily overlooked details that had previously defined their identities. Was Tante Rivel forced to give up her cigarettes, to surrender her elegant holders? Did Isaak tuck away his bow ties and three-piece suits in hopes of a time when they would be relevant again? Did Franya allow her bobbed hair to grow, looking at herself in the mirror to find someone altered staring back? Who had they become?

THE GHETTOS DID NOT STAY OVERCROWDED FOR LONG. THE PACE OF KILLings more than doubled from just under four thousand a month in July and August to eighty-five hundred a month in September, October, and November. Already on September 6, the day the ghetto was established, roughly six thousand of the city's remaining forty-five thousand Jews were ordered to report directly to Lukiszki Prison. Of these, just two hundred were later allowed to return to the ghetto, either because they could prove that they had a usable work skill or because they paid their way out, or both. The rest were taken to the forest and shot.

The Nazis continued to insist that Ponary was just another ghetto, housing workers. They even took the trouble to falsify letters written by "inmates" to their loved ones. Most people were not fooled; they knew better. After all, on September 4, a group of four women and an eleven-year-old girl who survived the shootings used their last ounce of strength to reach the ghetto hospital in Vilna and give graphic testimony about the pits in the forest and the corpses piled up there. Other women soon followed with similar stories. At Ponary, they explained, the men were shot first, while their families looked on, and the women and children were left for the end of the day. Sometimes, the killers lost their nerve with the women and children, or their aim would falter as the forest darkened and fatigue set in. Those who were not gravely wounded, or who escaped being shot at all, had a chance to crawl back out of the pit after the Nazis left and make their way to safety.

If those accounts weren't proof enough, Jews assigned to work at Gestapo headquarters were given the task of sorting through clothing recovered from the dead and determining which pieces were worth sending to Germany for reuse. One of their instructions was to remove the Star of David patches so recipients would never know the items had once belonged to Jews.

The Nazis' selection process started to become a bit clearer, too, especially after they started issuing work permits. You either worked or you were killed.

A survey conducted on September 18 indicates that all three of my family members were alive and still living on Dysnos Street. Isaak had a job with the city administration, most likely as a janitor, while Franya, not named on the survey, was listed as his dependent. Rivel, whose last name was Lichtenberg, not Punski, was listed separately as a "flower worker," perhaps a reference to her prewar job of making beautiful appliqués for hats.

Any sense of security these assignments gave them would have been tenuous at best. In the ghetto, life was a traumatic rattling experience, and even the best of circumstances were still the worst. Men in official uniforms could burst in without notice, day or night, to demand the surrender of money, jewelry, and other valuables, or to take beloved family members away without explanation, dragging them into the street. Grief and loss were a daily norm, coloring the experience of every single person at every single moment. People were forced to reckon with the reality that they too might be rounded up and sent to Ponary to be cruelly stripped and slaughtered—or to watch their own children die. They lay in bed at night and wondered how they might react when facing down the barrel of a gun: Would they plead for mercy? Would they hold their heads high? Did it matter, either way?

In fact, it did. Along with the accounts of the executions came stories of extraordinary courage in the face of the Nazis' attempts to demean and humiliate their victims in their final moments. When those sent to the forest were ordered to strip naked and stand in the cold until it was their turn to die, they dared not step out of line. If they grew restless or disobeyed, they risked a beating or torture. One remarkable young woman told her guards she refused to take her coat off no matter what. When one of them threatened her at gunpoint, she spat in his face. Wasn't she there to be executed, anyway? Such defiance was widely discussed and admired.

The ghetto inhabitants prayed that they'd never have to search their souls for such fortitude. To that end, they spent considerable time and energy building hiding places, known as *malines*, from tiny crawl spaces up chimneys to secret basements big enough for thousands. One of the few advantages of living in the old part of the city, once a medieval town, was that its buildings and courtyards contained underground passages, connecting doors between homes, walled-up rooms, and a variety of nooks and unexpected corners. The ghetto dwellers took full advantage, adding their own considerable ingenuity. They built false walls, erected secret doorways, dug tunnels—whatever it took to throw off their pursuers.

Some of the hideouts were elaborate, buried deep in the ground with heating and plumbing systems and two-way radios to alert the occupants if someone was coming or the coast was clear. Most, though, were physically uncomfortable and psychologically unnerving. There was the constant fear of discovery. Yitskhok Rudashevski described a large *maline*—perhaps one used by my family too—that became so crowded during police raids that people could barely move. The restless murmuring of people "lying on bricks like rags in the dirt" made him feel only more helpless and broken than before.

⁓

I CAN'T BE CERTAIN HOW LONG ISAAK AND RIVEL LIVED, BUT ALL SIGNS point to their luck running out on the evening of October 1, 1941, Yom Kippur, the holiest day of the Jewish calendar. Thousands of ghetto residents stayed home from work that day by bribing or circumventing their bosses. The German and Lithuanian police came looking for workers at nine in the morning and again as services let out at noon. At the sight of the security officers, panic spread through the crowd. A number started running and were gunned down. Hundreds more were rounded up and taken away.

That afternoon, Horst Schweinberger of the SS—"our lord of life and death," as Herman Kruk called him—ordered the Judenrat to produce another thousand people. He said that if they didn't cooperate, the Germans and Lithuanians would choose them themselves. So the Judenrat ordered the Jewish ghetto police to arrest anyone without a work permit. Since most people were in hiding at that point, they were able to find only forty-six individuals. Then the Jewish policemen took a different tack, this time going out with what they claimed was "a friendly warning." There's going to be an *Aktion*, or a roundup, they said, and there isn't a moment to lose. If you have a work permit, go to the main gate and get it stamped so you'll be protected.

Mark Dvorzhetski, who I determined lived directly across the street from Isaak, Franya, and Rivel, remembered a Jewish policeman coming into his apartment, where he and a group of fellow residents were breaking the Yom Kippur fast with potato soup, bread, and jam. Other policemen were running up and down the street, all with the same message. *There's no time to waste. Drop everything. Go to the gate.*

According to Dvorzhetski, most people with permits did just that. The only reason he didn't do it himself was that his wife grew suspicious. "Don't trust the Jewish police!" she said. "Don't go."

Before the Dvorzhetskis could hide themselves, two Jewish policemen and a Lithuanian militiaman burst into the apartment and chased all the men out. Dvorzhetski and a friend followed the rest down to the courtyard, but when no one was looking they dashed off into the darkness and ran up several flights of stairs until they reached the roof. They hopped from roof to roof, moving halfway across the ghetto until they were sure nobody was following.

The house searches continued late into the night. More than two thousand people ended up at the gate, because they either volunteered themselves or were dragged there. They were marched off to Lukiszki Prison. Most were never seen again.

As much as I hate to envision it, it seems likely to me that Isaak and Rivel followed the ghetto police to get their work permits stamped, while Franya, who did not have a job, stayed behind in hiding. I had begun to suspect that this might be the case, and Blecher's account in *Twenty-One and One* seemed to confirm this. "During the first days of the ghetto, her husband was arrested and put into prison," he wrote. "She was left lonely and alone. She had no one to be close to. So, she hid herself in the empty rooms and embroidered."

One man taken to Lukiszki Prison on the night of Yom Kippur, Simon Tubiaschewitz, recalled terrible scenes as the guards ordered everyone to give up their jewelry and watches. If they tried to hold on to anything of value and were caught, they would be killed. Rather than be at the mercy of their oppressors, several Jews hanged themselves in their cells. The next morning, hundreds of prisoners were herded into a courtyard and forced to look at their suicidal friends' broken bodies, bloated and twisted. Tubiaschewitz remembered gunshots and screams. Then everyone was searched, and most were taken away, presumably to Ponary. For reasons never fully explained, a few hundred, including Tubiaschewitz, were sent back to the ghetto. Life or death was reduced to a coin toss.

The Yom Kippur *Aktion* rocked the Jews of Vilna like nothing before. It was clear that even a work permit was no longer a guarantee of safety. Even worse, Jewish police officers had preyed on their fellow Jews' trust and led them to their deaths. "People believe that hell will never end," Kruk wrote in despair while the roundups were still happening. "We will be dragged to the slaughter in installments."

The episode gave even the Nazis pause, not because of its cruelty, but for the same reasons that had put the Wehrmacht (or the unified Nazi forces) at loggerheads with the security services in August. The war machine simply could not afford to have its valuable skilled or even unskilled workers killed off. This was a source of great frustration to the Einsatzgruppen (or paramilitary death squads), who wanted freedom to please Reinhard Heydrich and Heinrich Himmler. Their goal was to "solve the Jewish problem for Lithuania," as Karl Jäger, one of the death-squad leaders, wrote in an official account of the mass killings a couple of months later. "I was willing to go ahead and eliminate these Jewish workers and their families too," Jäger continued, "but I ran into strong objections from the civil administration and the Wehrmacht, who decreed: these Jews and their families must not be shot."

Indeed, to avoid ruffling feathers up the chain of command, Jäger omitted the Yom Kippur killings from his report entirely. My cousin and my great-aunt had most likely been murdered along with thousands of others, but to the nervous Nazi bureaucrats, it was as though nothing had ever happened.

⁓

ON OCTOBER 15, THE JUDENRAT ANNOUNCED THAT IT WAS OVERHAULING the work-permit system and would issue new certificates guaranteeing the safety of each holder and as many as three family dependents. That meant those work-permit holders with more than two children were forced to make the cruelest choice imaginable: which two of their children would live and which would die. People became frantic in their efforts to secure one of the so-called yellow permits. They attempted all manner of bribery and subterfuge and became incensed when they suspected the Judenrat was playing favorites.

A number of single people who obtained permits found creative ways to put together a family grouping of four, no matter how incongruous it seemed. Kruk, who as head of the ghetto library was a Judenrat employee and therefore eligible for a permit, joined up with a seventy-five-year-old widow, Pati Kremer, and together they claimed two orphaned children. No matter that Kremer, whose husband had been one of the Jewish-Socialist Bund founders, was thirty-one years older than Kruk and looked older still. They walked arm in arm to the registration office like it was the most natural thing in the world. Others were reduced to running around "as though in a fever"—as their neighbor Yitskhok Rudashevski later described his permitless parents—with no solution.

Surely, Franya would have needed help. She was, by then, listed as a dependent of her husband, who according to Blecher was sent to Lukiszki Prison, presumably in the Yom Kippur Action, and either died there or was shot in the pits of Ponary. Blecher wrote of the time after Isaak was killed, "But in a calm minute, she sat down and sewed little dresses for the children of her fellow actors who came to the ghetto tattered and torn."

I learned that by mid-October, she was no longer living on Dysnos Street, but had moved alone into a new apartment in one of the coveted courtyards near the Judenrat offices, alongside the ghetto police officers and other influential people. No doubt this offered her some protection, but there was only so much her friends and neighbors could do in the face of this latest crisis.

Jakob Gens, the head of the Judenrat, had spread word that bribing the Germans would not work. He had offered large sums of gold himself for certain allowances, and they had refused it. They did, however, relent on the number of permits, which increased from three thousand to thirty-seven hundred, plus another eighty for workers assigned to Gestapo headquarters. The population had dwindled at this point, but that didn't seem to make a difference. Gens's advice to those without permits, perhaps delivered to Franya directly, was to escape and seek shelter outside the ghetto.

And that is exactly what Franya tried to do, according to Blecher's account. I leaned in closer as I read what came next, as if, irrationally, she would somehow be saved. "One gray dawn," Blecher writes, "a friend of hers took her out through the ghetto fence and gave her over to her own one-time servant, Manke, who was living at the family home and . . . now gave her a room in her own house." In what must have been a surreal moment, she returned to the grand old family home on Ostrobramska. I could only imagine the emotion, the combination of nostalgia and pain that must have consumed her as she sneaked through those doors, a stowaway in the attic of her own former home.

Franya was by herself, left alone with her thoughts—of fear, of sadness, of isolation. She hid there for several days before finding transport to a house in the suburbs. Neither Rubina's account nor Blecher's explained who exactly took responsibility for helping her. Blecher did write generally about a number of "Aryan" or non-Jewish business connections that Isaak established before the war, about Greek Orthodox and Catholic priests whom Franya hosted for dinners, and about Christians now living in the old Punski house and enjoying all the possessions they had left behind. There was a sense that, at the time, he was cautiously hopeful that Franya would find her way to safety. Of course, none of them knew how long this horror would rage on.

Both accounts concur that Franya's "protectors" kept her only as long as they could benefit from her money and jewelry, and when the well ran dry they kicked her out, leaving her "in God's care."

Where could she go now?

For a moment, as I was reading Blecher's words, I paused to imagine an alternate reality in which Franya returned to her home at Ostrabrama and stayed hidden in that attic until the end of the war, just as Bolesław Boratyński had hidden the Etingins. But, of course, that was not to be.

Instead, Franya scrabbled around for a survival strategy without anyone to put her faith in—not the Germans or the Lithuanians, certainly; not the "friends" she'd turned to in vain; and not the Jewish leaders of the ghetto, who had demonstrated how easily they bent to the will of the Nazi death squads.

Some simply gave up the struggle, including Leib Shriftsetzer, the revered comic actor who had directed Franya in *The Virtuous Susanna* and appeared with her in *Dos Groyse Gevins* on the night before the German invasion in 1941. "I have no more strength to fight," Shriftsetzer told friends who begged him to follow them into hiding. "Let whatever is going to happen, happen." He was only fifty-five, Blecher wrote, but like many who had endured the horrors of the previous years, he felt decades older. He and his family were dragged to Ponary.

Franya did not give up. She had nowhere left to turn, but she was a fighter at heart just as I had always suspected, and she wasn't going to give the Germans a second chance to catch her without a work permit. Blecher wrote, "She was very calm, in order to be strong within herself for when the bad times would come." This was a reaction that I understood, calm in the face of chaos.

Where, though, could she go? The Soviet Union would have been the safest place, but to get there required slipping across the military front lines, a near-impossible task. Anywhere else in Lithuania was out of the question, because Jews in rural communities had been wiped out entirely, and in Kovno and Shavli, the two other major cities, killings were occurring with the same merciless regularity as in Vilna.

She must have seen only one way to go, to a region southeast of Vilna that the Germans had reassigned to Byelorussia (or Belarus), and from there,

maybe to Byelorussia proper. These areas were not under the same administration as Lithuania and were said to be quieter. This was only a temporary
lull, and an illusory one, but Franya put her faith in it and set out on the
road to Ashmyany.

———

ASHMYANY, BEFORE THE WAR, HAD BEEN A QUIET POLISH COUNTRY TOWN
of about 8,000 people, split more or less evenly between Polish-speaking
Catholics and Yiddish-speaking Jews. By the time Franya got there, though,
all vestiges of peaceful coexistence were gone. According to eyewitness accounts, local Polish leaders had "a fire of vengeance" burning inside them.
The Soviet authorities had exiled many of the town's most respected Gentile
figures about a week before the Nazi invasion, and the town's inhabitants
somehow blamed the Jews for aiding in this. As in Lithuania, there was no
evidence to support that belief, but aggrieved Polish families, needing no
proof beyond the absence of their community leaders, were happy to point
out Jewish households to Einsatzgruppen officers and to participate in hu-
miliation rituals as the Jewish men were dragged away to their deaths.

The worst incident in the wake of the invasion came at the end of July
1941, when the Nazis created a sort of game: Hundreds of Jewish men were
ordered to lie facedown in the Ashmyany market square and eat grass while
German officers revved up their cars and drove at full speed toward them,
stopping only at the very last minute. If the men lifted up their heads at the
sound of the approaching cars, they were shot. After many hours of this
torment, cheered on by local Poles, somewhere between 500 and 700 men
were taken away and never seen again. For a while, the Germans maintained
the pretense that they had been taken for a work assignment, but their devastated wives, mothers, and daughters suspected otherwise and eventually
recovered pieces of their mutilated bodies from a mass grave in a nearby
village.

By the time Franya arrived in Ashmyany, the killings had largely ceased.
But the remaining Jews—about 1,800 women and 150 men—were locked
up in a ghetto. It was surveilled by a military commandant described by a
local teacher as "a wild, bloodthirsty beast" and by another man who was

known as a criminal and sadist with a taste for tormenting and humiliating women. The residents had been instructed not to let outsiders in, on pain of death. Food was desperately scarce. There was very little to share, even if families were brave enough to take in any of the hundreds of refugees from other parts of Lithuania who came knocking that autumn.

According to *Twenty-One and One*, Franya offered to sing and organize concerts to help raise money for the needy, but the ghetto leaders wouldn't take the risk, especially after a deployment of German paramilitary police from the SS intelligence arm arrived in early November. They were there for the express purpose of hunting down people without the correct registration papers and shooting them.

In other words, Franya's timing could not have been worse as she tried and failed to gain admission. A few months later, the Ashmyany Judenrat was able to take advantage of a change in German personnel to cut a deal with the town mayor and add about two hundred refugees to the registration list. But for now, their hands were tied, forcing Franya to keep moving.

By that point, she had taken up with a group of about fifteen to eighteen other similarly luckless refugees. Strangers transformed into fast friends as they sought refuge together on cold nights and long, strenuous, terrifying days. Together, still clinging to hope, they traveled to the next town, Olshan, only to run into the same objection. The situation was growing desperate. A group that size couldn't hope to continue moving through open country without being spotted, and temperatures were beginning to dip below freezing. Experiencing my own kind of chill, knowing that I was truly reaching the end of Franya's story, I was suddenly reminded of a verse by Paper Brigade founder and poet Abraham Sutzkever:

> *Have you seen, in fields of snow,*
> *frozen Jews, row on row?*
> *Blue marble forms lying,*
> *not breathing, not dying.*

Any thoughts of continuing deeper into Byelorussia or even making a break for the Soviet border had now been abandoned. Most likely, Franya and her friends recognized Vilna as their best option after all, because they turned around and started the perilous journey back north.

They made it only a few miles before falling into the hands of the Nazi paramilitary police, who, by one account, took them to the Jewish cemetery in Ashmyany, handed shovels to the young men traveling with Franya, and ordered them to dig.

Franya knew the end had come, but she refused to go quietly.

"She wanted to live," Blecher wrote.

"She struggled with her last abilities," Dora Rubina said.

Franya was a fighter.

This was the passage of Rubina's testimony that I had struggled to read to my fellow writing students in Iowa, the part that moved me to slam my laptop shut before I was able to gain the strength to continue.

"With her teeth, she bit the SS man . . . ," the Rubina account continued. I imagined the actress's voice faltering as mine had in that classroom.

My eyes had welled with tears as I reopened my computer, exhaled, and, through a blur, read these words to the class: " . . . the SS man, who, out of anger, saved on a bullet to shoot her, and ordered that she be buried alive."

10

The Aftermath

"ONE CAN TRULY ONLY SCREAM. BUT IT IS NOT POSSIBLE TO COMPOSE
SUCH MEASURED, RHYTHMIC SENTENCES"

I SAT STUNNED on my couch, the translation of *Twenty-One and One* open on my laptop. I shifted to the edge of my seat as if I should stand up and do something, but I couldn't think what. I had been hearing about and avoiding this book, the final details of Franya's story, for almost thirty years. Did I feel catharsis? A sense of completion? Of a mission accomplished? Did I feel closer to Franya, or did I feel her fading away, her image disappearing like she had, evaporating into dust?

My heart was still pounding from the read. I was sad, undoubtedly, despite having already known the ending. About Franya's savage death, of course. About Tante Rivel and Isaak and all of the others who had simply wanted to live their lives. About hatred so strong that it fueled unspeakable violence and brutality, though it was rooted in lies and imaginary evils. About the unchecked murder of six million people, each an individual with likes and dislikes, responsibilities and pleasures, and families just like my own.

But also, I realized, I felt at loose ends. Was I feeling enough? Too much? Did I have a clearer sense of what to tell my children about this tragedy?

How many years had I been chasing this truth? How many decades had I been using the quest to lend a sense of control, a way to impact what could not be undone?

What was my life when the mission was over? And if I had satisfied the responsibility bestowed upon me by Aunt Mollie as the memorial candle, why didn't I feel done? I had a gnawing sense of something more.

Even before reading Blecher's forbidden text, I had chosen to learn about Franya's death in a room full of near strangers. It was emotional, bordering on bizarre, to be sure. But I wasn't sure, given the chance, that I would have done it differently. I wanted my classmates to be witnesses to the story as it unraveled and see firsthand how the horrors still resonated generations later, how they impacted lives. Like Aunt Mollie, I wanted the story to serve some useful purpose. I wanted the account to open their minds. I wanted the class to *feel* the reverberations of hatred on the generations.

And they certainly did. I recalled how after I'd finished reading, closing my laptop (slowly and reverently this time), I looked out over the faces staring back at me with empathy. They appeared to be in as much shock as I, tears in their eyes, lips wide open.

I could feel the shocking betrayal of the push out the door by a onetime friend, having taken everything, her gold and jewelry.

I could feel the desperate struggle, punching and kicking and screaming for life. I could feel the strength of her jaw on his arm and the taste of his flesh.

My teacher said, "Meryl, this is a book. You need to write this as a book."

I looked up at his face, his expression kind, and shook my head. "I don't think I can find the words."

It wasn't false modesty. A hurricane had just blown through my mind, leaving my thoughts and feelings in a hopeless jumble. How could I ever make sense of them on the page?

"Just write," he said. "Imagine what *she* felt."

As if I hadn't been hearing Franya's voice in my head, sensing her at my shoulder, my whole life.

He was trying to encourage me, of course, but I was in no mood to hear it.

"What am I supposed to write?" I retorted, suddenly exasperated. "How the dirt tasted?"

—⁓—

FOR A FEW MONTHS, I DIDN'T FEEL LIKE DOING MUCH. WITH MY PROTEC-
tive layer now lifted, I was vulnerable to the full impact of what I'd discovered. I stopped writing.

"I am not sure when or if I will return to this project," I wrote to a confi-
dante. "I don't know how. I need to find a way to live with it, and I am not
supposed to close off to the pain, right?"

And though I shared both Rubina's and Blecher's testimonies with my
husband and children, I could not force words for what happened to Franya
out of my mouth.

No doubt the lingering shock was one of the reasons I postponed my
reading of *Twenty-One and One*. Now that I knew the truth, I finally understood Aunt Mollie's admonition better. She knew how much I idolized
Franya just based on the photos and prewar stories. What responsible adult
could tell a little girl, or even an adult version of that little girl, that the Nazis had tortured her celebrated actress cousin to death? That they had flung
her precious body into a freshly dug pit and forced her to choke on the dese-
crated soil of a Jewish cemetery?

The language of my childhood household now echoed in my ears: *They're
gone. They didn't make it.* That was, in some ways, the beginning and the end.

My bewilderment was not helped by the fact that I wasn't sure if I would
ever know who these men were who were responsible for Franya's death, as
well as Isaak's and Tante Rivel's. I surely couldn't bring them to justice, but
at least I could tell their truth.

So, I set out on yet another journey.

All of the potential suspects were unquestionably war criminals and
agents of genocide, yet the record showed that most—the perpetrators I was
certain of and the ones I researched as likely matches—had wriggled free of
the punishments they deserved. Only Martin Weiss, the overlord of Ponary,
received anything close to justice. He was tried in Würzburg in 1949, found
responsible for the murder of at least thirty thousand Jews (including seven
he murdered personally), and sentenced to life imprisonment. Yet even this
definitive judgment failed to stick completely. Abraham Sutzkever wrote
that Weiss "loved his art like a musician loves his violin; his greatest joy
was to strangle children with his own hands." Yet, by 1970, he was deemed

eligible for parole. Seven years later, he was released. He died peacefully in Karlsruhe, the city of his birth, at the age of eighty-one.

Most dispiriting, perhaps, was the story of Franz Murer, the Vilna ghetto's cruel guardian who forced parents to choose between their children. A Soviet military court in Vilnius sentenced him to death in 1948, but the sentence was commuted to twenty-five years of hard labor and then suspended altogether when, under the terms of a 1955 treaty between the postwar occupying powers, he was shipped home to Austria. Murer was supposed to serve out the rest of his sentence there, but the Austrians instead let him return to his farm in Styria. There, he was given a hero's welcome and soon became a prominent figure in local agricultural politics.

Under considerable international pressure, he was retried in 1963, but the jury showed little interest in the devastating testimony of fifty prosecution witnesses who recalled their suffering with pinpoint precision. The jurors weren't interested in the prosecutor's attempts to show the world that Austria had moved on from its past pro-Nazi inclinations. They didn't just acquit Murer, to loud applause from the gallery; a number of them took him out for a celebratory drink afterward, during which he was presented with flowers and driven home in a swanky black Mercedes.

Clearly, anti-Semitism was far from eradicated.

Could Austrian SS officer Bruno Kittel have issued the order that ultimately condemned Franya when he was in charge of the Vilna ghetto? Psychologically, there's no question he had the capacity for it. But there never was a thorough investigation into his crimes. At the end of the war, Kittel vanished and was never seen or heard from again.

The record on accountability was a shocking mess. If I was looking for comfort there, there was none to be found. Still, it was essential to look the reality of what these men did straight in the eye, all part of "never again." I could look at what they did and extrapolate about what was possible, if hatred took the reins. That was an essential lesson.

Practically, part of the problem stemmed from gaps in the Nazis' records, some of which were lost in the chaos of war or deliberately destroyed to protect the guilty. Part of the issue, though, was the result of specific policy decisions made by both the West Germans and the Allied occupying powers that undermined efforts to prosecute war criminals below the very top tier. That brought the energetic push for accountability at the Nuremberg Trials to an abrupt halt.

The West German government, for its part, quickly abandoned denazification efforts in just about every area of public life, including the criminal justice system. The way Konrad Adenauer, the first postwar chancellor, saw it, there were simply too many ex-Nazis in key positions holding up the institutions of state. This was the price a shattered country had to pay if it wanted to stay united on a path to democracy. The supposed hope was that, in exchange for being left alone, most former Nazis would "atone" and act like democrats going forward. "You don't throw out the dirty water," Adenauer reasoned, "if you don't have any clean."

The Western allies, especially the United States, could have pursued the prosecution of war criminals themselves, but their attention was soon diverted by the Cold War. Instead of chasing Nazis, they found uses for them in combating their new top adversary, the Soviet Union. The Central Intelligence Agency had no hesitation about working with former Nazi allies in Ukraine and other parts of the Soviet Union, groups as bad or worse as the one that killed Cheyna's cousin Schloyme Boyarski in Vasilishok. Without qualms, the US government smuggled Nazi scientists and military experts out of Europe and gave them high-profile positions within the rapidly growing national security establishment. This was closer to home than I liked.

It wasn't until the Eichmann trial in 1961 that many people around the globe woke up to the reality that hundreds, maybe thousands, of the worst Nazi war criminals were walking free. In West Germany, the renewed prosecutorial efforts of the 1960s and 1970s were in part a reflection of the disgust many younger people expressed at the compromises of their parents' generation. Still, the effort proved to be too little, too late. The judges and juries with lingering Nazi sympathies were still willing to make excuses on behalf of ruthless killers. The men who tormented and murdered my family were allowed to live and die in peace.

If I had been looking for justice on this quest—and I'm not sure I was—I realized then that I would never find it. The scale of the Holocaust's devastation was just too great.

11

The Final Piece

I HAD EXHAUSTED my search for Franya's story. My work was done—yet I had this nagging feeling that something was still missing. For a while, I explained that sense away, blaming how accustomed I was to working toward this goal and how unnatural it felt to stop. I was adjusting to a new perspective.

But then it hit me: I had never figured out how the photographs of my family had ended up in an abandoned house in Choisy-le-Roi! I had guessed and theorized, talking through possibilities with Aurore, the Mémorial de la Shoah archivist, and Serge, but nothing ever made complete sense. This was a question that the forbidden book couldn't answer.

I couldn't just let this dangle. If I wanted full closure, I had to figure it out. And, after all my searching, I felt confident that I could.

I had learned through my genealogical research that Franya had other relatives who lived in Paris, including an uncle Lezer, who owned a leather factory and may have encouraged her brother Nisen to enter the business, and Lezer's two grown children, who were born in Poland but went by the French names Charles and Berthe, married to Henri Gajst.

Hopeful that I might find someone who made it through the war, I began searching for any record of Franya's cousins. I found a jarring photograph of Berthe and her son Jean online. Jean, born in 1929, appears to be about twelve years old. He is wearing a jacket, tie, short pants, and knee socks, with shoes clearly too big for his feet. He stands with his hands in his pockets and a sweet smile on his face. To his left is his mother, with a blank stare, dressed in a skirt and jacket, which on its left breast is sewn a Star of David with the word "Juif." This was not a portrait or pleasure shot. There was no background. Perhaps, I thought, this was some sort of ID photo taken for papers to leave France at the last minute.

Unfortunately, neither Jean nor his mother, Berthe, nor any of this branch of the Rosenrot family made it out alive. They were all rounded up and sent to Auschwitz in the summer of 1942. Once again I was at an impasse. I read and reread all my notes and records, reviewing every piece of relevant evidence again and again until I'd practically memorized them. What was I missing?

Finally, as I sat in my sunroom in the late spring of 2021, staring at the photographs for the thousandth time—like I had as a child—silently pleading with the subjects for a clue, I realized that I had missed something.

Aurore Blaise and her colleagues had left one inscription on the back of the photographs undeciphered. It was in a language they couldn't identify, and, in the flurry of excitement following my first visit to the Mémorial de la Shoah, I had completely forgotten to set about translating it myself.

Now I took a closer look and realized the photograph the Mémorial had tagged as number 30 was of a strikingly elegant young man, slim shouldered with a round face and deep, expressive eyes that reminded me of Franya's. He wore a beautifully tailored three-piece suit, a watch chain dangling from his waistcoat, and an equally sharp dark overcoat with a large oval cuff link poking out of the right sleeve. On his head was an unusual round felt hat, possibly a *kaskhet*, which Hasidic Jews had taken to wearing during the czarist era when the law prohibited more traditional Jewish headgear.

Aurore guessed in her notes that the inscription on the back of this photograph was in Lithuanian. I sent it off to a friend in Lithuania who told me that the writing was Polish, not Lithuanian. I had it translated right away. When the English version arrived in my inbox, my eyes welled with tears. It was the missing piece, and it had been here all along. It was meant to be a final message from a brother to his dear sister.

It read:

When I die, when I pass away, when I
am no longer here, this postcard will remind
you of a brother who loved you.

—Abramek Rosenrot, to his beloved sister Franya

Everything suddenly fell into place. As it turned out, Franya had *an-other* brother in Paris besides Nisen, one who loved good clothes and had the money to pay for them. Abramek—using the Polish diminutive for Abraham—had plainly scrawled this note while fearing for his life after the Nazis overran first France and then Poland in the summer of 1940. And plainly, too, he thought Franya, of all the Rosenrots, stood the best chance of survival. She was after all a famous actress with friends and connections all over Europe, she had a rebellious spirit and a determination that Abraham would have known from childhood, and Vilna had not yet been invaded as France had. If Abraham wrote the note before June 1941, he might have reasoned that Franya was safer in Vilna, on the Soviet side of a partitioned Poland, than in Nazi-occupied Warsaw or Paris. Few foresaw the German invasion of the Soviet Union. Indeed, many in Western Europe believed that when Polish refugees made it to Vilna in 1939 and 1940, they had reached a place of safety.

Clearly, Abraham, not Nisen, had assembled the photographs and arranged for their safekeeping, with instructions that if anything happened to him, they should be sent on to Franya. What, though, had happened to Abraham? He was already worried, though the first transports of French Jews to Auschwitz did not take place until the summer of 1942.

To answer these questions, I set about learning more about Abraham. Shaking my head at my own mistake, I realized I had seen his name before: photograph number 31, the next one in the collection, was of two very young men, maybe teenagers, who were small and slight and had similar shocks of curly dark hair. From Aurore's notes on the Yiddish inscription, I had not two but *three* names to go with these two boys—Simcha Lezer,

Nisen, and Abraham Joseph Rosenrot—with little clarity as to which of them was pictured or how they were related. Something about the translation was off, leading me to suppose that Simcha and Abraham were cousins of Franya's and, thus, of less interest to my search. The genealogy was so important to me because it could lead to the answers that I was seeking. Why were these photos found in Maison Danton? Who was the owner of these photos? Were any of the siblings or the descendants of the siblings still alive, who could contribute some additional information on the life of Franya? Was there more to know?

I requested my own translation of the second inscription, and it turned out that the first translation had to be corrected. It cleared up the confusion immediately:

As a keepsake of your two dear brothers, Simcha Lezer and Nisen, we offer this portrait to you, Abraham Joseph Rosenrot.

So, they were *all* Franya's brothers. Later, I would establish a rough birth order, with Franya, born in 1896, as the oldest, Abraham the second oldest (1898), then Simcha (for whom I did not have a birth date, but he appeared older than Nisen in the photograph), Raisel (1909), Nisen (1911), and then maybe another sister, or someone who looked like a sister in a photograph with Franya and Franya's mother from Serge's collection. I also assessed that one photograph I had of the two youngest brothers was taken while they were still growing up in Warsaw and far away from Abraham, who had already moved to Paris.

I checked the available records, but could find no trace of Abraham at Pithiviers, the internment camp outside Paris where Nisen was taken in May 1941, following the so-called green-ticket roundup. This had been the first mass arrest in Paris, aimed specifically at expatriate Jews, particularly Poles. Nor could I find a trace of Abraham at Auschwitz, where Nisen and his cousin Charles met a bitter end in 1942. Still, I could feel that familiar drive taking over, and I knew it was only a matter of time until I figured out more.

Eventually, after days of searching online, I found a death notice. Though he was now gone, Abraham had found a way to slip through the Nazi net and live a long life after the war! He died not in Paris, but in Annecy, in the French Alps, at the ripe old age of ninety-three in 1983. I was overcome by unexpected elation at reading those words. After all the tragic and horrifying endings, it was so wonderful to discover a story that ended differently. One of my relatives—one of Franya's closest family members—had lived!

How could I find out more? The French have strict privacy rules around the disclosure of family records, so it was impossible to collect information from official sources about whether Abraham had been married or if he had children or grandchildren. Instead, I decided to look for evidence of a Jewish community in Annecy, searching out a website for the town's single synagogue. Since I speak limited French, I asked a native speaker to put in a call on my behalf, unsure of what to expect. I waited on pins and needles.

The rabbi's wife, Esther Suissa, turned out to be the wildly enthusiastic Canadian mother of seven and grandmother of twenty-six, who was more than happy to speak to me in English. Beyond that, she understood exactly what I was looking for and was thrilled to help. Esther, who did not learn that her own father was interned in Dachau until she was twenty years old, understood the silences and the importance of keeping memory alive. Yet again, I'd found an invaluable partner for my search, my *schvester* (Yiddish for "sister") Esther, as she signed her emails to me.

"Of course, I remember Monsieur Rosenrot," she exclaimed. Speaking so rapidly I had to listen carefully to follow, Esther recalled from thirty years earlier that he attended services, in fact he was given a seat of honor on the bima, and, she added, "he was always dressed impeccably." But that wasn't all she had to share. She had already made additional phone calls on my behalf, beginning to piece together the story of how he survived the war.

After six years of false starts and dead ends, these last details came together with surprising ease. With a confidence I couldn't quite explain, this, I felt, was where I had been headed all along.

~

ABRAHAM DIDN'T JUST LOVE CLOTHES, I WOULD LATER LEARN. HE WAS IN the garment business as a hatmaker, with a millinery workshop established in the early 1920s on the rue de Charenton in Paris's Twelfth Arrondissement.

In 1925, when he was twenty-seven years old, he married a seventeen-year-old
from Philadelphia, Susie Otchakovsky, and together they had a son, Jacques,
in 1929. A photograph from the early 1930s shows Susie with a round face
and dark hair, holding a smiling Jacques aloft at about eighteen months old.
Abraham, dapper as always in a worsted suit, leather dress shoes, and striped
socks, is sitting across from them, while Nisen and a woman I can't identify
stand behind. A feeling of easy contentment abounds, free from stress. I
knew Abraham was doing so well financially that he'd moved his family to
Bagnolet, in the eastern suburbs. Nisen, who had arrived in Paris two years
before, was making a name for himself at Lezer's leather business on the rue
Sainte-Croix de la Bretonnerie, in the heart of Paris's Jewish quarter.

The war disrupted their lives with a shocking abruptness. They would
never feel quite so safe and settled again. Within weeks of the Nazi invasion
of Poland in September 1939, Abraham enlisted with the French Foreign
Legion. He no longer had a country or a nationality—documents from the
time list him as *apatride*, stateless—but like many other Polish Jews living
in France, he was motivated to do whatever he could to counter the Nazi
threat. It's not clear exactly what happened next, as most of Abraham's military files have been lost, but he, like many other Polish legionnaires, was
likely sent to a training camp near Perpignan, close to the Spanish border. I
uncovered a police document from March 1940 that shows he was obtaining
a waiver that would permit him, as a noncitizen, to switch branches. Apparently, he'd opted not to stay in the Legion, but to join a standard French
army regiment, an indication that he was considered a promising recruit.

Records suggest that Abraham fought to defend France from May or June
1940. This was not an unusual phenomenon. Many foreign fighters risked
and lost their lives on France's behalf, both because they had no other al-
legiance due to geopolitical shifts and because the Nazis were a common
enemy. Based on the photographs, this was probably also the period when
Abraham made contingency plans in case he did not survive. The prospect
of combat raised the chances of him being "no longer here," as he wrote to
his sister Franya on the back of his portrait. And the danger would not have
ebbed that much after the fighting was over. All Jews were at risk after the
fall of France, but Abraham had a bigger target on his back. The Foreign

Legion had been infiltrated for years by Nazis posing as ordinary German recruits. These spies compiled lists of Jews in the ranks with the intention of hunting them down and targeting them for death later.

In 1942, when Nisen, Uncle Lezer, and his two children, cousins Charles and Berthe and their families, were arrested and sent first to Pithiviers and then to Auschwitz, Abraham made some tough and irrevocable decisions. He had in the interim become estranged from his wife, Susie, who had an American passport that might have allowed them to leave. Instead, he struck up an affair with a young widow who worked at his millinery, Camille Brondel. This relationship was to be something more than a passing infatuation. Before long, Abraham and Camille, who was not Jewish, put their heads together and hatched their own survival plan.

Abraham and Camille each had a son the same age. Together they decided that Abraham's son, Jacques, would pose as Camille's son, Bernard, and spend the rest of the war in safety on a farm in the Pyrenees, using Bernard's identification papers as a cover. Bernard, meanwhile, would obtain duplicate papers and stay in Paris with his mother and Abraham. Once the mass deportations began and it became too dangerous for Jews to appear on the street, Camille devised a hiding place for Abraham inside a wardrobe where he could retreat when the Germans or the French police approached with their heavy boots, banging their fists on the door and demanding documents. Being a non-Jew, she was able to keep working and bring in whatever supplies and goods they needed. Meanwhile, Abraham existed as an invisible man.

I was overjoyed to learn that the plan worked: Abraham, Susie, and Jacques all lived to be liberated in the summer of 1944 and were able to reunite after the war. Abraham finalized his divorce from Susie just a week after the Nazi surrender in May 1945 and married Camille two years after that.

The psychological damage incurred by these wartime experiences, though, was profound. Abraham had to reckon with the loss of almost his entire family, including both his parents and all his siblings, without knowing anything about how they died. Like so many, it was as if they'd just vanished. I'd spent decades researching, with the benefit of travel, telephones, established archives, and the Internet, and still had large gaps in my knowledge. Abraham had none of these channels. The fate of my family members trapped in Warsaw—Abraham's parents, his brother Simcha, his sister Raisel, Raisel's husband, Soma Punski, and their adorable daughter, Basha (beloved by Franya)—remains a mystery to this day.

Abraham's son, Jacques, had his own trauma to process too. What a strange, isolating, and frightening way to grow up! He spent his formative teenage years away from his parents, pretending to be someone he was not, in a place that was wholly unfamiliar. If that wasn't bad enough, he also had to wrestle with the fact that another boy, the real Bernard, was living *his* life in Paris, with *his* father, and all the comforts of home.

By the time the war was over, Jacques was, understandably, a mess. His fury toward Abraham knew no bounds, but so did his deep-seated desire to connect and belong. He expressed his animosity by setting himself up in perverse competition with and emulation of his father. He too married a seventeen-year-old, had a child with her, and left her. He too joined the French Foreign Legion—in his case serving in Algeria and Indochina during their wars of independence. Eager to prove himself, he came home with eleven medals, more than his father had managed. But he also suffered a head injury that led to lifelong medical problems. He spent most of his subsequent career as an assembly-line worker at a Renault car factory.

It occurred to me again, as I learned his story, that the reverberations of genocide stretch far beyond the obvious and immediate. Even in the midst and wake of war, a period of so much loss, families are complicated entities struggling for equilibrium. I thought about my own role in my family, designated by Mollie, about the countless times I'd felt both honored and resentful of being the memorial candle. Now I realized that those were both valid reactions, not mutually exclusive. Yet, in many ways, the role defined my life.

Abraham responded to his own calamitous experiences by shrouding them in silence. He and Camille—the same Camille, I now realized with shock and recognition, whose photos from the 1920s had found their way into Serge's stack, confounding us in our search—spent the rest of their working lives in Saint-Denis, just outside the northern Paris city limits. Eventually, they retired to the South of France to be closer to Bernard, living first in Tallard, a remote mountain town between Marseille and Grenoble, and then in Annecy.

Esther talked and introduced me to multiple people who knew Abraham in his later years. They all described him the same way: very discreet, very quiet, impeccably dressed, polite, but utterly unforthcoming. Every week, a neighbor of his in Annecy, Monsieur Hassoun, would walk with Abraham from their apartment building to the synagogue a mile away. They repeated that same journey hundreds of times over the years, but Hassoun never learned a thing about him. "I don't have any information" was all Madame Hassoun, now widowed and living in Israel, told Esther Suissa over the phone.

The only story that circulated about Abraham was related to Camille hiding him in a wardrobe during the war. Perhaps he shared this much to explain to a highly conservative Jewish community why he was married to a non-Jew. Or perhaps Camille shared the story from her own perspective. Regardless, Abraham owed his life to her, which the synagogue elders accepted without question or hesitation. But it was also unclear where exactly the story originated. As Esther's husband, Rabbi Naftali Suissa, said with delightful vagueness, "It's a story that was told."

In the fall of 2021, my husband, Steven, and I boarded a plane and flew to Annecy to meet Esther in person and see the Alpine town for myself. The city, sometimes referred to as "the Venice of the French Alps" thanks to the crystal canals that run throughout, was so idyllic that it seemed almost unreal. With glorious mountains rising above, in the charming old town, medieval stone structures and sun-bleached pastel buildings lined the water, cafés spreading into the streets. There was an autumn chill in the air, fresh and crisp. The first wave of the pandemic had passed, and it was possible to travel with proof of vaccination. If you wanted a place to forget the evils of the world and your past, Annecy seemed perfect. Upon seeing it with my own eyes, I felt buoyed by the fact that Abraham and Camille had found their way here, to a kind of Eden.

Esther Suissa welcomed me with open arms—in a pandemic mask and shoulder-length wig (as per her tradition)—and introduced me to her husband so he could share his perspective. Immediately, it became obvious that

Abraham had commanded great respect as a Holocaust survivor. Most of the founders of his synagogue were not Eastern European Ashkenazi Jews but French Algerians who settled in Annecy after Algeria won its independence in 1962. Still, they welcomed Abraham as one of their own. Rabbi Suissa gave me a tour of his modest brick synagogue, which followed the typical Orthodox practice of separating men from women and placing a *mechitza*, or partition, between their seating areas. The rabbi also pointed out a blue-cushioned chair reserved for Abraham week after week directly across from the temple president's seat—a great honor.

Inside, the synagogue featured a green marble plaque dedicated "to the memory of the dead, the deported, and the disappeared who fell victim to Nazi barbarity." Every year, Rabbi Suissa held a ceremony to acknowledge those lost in the Holocaust. If Abraham had any thoughts or feelings about this, he didn't share them. "He never said a word about his experiences or showed any emotion during the ceremony," Rabbi Suissa recalled.

I'd hoped, perhaps naively, that if I personally talked to enough people in Annecy, I might learn more about Abraham's wartime experiences and understand how the photographs that Serge unearthed had played into his story. But that was not to be. Abraham remained an enigma, private and reserved. This was not a surprise. How difficult it must be to find words to convey the reality of the horror.

I regularly ran through the possible scenarios in my head: Perhaps Camille hid Abraham in the house in Choisy-le-Roi, either because that was where they lived during the war or because it was simply an alternate hiding place for their most desperate times—and the photos followed him there. Another possibility was that Abraham knew about the abandoned Maison Danton much earlier—one of the witnesses at his wedding to Susie had an address in Villejuif, an adjacent suburb—and he stashed the photos there in 1939 or 1940, while he was in uniform and getting ready to face the German army. I couldn't know for sure, but there was a part of me that felt as if the location of the photos was simply meant to be—like the journey of the forbidden book or stumbling onto Karen Etingin's poster shop. Without those accidents of fate, I would never have found Serge and his beautiful family, now part of mine. I would not have been standing there today.

Remarking on the many synchronicities that fueled this journey, Esther remarked, "It's a very well-managed world!"

—⁓—

BUT THERE WAS AN EVEN MORE SIGNIFICANT DISCOVERY I HAD MADE THAT had prompted my trip to Annecy: it turned out I was not the first relative to come looking for Abraham, hoping to penetrate his thick walls of silence.

In researching, Esther Suissa, who turned out to be quite the sleuth, realized that the contract to maintain Abraham's grave in the Annecy municipal cemetery was about to expire, as it had been almost thirty years since his death. Would a relative come forward to renew it? Esther contacted the municipality to find out who had signed the original contract. It was Jacques, Abraham's son!

As soon as Esther shared that lead, I had set to work trying to track him down, only to learn that a Jacques Simon Rosenrot had died in 2010 in Rambouillet, just outside Paris. Was this the right Jacques Rosenrot? And if so, who was his next of kin? Esther called the city of Rambouillet, explaining her concern about the upkeep of the grave. The administrator on the other end of the line let slip that Jacques had a daughter named Léa, about whom I had no idea. When Esther called me, breathless, to share this huge development, I gasped with excitement. I knew instantly that we had the right person: Jacques's daughter had been named for Abraham's (and Franya's) mother, who was also Léa. This was the daughter Jacques had abandoned when he went off, like his father, to fight with the French Foreign Legion.

The administrator was nervous about having disclosed Léa's name, a violation of the law, so he'd begged Esther not to reach out to her directly. "Let me call her," he suggested, "and if she wants to get in touch about the grave concession, I'll give her your number." We agreed.

In the meantime, armed with her name, I began my own research—with Esther's help, of course. Léa Rosenrot Guinet had grown up in the 1950s and '60s with no clue that she had family connections to the war or that she was descended from a line of Eastern European Jews who had been almost entirely wiped out. Léa's mother, Jacqueline Hemond (a Gentile), was so furious about her husband leaving her that she refused to tell her daughter anything about Jacques or his immediate family. They left Paris when Léa was still quite young and moved to a rural area near Angoulême in southwestern France, obliterating any possibility of running into Jacques or Abraham by accident and making themselves more elusive if someone came looking.

Jacqueline did disclose that Léa's first name—unusual for a Christian child at the time—came from her great-grandmother, but all explanation stopped there. As Léa grew older, she felt a gaping hole where her father's side of the family should have been, one that proved impossible to tolerate. She begged her mother to show her photographs, but was met only with resistance. She asked for a way to contact her father, but Jacqueline refused.

Once Léa turned eighteen, she was legally empowered to seek information herself. She could apply for her own birth certificate, which gave her father's full name and place of birth, and her parents' marriage certificate, which gave the names of each of her grandparents.

The first person she was able to track down was her American grandmother, Susie Otchakovsky, Abraham's first wife and Jacques's mother. Susie, as it happened, had spent years trying to find her too, as her granddaughter, and had written a number of letters that Léa's mother had hidden. When Léa was nineteen, she managed to intercept one of the letters, holding on to it just long enough to write down the return address in Miami Beach. She and her grandmother struck up a long correspondence. Susie even came to France to visit in 1970, expressing shock to see Léa, at twenty, living in abject poverty with a husband she'd married shortly after leaving home and a six-month-old daughter. Susie told Léa about the Jewish origins of the family, but refused to talk about either Abraham or Jacques. It was too painful.

Thinking about my own experience and that of my immediate family, it seemed like too often we fell into the trap of either silence or obsession, two sides of the same coin. Part of this journey had become about trying to find a balance between the two. I wanted to be able to acknowledge and share the history without living inside of it, for myself, my children, and, even more recently, my two grandchildren.

The communication between Susie and Léa eventually lapsed in part because Léa went through an acrimonious divorce in the early 1980s, and her ex-husband destroyed her letters and address book. She tried to re-create Susie's address from memory, but every time she thought she finally had it right, a blue airmail envelope would return unopened.

All Léa knew about her father at this point was that he'd been born in Paris. At some point in the late 1980s, she learned that if she could figure out which arrondissement Jacques had been born in, she could access his birth and marriage records. So, she wrote to each of the arrondissements in turn, starting with the first and going in numerical order, until she reached the twelfth and found what she was looking for.

Suddenly, she had details. Jacques, she learned, was now remarried to a woman named Celeste, and their wedding had taken place in Issy-les-Moulineaux, a suburb just outside the city limits, best known for its Renault factory, where he worked on the assembly line. The city of Issy-les-Moulineaux wouldn't give out Jacques's address, but an administrator there happened to know Jacques personally and agreed to forward a letter.

That was a major stroke of luck. Jacques had retired from Renault by this time and was living twenty-five miles away in Rambouillet, something Léa would have struggled to learn on her own.

Not long after that, Léa's phone rang. It was her father calling. This was the first contact Léa and Jacques had since she was eighteen months old. Her heart beat wildly. The pieces of Léa's identity were falling into place. Her pulse thumped as they spoke tentatively at first, touching on basic details about their everyday lives, carefully skirting the reality of their divide. Then, as they began to grow more comfortable, they delved deeper, sharing truths about those missed years, as well as comparing likes and dislikes. They exchanged phone calls for several months. Then Léa and her second husband, Francis, took a train to meet Jacques.

As they pulled into the station, Léa was shaking so badly that "the hands of her watch" danced on her wrist. Her father, though, was in the mood to celebrate, thrilled to have his daughter back in his life. He showed up with Foreign Legion music blaring from his car and Legion flags hanging from the windows like he was preparing for a Bastille Day parade.

Instinctively, Léa addressed Jacques as *vous*, the formal French "you." "I'm your father, you should use *tu*," Jacques admonished her. But Léa couldn't make that shift, not right away. Jacques might have been her father, but he was also a stranger.

The duo did form a bond, though. Over the ensuing years, they became fixtures in each other's lives, traveling back and forth from Rambouillet to Hiersac, the town where Léa and Francis lived.

Léa's mother couldn't understand why she'd want anything to do with a father who had abandoned her, but Léa harbored no ill will toward Jacques and pushed back. "Your relationship with him is your relationship," she told Jacqueline. "It doesn't concern me. I want to know who he is." She had been able to find the connection to her past that had eluded her for so long.

Reuniting with Jacques only made Léa want to learn more about her heritage. What about her grandfather Abraham? Could she find and meet him, if he was still alive? She had a joyful early memory of visiting his millinery when she was little, but contact had been lost when she and her mother moved to the country. As an adult, she learned that her "Papy Joe"—what she called Abraham—had continued to send money to help support her, but Jacqueline had concealed this, as she concealed anything to do with her ex-husband and his family.

For years, whenever Léa and her husband, Francis, traveled anywhere in France, they would look up the name Abraham Rosenrot in the local phone book. Léa even wrote to the authorities in Warsaw, hoping they'd know where to find him, but the civil records of Abraham's generation had not survived the destruction of the city in the closing stages of the war.

It was Jacques who ultimately provided Léa with the break she needed. Though he hadn't spoken to his father for years, he did remember that Abraham and Camille had been married in Saint-Denis. From that city, Léa was able to access their civil records. Sadly, Camille had died a few years earlier. Her place of death was listed as Annecy.

Léa raced to the nearest post office to find an Annecy phone directory, then flipped through the pages quickly. There he was: Abraham Joseph Rosenrot, living at number 31, rue Henri Bordeaux, with a listed phone number.

As soon as she could compose herself, Léa dialed his number.

When a man picked up, she asked if he was Abraham Rosenrot.

"*Non, non, madame, ce n'est pas moi*" was her grandfather's instinctive reply. No, not me. You must have me confused with someone else.

Instinctively, Léa understood that her grandfather had lived much of his life in danger and needed to be approached cautiously, so she tried another approach. "Papy," she said gently, "it's Léa."

At the mention of her name, Abraham's defensiveness melted away. He could not have been more delighted to hear from his granddaughter, though he had hardly known her and had given up on ever seeing her again. Having lost Camille, he was living a mostly solitary life, alone with his thoughts, memories, synagogue visits, and exquisite hats. Here was the offer of kinship without strings attached, especially meaningful to someone who had lost so much of his family.

For the next four years, Léa and Francis visited Annecy regularly. In that time, Léa periodically talked to both Abraham and Jacques about putting aside their differences and reuniting. After some initial reluctance, they made their peace and spent time together several times before Abraham's death in 1992.

"I can't tell you, dear Léa, how happy I am about the great reconciliation," Abraham wrote on the eve of his first meeting with Jacques in 1989. He went to his grave calmer and more resolved than he had been in many decades.

~

LÉA DIDN'T GET IN TOUCH RIGHT AWAY, THINKING WE WERE SIMPLY FOL-lowing up on a cemetery bill. But eventually, she called back. When she reached Esther, the rabbi's wife told her about how I, her American relative, had been looking for her.

I received my first enthusiastic email from Léa shortly thereafter. As if finding Serge's incredible family hadn't been enough, now I was connecting, across the Atlantic, with an actual family member who was equally thrilled to be in touch. I told her that I had been searching for her for six years. She said she understood. She had searched for twenty years for her father and grandfather.

Léa understood little English, and my French was nearly forgotten, but we muddled through and understood each other well enough thanks to Google Translate and a Zoom call in which Esther acted as translator. Léa had a round face—like Franya's, I thought—with brown hair and light eyes. She had the manner of a shy woman, but I knew that beneath her exterior she had a fierce determination, one that drove her to search for her family for twenty years.

Soon we were making plans to meet up in Annecy so we could tell our stories more fully and share the documents and photographs we each had in our possession. Together we would be able to reconstruct something fuller—a history with missing pieces, yes, but also stories with dimension and history to help us understand ourselves better. I was so touched when Serge, who had long been in remission from his cancer, also offered to come, taking the long train ride from Plouha to Paris and then on to Annecy to witness our meeting.

Just a few weeks later, we were standing side by side around the grave of Franya's brother Abraham, a clear blue sky above us and blazing fall colors all around. As Rabbi Suissa, Esther's husband, recited prayers over the black granite tombstone, I stood, arm in arm, with Franya's niece. For the first time, there was human contact with someone who was an actual player in the story, a blood relative of Franya's, someone who spent her life searching as well. I felt as if the ghosts of Franya and her brother Abramek were flying above. His message of love to his beloved sister written on the back of his photo so long ago was delivered.

And if we were not blood relatives, that didn't matter, as I told Léa; we were *mishpucha*, a Yiddish term that means family in a broader sense, a term for which there is no English translation.

Together, Léa and I were closing the loop. We were bringing the Rosenrot family, and even the Punskis, who had lost each other, back together, representing Abraham and Franya and so much more.

Léa's life had not been easy. But she was modest and kind and utterly devoted to her husband, who was never more than a step or two behind her. But it was evident as I walked her through the research I'd done and told her stories about relatives we had in common over drinks in a hotel lobby that the family connections she'd been denied as a child still weighed heavily on her. She never knew that Abraham had siblings since he never talked about the past or that one of them had been a celebrated actress, a prima donna, before the war. I was so glad to be able to share that with her.

Léa was clearly emotional about finding the family she so longed to know, a feeling that I innately understood. I gave her a framed photograph of her great-grandmother Léa, the woman for whom she was named, saying, "La mama de Papa Joe . . . Léa Rosenrot pour vous." Although she spoke as little English as I spoke French, it was a moment that didn't require translation. Then I placed a symbol of our connection in her hand: a ring from our collection of family jewelry, a platinum deco-era piece set with a blue sapphire. As she teared up in recognition, she told me she regretted not asking more questions of her father and grandfather before they died and blamed herself because she didn't have it in her to insist when they evaded.

"It's the way I was raised," she said.

Her upbringing was only one part of the story, though. Abraham had chosen silence. It was the only way he could bear to live the rest of his life. In doing so, like my family, in some ways he had amplified that same history, until it loomed enormously in Léa's mind. I knew this all too well. In a way, she was also a memorial candle, though she'd met with resistance all along.

Still, looking at Léa, I couldn't help but feel grateful for whatever had brought us to meet at this place. It was not possible to find much of the family for whom I had been searching, at least not in the flesh. I couldn't resurrect the missing or the dead. But I had found something equally valuable: the new family I hadn't known I needed.

⁓

KNOWING HOW MUCH IT MIGHT MEAN TO LÉA AND EMBOLDENED BY THIS latest discovery, I took one last dive into our French family history. For five years I'd known the name of Nisen's wife, Midza Grunfass, because the Auschwitz-Birkenau state museum had it in their records. I also knew from Aurore Blaise's research that Nisen and Midza had a son. What, though, had happened to his wife and child after Nisen's arrest and deportation?

Aurore, the Mémorial archivist, found an important first clue by consulting the archives of the French Defense Ministry and piecing together the fact that Midza (listed by the French as Mindla Mysza Grinfas) married a man named Ingelman after the war and moved to Normandy, not far from Mont-Saint-Michel. Aurore also found a record of Nissen and Midza's son, Marcel. He was born in 1939, which meant he would have been in diapers when his father was taken away. All signs pointed to the fact that, like Abraham, Marcel had survived. As I neared the tail end of my search, I was thrilled to find life amid the loss and rubble.

I looked long and hard for Marcel and the Ingelmans. At one point, I wrote to every French family I could find with the last name Grunfass or Grinfas. What clinched it, in the end, was sheer luck, which was so often the case in this process. I searched for the name Ingelman on LinkedIn and sent a message to a woman named Sandrine Ingelman in the Paris suburbs. I figured it was just another shot in the dark.

She turned out to be Midza's granddaughter.

Sandrine put me in touch with her daughter, who, she said, knew both English and the family history better than she. Soon enough, I had pieced together most of the story: In July 1942, just a few days before the French authorities launched their biggest and most notorious roundup of Jews, Midza ran into a policeman in the Paris metro who saw her holding Marcel and warned her to get out of town as fast as possible. "They're going to arrest everyone—men, women, children, even babies," he told her. None of the family or friends with whom she shared this warning wanted to believe it, but Midza had already lost her husband and did not hesitate to take the policeman's advice. She was right to do so. Over the next few days, the French police, under the control of the German-installed government, arrested more than thirteen thousand Parisian Jews, including four thousand children, and penned them in an indoor cycling stadium near the Eiffel Tower. Soon after, they were shipped off to internment camps outside Paris and then to Auschwitz.

Midza chose to flee south so she could leave the German-occupied zone and reach the part of France controlled by the nominally independent Vichy government. This was hardly a guarantee of safety, since Vichy was also doing the Nazis' bidding. Indeed, she was arrested as soon as she reached the demarcation line between the two zones, saving herself only by convincing her captors that Marcel, who had light hair and blue eyes, had a German father. She had escaped.

The man Midza married after the war, Samson Ingelman, was a survivor himself, and the son they had together, Henri, may have suffered many of the traumas typically associated with children of the Holocaust. One relative described him as a "replacement child," burdened with filling the gaps left by family members who had died before his birth. Other relatives described conflicts between Henri and Marcel, half brothers brought together as much by tragedy as by love.

It all came to a head in 1988. Henri committed suicide at the age of forty-two.

In the aftermath of the tragedy, a rift developed between Marcel and the surviving Ingelmans over who was to blame. They fell out of touch so completely that by the time I started making inquiries, none of them even knew where Marcel lived. He'd worked as a security guard, they told me, at the Musée des Arts et Métiers in central Paris, but was presumably retired now. He had no wife or children.

At this late point, my research skills were finely honed. I sat at my laptop, staring at the ceiling for inspiration. I couldn't find Marcel in any phone or online directory, and a letter I wrote to the museum had gone unanswered. Ever helpful, Esther Suissa made countless calls on my behalf, trying pharmacies, doctors' offices, even opticians in Paris known to cater to a Jewish clientele. Miraculously, she tracked Marcel down in a Jewish nursing home and hospital in the Thirteenth Arrondissement. And, after charming nurses and social workers alike, Esther was able to arrange a visit.

The hospital was nondescript, with beige walls and beige floors. It was plain as soon as I set eyes on Marcel that he'd been neglected and lonely for a long time. The nurses said he never had visitors and had no possessions to speak of, not even clothes to wear out of bed. In preparation for my arrival, the staff had rustled up some pants, a T-shirt, and a sweater, all beige like the walls. They got him out of bed and into a wheelchair and made a point of cutting his hair and trimming his beard. Still, he looked disheveled and sad, unused to the most basic expressions of human kindness. The staff gathered around to see his reaction to his rare visitor.

At eighty-two, he was still a good-looking man, with soft skin and piercing blue eyes. He bore little resemblance to the photos I had of his father, Nisen, but he looked remarkably like his maternal grandfather, Franya's father, David Rosenrot. Esther had arranged for a friend to act as translator for me, and, through her, I told him who I was and how I was related to him. I showed him the photos I had in my possession of his father and mother and grandparents. I opened the box of fancy Damyel kosher chocolates that I brought him, and he picked up one happily, then two, then three.

He barely communicated, but, as I held his hand and looked into his eyes, I felt we were establishing a connection all the same.

Esther had also arranged that his doctor and a former Torah study partner, Stephan Botbol, meet us to talk. Sitting across the table and speaking as if Marcel were not still in the room, Dr. Kissous told me that Marcel "was a tsaddik with an extraordinary ability to see things in the texts and the prayers that others did not see." Botbol added that when Marcel was a bit younger, he wrote hundreds of poems and thought of his writing as his true vocation, but no longer. Again, I could not ignore the parallels that kept emerging, the tug-of-war between silence and compulsion. It was impossible to forget and torture to obsess. Looking at this shell of a man, I thought, whatever had happened between Henri and his brother, they were both victims of something much greater, trauma carried in their bones.

12

The Taste of Dirt

"AND WHAT IS THE POINT OF WRITING?—
TO SIGH! TO WRITE! TO PAINT!"

NOWHERE IN THE course of their genocidal frenzy between 1941 and 1945 were the Germans more thorough, more systematic, more ruthless than in Lithuania. In all, they wiped out 95 percent of the country's Jewish population, around two hundred thousand men, women, and children, of whom roughly three-quarters were rounded up and shot within the first six months of the invasion of June 22, 1941.

Eastern European Jews carried within them the passions, traditions, creativity, dreams, and aspirations of a dynamic culture, including the Yiddish theater, whose influence stretched around the globe, a culture so comprehensively crushed that its loss has sometimes been described as another Holocaust.

And Jews were not the Nazis' only victims. As a direct consequence of the Germans' obsession with agricultural resources and their willingness to deny food to entire populations, they deliberately starved to death more than three million Soviet prisoners of war. In all, the Nazis shot, gassed, froze, or starved more than ten million noncombatants on the eastern front, including political prisoners, Poles, Romani, and LGBTQ+ people; some believe as many as thirteen million. Add military casualties, and that figure tops twenty million.

Twenty million people.

How can anyone absorb such appalling numbers? How are we to digest the endless horrors that lie unspoken inside them? If the point of delving into the past, of investigating what our parents' and grandparents' generations didn't want us to know, of taking care to dismantle all the mythologizing so we can face the horror of the Holocaust, is to learn something, then what is the lesson, exactly?

Is it about striking a balance between remembering and moving forward? Is it about the history living inside us, but not controlling us? Is it about invoking the horrors without allowing others to appropriate and dull its meaning (as the lazy often do these days in petty political riffs) to continue to shock people with its heinousness without making them turn away?

The problem is multigenerational. Even if we do manage to wade through the atrocities and figure out what is most important to remember about the Holocaust or any other human tragedy, how are we to pass on what we've learned to our children and grandchildren so that they, too, keep memory alive? How do we help them heed the lessons and warnings without forcing them to be overwhelmed with fear? I grapple with these questions daily as I watch my own children and grandchildren navigate the modern world.

The challenge is not only to keep the stories relevant in a drastically different world—unfortunately, the rampant bias and hate in our culture make that part easy—but it's to impart the truth about anti-Semitism and human suffering without burdening the next generation with our anxiety, forcing them—like I did—to carry the torch of not just responsibility, but terror. As I look back, was it really Aunt Mollie's disappointment that I feared in reading the forbidden book, or was it a greater fear lurking just below the surface? Was I afraid of opening myself up to the pain of the whole truth, the full weight of what happened not just to Franya, but to millions of Jews? Did I have a sense, perhaps, that the silence persisted for a reason?

When my daughters were young, they used to play something they called "the Nazi Game." When one of them gave a signal, they'd all clamber as fast as they could into a single bed, piled with stuffed animals. They'd pull the covers over their heads as they waited for a thump on the door and hostile shouting from the other kids. "You have to be quiet," they'd whisper to each other. "They're coming!"

When I first found out they were doing this, I felt sick with guilt and worry. Had I damaged or traumatized my sweet girls with my own preoccupation? Had I done them a disservice by teaching them that everybody in the world hated them—or would, given half a chance? Now that my children are grown, though, I take comfort in the fact that they view my Holocaust obsession like any other quirky character trait, something synonymous with "Mom," for better or worse. They even tease me about it.

"Please, Mom, no Holocaust books on vacation!" Eve says. And we all laugh, knowing that much of the time, even when we went on trips to places the Nazis *hadn't* terrorized, I couldn't stop myself from drawing parallels.

Not so long ago, I made a point of talking this over with my children. Belle, my youngest, who came with me to Paris to meet Serge for the first time, admitted that she had vivid memories of how candid I'd been when she was little, about awful details. Apparently, she'd overheard me describing mothers so afraid of being discovered in their hideouts that they smothered their own babies. I covered my eyes, feeling like an awful mom. But I suppose that this is part of what happens when you're the youngest of four with inquisitive siblings all around, overhearing and watching things that your parents would never have let the first child see. Regardless, Belle didn't think there was anything wrong with the Nazi Game, and neither did her older sister, Eve. To them it was fun, like any other boogeyman.

They and their two brothers recognized my preoccupation with the Holocaust, without a doubt. They often rolled their eyes when I made constant references to it. But in retrospect, they all incorporated it into their worldviews and didn't think my harping made them overly fearful or paranoid. Rather, as Eve put it, they felt "prepared" and not just for dangers faced by Jews. Rather, they said, I had taught them to be alert to signs of hostility toward *any* minority group—immigrants, people of color, Muslims, or any other people who have been recent targets of hatred and violence. Belle said her upbringing and the "ever-present" talk about the Holocaust had given her "a sense of injustice in the world." Isaac, my eldest, said that all the talk about the Holocaust taught him that people can be too complacent, too comfortable, to face the dangers that are happening even now. "People didn't believe that it was real and didn't do anything," he lamented.

Eli, my second son, told me that he had similar thoughts about how what he learned as a child colored his world. He uses his understanding of the Holocaust as a tool for empathy. People need to ask themselves if they're just about talk or if they'll take action. He said that they need to ask themselves, "Who are you really?"—but he added that his connection to Judaism isn't tied to the Holocaust, which was exactly what I hoped to hear.

These reactions may say more about the admirable character of my children than they do about my parenting skills. But they do also make me think that a little paranoia, a little fear, may not be such a bad thing. In the end, it seems like acknowledging the reality of the ugly past and present is better than deafening silence.

Often, others who have suffered persecution seem to understand that outbursts of anti-Semitic prejudice and violence—attacks on synagogues, the desecration of cemeteries, the white supremacists in Charlottesville chanting, "Jews will not replace us!"—are not isolated incidents, but indications of a broader social unraveling that implicates everyone. "When you hear people speaking ill of the Jews," the Black French anticolonialist writer Frantz Fanon described being told as a young man, "pay attention, because they're talking about you."

We live in a world of extraordinary challenges—to the climate, to equity, to civil rights, to health, to basic notions of truth and decency, to democracy itself. None of us, white or Black, rich or poor, Jewish, Christian, Muslim, or atheist, can afford to be complacent. If there's one thing I hope my children have absorbed, one thing they have learned from the harrowing experiences of our Eastern European cousins at the hands of the Nazis, it is that the comforts and privileges they have grown up with can be taken away in a moment. That people are facing these challenges all over the world, every day, and we must be vigilant and willing to cry out and fight back against oppressors.

I don't want my children to be like those Jews in Vilna who told themselves, *The Germans are civilized people.* The hard truth, which no parent *wants* to tell a child, is that the world is not always a beautiful place. Our history tells us that horror exists, democracies can fall, economies can fail, and hatred and violence can erupt on a scale that defies imagination. Accepting that means realizing that, sometimes, we will be afraid. If anything, we need to worry if they are not afraid *enough*. As poet Amanda Gorman put it more beautifully than I ever could, "If you're not afraid, then you're not paying attention. The only thing we have to fear is *having no fear itself*—having no feeling on behalf of whom and what we've lost, whom and what we love."

To be able to move forward, we also need to look back. If there is one thing I have internalized from my Jewish tradition, it is the exhortation repeated over and over in the Torah to *teach your children*. They need to know that the Israelites were enslaved in Egypt before they crossed the Red Sea to the Promised Land. They, as privileged Americans, are afforded a certain level of comfort and security. They need to know that Jews suffered discrimination and marginalization throughout the Christian era, that they were slaughtered in the millions during the Holocaust, and that the danger is far from over. When white supremacists storm the Capitol, or march in Charlottesville, or shoot up the Tree of Life Synagogue, or when extremists equate the Star of David with the swastika, there is a risk that we must recognize. We must be vigilant. We must take action. I would be remiss as a parent if I *didn't* teach them these things, just as I would be remiss if I didn't teach them about the richness of their heritage, our contributions to civilization, the emphasis on scholarship and study, the depth and splendor of the Jewish lives their ancestors led while they still had the freedom to do so, and the way this richness sustained them in their darkest hours.

⁓

OF COURSE, DELVING INTO THE PAST ALSO MEANS GRAPPLING WITH THE complicated issue of memory. Mollie didn't always know the real story, and it was certainly important to me to nail down every detail I could uncover of my family's history. But in the end, I think perhaps the forbidden book gets it right when, in the introduction, Abraham Morewski wrote, "Because motives obstruct the facts, and even if any details are altered, it still does not become lies. But with words, one letter can set the truth on its head." On my journey, did I find truth, or did I find something more nuanced and even more important?

My children all adored Aunt Mollie, as I did, and I've always thought it was important, for their sakes as well as mine, to be able to account for the things that she either wouldn't tell me or misremembered. How did these omissions square with her admonition that I mustn't forget a thing? Or her even graver admonition that if I didn't retain all the old stories *exactly*, I wouldn't be properly equipped for the responsibilities I bore as a citizen in the world?

I recognize now that Mollie was also just trying to fulfill her own role as a memorial candle, ensuring with painstaking exactitude that she would not fail her lost family, her future generations—us. She was doing the best she could. Seen in this light, Aunt Mollie's approach to historical memory makes more sense. She believed in a version of our family history that was, in its way, a sacred text rooted in her unique Jewish soul, like folktales passed down through the ages—*zachor*. She believed that this text connected us not only to our family who died in the Holocaust, but also to the whole collective community of Jews who mourned together.

For Mollie, in other words, it was always about collective memory more than historical memory. And collective memory, by its nature, is an interpretation of the past upon which a group of people—a family, an ethnic group, a religion, a country, a community of nations—can agree because they all find the same basic significance in it. Collective memory is not, ultimately, about the past at all. The people it concerns are not those who experienced the catastrophe directly, but those who follow. People like me. The way events are remembered is a reflection of how the group defines itself now and who they decide they want to be moving forward. Mollie wanted us to articulate our family's story in a way that would link it to our people and also to the experience of others, all the better to celebrate the positive and fight to ensure that this never happens again.

Of course, as important as it is that our history lives inside us, it's also essential to move forward. To stay locked inside the memory of the Holocaust is to rob our lives of a crucial joy, of carefree moments, of art and love. "Even a conversation about trees," Bertolt Brecht wrote in a famous ode to "those born after" the Nazi era, "is almost a crime because of the silence it implies about so many misdeeds." Yet, in the aftermath of tragedy, people need to talk about trees again.

It's not a binary choice, what to carry and what to leave behind. There are pieces that we leave and then return to when the time is right. My sense is that Mollie understood this. Just because certain facts are too disturbing to reveal, especially to children and young adults, doesn't mean there will *never* be a time when successive generations can absorb them and put them into perspective. Children sense there is a conversation in silence. Maybe that's why I decided not to stay silent with my own kids. It's only natural for children to want to ask questions of their parents and grandparents and draw their own conclusions. That's not just true of the Holocaust, but it is *especially* true of the Holocaust, which has undergone near-constant reappraisal and reevaluation over the past eighty years as our historical knowledge has deepened and the symbolic importance attributed to it has shifted.

Now, in the 2020s, we see signs that the collective will to remember is itself cracking. For all the optimism that prevailed after the end of the Cold War, hopes that a reunited Europe could permanently inoculate itself against the divisions and virulent hatreds of the past, we are now struggling with the aftermath of Russia's invasion of Ukraine. The continent has not experienced this resurgence of brutality directed at civilians since the Nazi era. Authoritarianism and ethnic nationalism are on the rise in all corners of the world. In many of these newly autocratic countries, governments have encouraged an anti-Semitic backlash against the commemoration and memorialization of Jewish suffering. This hateful movement not only has put a target on Jewish backs, but is also exposing immigrants and other ethnic minorities to abuse and violence.

We now face multiple threats of our own to the liberal democratic consensus that has prevailed since the defeat of Hitler. White supremacists are moving rapidly from the political fringes to the mainstream, especially in the United States. In this country, the Holocaust graphic novel *Maus* is being banned in schools and at libraries, preventing people from accessing a resource to learn our history. Many of our bedrock principles—freedom of speech, the right to vote, the peaceful transfer of power, control over our own bodies—are coming under heavy attack.

Under happier circumstances, we might have expected the Holocaust to start fading into the pages of our history books by now. That's not to suggest we would have stopped treating the subject with solemnity, only that we could begin to view it with greater detachment, especially now that the last survivors and eyewitnesses are reaching the end of their lives. After all, we are about to lose our direct human link to what happened. But by necessity, the Holocaust remains vividly with us as a challenge and a warning.

I know it is still with *me*. For many years I yearned to make my peace with it, to exorcize its demons and quiet the perpetual anxiety it has stirred in me since childhood. As I look at our world, I know that I can't ever afford to be done with the Holocaust, because it's far from done with us. But I do think my journey changed my outlook on it. It forced me to look the realities straight in the face without the benefit of numbness; it broke down my vulnerability while also showing me the beauty that can still be found in the world if we open ourselves up to the future as well as the past.

The trick now is to maintain that balance. How can we continue to keep the flame of memory alive without being consumed by it? How can we learn to carry the burden of the past and still live our lives in the present?

What do we need to remember, and what can we afford to release?

For a long time, I hoped that finding Franya would answer these questions. As long as I was grappling with the mysteries of her life and death, I had the sense that I was delving into the past in order to *fix* something, that there was an unquiet spirit out there who needed to be laid to rest and that I was the one to do it. Perhaps by reaching through time, I could grant my cousin a peace that eluded her. I see now that the unquiet spirit was also me.

It wasn't easy. Even after I'd broken Mollie's rule and read *Twenty-One and One*, even after I'd completed the rest of my research and reconstructed the record as fully as I could, even after I'd learned how Franya wound up in a cold and lonely town far from the city she called home and went to her death with defiance, I *still* didn't feel fully resolved. There's no question that my long journey into the past deepened my love for Franya and the rest of my family, and even helped me discover a new family in the present. There was no question that I was a different woman now than when this began. But I felt I needed one last good-bye.

So, I organized one final trip to Vilnius. I wanted to revisit the places where Franya had lived and loved and suffered. And, as painful as it was, I also wanted to see Ashmyany for the first time, where she had wandered when her options were running out. If she had the power to speak to me one last time, this surely was where I would hear her.

~

VILNIUS HAD CHANGED DRAMATICALLY IN THE SEVENTEEN YEARS SINCE MY first family trip. Almost all traces of shabbiness were gone from the city center, now filled end to end with restored architectural treasures, designer stores, chic restaurants, and artisanal coffee shops. People were unfailingly friendly and helpful to tourists, a dramatic change from 2002, and the fashions and design aesthetic were positively Parisian. Every night, the baroque churches and palaces were illuminated from the inside out, creating a magical tableau.

My husband said the city looked to him like a "hipster Baltic Brooklyn," and he began searching out the best latte and chocolate treats, as he might have in Williamsburg or Park Slope. I suppose this shift in European cities is why the French now have a verb, *brooklyniser*.

Many of the stores featured signage in English, or some approximation. One, specializing in cashmere, was endearingly called "Coaty Coat." One of the railroad station platforms had a café called "Take Eat Easy," and right next to it was a larger-than-life painted statue of Tony Soprano in purple trunks and a ratty white bathrobe, a taste of my very own New Jersey. An entire area of the city, once downtrodden, had now been devoted to the tech boom, featuring sleek new complexes to house some of the more than two hundred fintech start-ups in the country. Even the old ghetto area had undergone a spate of gentrification, several of its narrow streets and archways now dressed in twinkle lights and colorful pennants to charm the international tourist market. The high-profile building where Franya had lived out her last weeks before heading to Ashmyany was now occupied by "Curly and Bald," a tongue-in-cheek barbershop. On a single stretch of what had been Szklanna, now Stiklių Street, I found a boba tea shop; Nick & Nora's cocktail bar; a French bakery decorated with gaudy, oversize green, purple, and brown macaroons; and a five-star hotel proclaiming in English: "Your luxury starts here."

I shouldn't have been surprised. In 2018 the city launched a tourism campaign, labeling itself "the G-Spot of Europe," prompting the likes of John Oliver to spend valuable minutes of his show riffing. I couldn't blame him. The clincher was the tagline: "Nobody knows where it is, but when you find it—it's amazing!"

The irony was that for me, a "G-spot" in Vilnius could only stand for "ghetto."

This, I told myself, is what happens when history moves on, especially in Europe where the remembering is different somehow, more lived in. And it was a good thing, wasn't it? How benign and normal it all seemed? How safely run-of-the-mill?

The change was startling at first, and I might have minded more were it not for the fact that the streets and buildings were lovingly restored to their former glory in a way that would have made my grandmother Meryl and Tante Rivel proud. Plus, even amid the cupcake and candle shops, there were respectful nods to the past. On several streets, as I wandered, I came across sculptures or plaques referencing life in the ghetto after the Nazi invasion. There were also brass memorial squares embedded in the streets underfoot, known in German as *stolperne Steine*, or "stumbling stones," designed to prompt passersby to stop in their tracks and remember the dead. I particularly loved the rectangular cutouts in the facades of many of the restored buildings, which offered a glimpse of their original stone and brick materials. Similar cutouts in the repaved roads and pedestrianized alleyways exposed the paving stones of the prewar period.

Of course I went to go see the old family house and found it had undergone its own transformation, which I had suspected would be the case. After 2013, when I first identified it correctly, I'd gone to see it on every one of my trips and had familiarized myself with its stately elegance: the slightly rounded archway leading in from the street; the odd corner where the Trinity Gate cut into the building at a sharp angle, giving a fifth side to the otherwise perfect rectangle of the cobbled courtyard; the ground-floor rooms on the north side, which had presumably been the domain of the tinsmiths a century ago but were now occupied by a restaurant with plateglass windows and a terrific view down the avenue toward the old city hall.

The character of the place was unaltered, but the building itself was in the process of being converted into modern apartments, including one I saw advertised on booking.com as a "Classy Old Town Apartment." At first, I was reluctant to sleep under the same roof as so many of my doomed family members. Too many ghosts. I was afraid that all I would think about was Franya hiding out in the attic in the days after she fled the ghetto in 1941, alone and afraid. That sounded like more than I wanted to bear.

At first, so many years before, I had felt unsettled in Vilnius, agitated and on edge. Now I felt at home. If any ghosts remained, rather than haunt me, I felt that they were there to spur me on, to reassure me. They would have been proud of what I had done to recognize them as real people with real lives. So, I booked my family home, which had been beautifully renovated, modern but with touches of the Old World, the original floorboards and exposed beams. As I walked upstairs to the apartment, my hand swept up the banister, which was clearly original, and I imagined their hands running over it the same way.

I was heartened to see that the changes in Vilnius went beyond the city's physical appearance. Younger members of the city's Jewish community, children of those few who'd survived the Holocaust, were pushing hard to rekindle interest in the *Litvak* culture that had flourished before the war. And the mayor, along with a number of allies in the national parliament, was outspoken about recognizing the full extent of the Holocaust, including the role played by Lithuanians in aiding and abetting the Nazi genocide. This was a big deal, since some of the worst Nazi collaborators had risen to prominence in the anti-Soviet struggle at the end of the war and were regarded as national heroes. It spelled controversy, not unlike when the United States began to confront and tear down its Civil War monuments celebrating southern Confederate generals who fought in defense of slavery.

A riverside path in the heart of Vilnius, honoring Kazys Škirpa, the leader of the pro-Nazi Lithuanian Activist Front that had pushed to rid the country of its Jews from the moment the Germans invaded, inspired similarly impassioned debate. Eventually, the city changed the name to Trispalvė (tricolor), after the three colors of the national flag. "It's not about plaques or street names," Mayor Remigijus Šimašius said, "but about principles." It's about the way we honor history and memory. And the guiding principle now was to steer Lithuania closer to the mainstream European Union of which it was an enthusiastic member and away from the lurking menace of Russia and Belarus to the east. Life had returned to Vilnius.

To mark the seventy-eighth anniversary of the yellow-permit roundup, on October 24, I had the idea of re-creating Franya's final journey, making our way to Ashmyany on foot. In the end, the three of us—my husband, Steven; Regina Kopilevich, our boundlessly resourceful translator and fixer; and me set off toward Ashmyany, Belarus, about a thirty-five-mile trek southeast of Vilnius. We stocked our backpacks with KIND bars and kale chips, hardly the provisions Franya would have taken. Of course, the view looked quite different than it would have to Franya, and we had many more layers of athletic wear and creature comforts. We walked alongside the highway, past supermarkets, beneath underpasses, and then past birch forests and open fields. Above us, the sky seemed wide open, blue with streaks of white cloud.

We made it about ten miles outside of town before deciding we'd had enough walking. We started flagging down cars and managed to hitchhike the rest of the way. Since pedestrians were not authorized to enter Belarus on the road we were taking, Regina had to work her magic down a line of cars and trucks at the border until she found a minibus driver transporting workers back to their homes, who agreed to let us hop on board.

We finally reached Ashmyany, a city of about fourteen thousand inhabitants. A statue of Lenin stood at the town center, which was surrounded by farms and a nuclear power plant. By this time, the sun was setting. We registered at the city's only guest lodging, a simple Soviet-style hotel with basic accommodations. We immediately set off for pizza and borscht at Cherry Secret, a nearby karaoke bar with a chalkboard menu. That night as I closed my eyes to go to sleep, I thought about how strange life is. Was this how I had pictured this leg of the journey? Dinner at a gastropub with '80s music playing on repeat? Maybe not. But I could only take it as it came.

The next morning, we met with the staff of a small city museum, who told us what little they knew about the Jewish community. I'd contacted them after viewing a children's play on YouTube that depicted the history of Ashmyany—of course without mentioning the Jews who constituted 50 percent of the town's prewar population. As we sat with these lovely women, I could not help but think of what their parents or grandparents were doing during the war. Did they help their neighbors or betray them? Were they living in homes that once belonged to the city's doomed Jews, using dishes or candlesticks that had been sold off for a few rubles?

They arranged for us to meet with one Jew who remained in the area. She was proud of her Jewish heritage, but also ashamed of how little she knew. Having been brought up during Soviet times, Jewish history was not something that was discussed. There was that silence again, but, in this case, enforced.

Finally, they introduced us to an elderly woman who remembered the ghetto, hoping in vain that she might recall a famous actress there in Ashmyany. She did not, but wept real tears as she told us about those horrible times.

We were guided through the ruins of the Ashmyany Synagogue, one of the last in Eastern Europe with its original wooden roof and a magnificent painted ceiling of a yellow sunrise leading along the outer rim to a center dome, complete with golden stars in the midnight-blue night sky.

We then headed to the Jewish cemetery where Franya had taken her last breaths. My expectations were low, but the reality was even worse than I'd imagined: a sad, uneven, weed-strewn field sat next to a large Soviet-era apartment complex. The cemetery had no map or memorial plaque to indicate where Franya's group or the Nazis' other victims had been forced to dig their own graves. Several hundred tombstones were dotted at irregular intervals, but most of these were dated from well before the Nazi era. Some had writing still visible in Hebrew, while others were eroded, overturned, or barely visible beneath the undergrowth.

I wanted to be able to feel Franya's presence here, but all I picked up on, beyond the decades of obvious neglect, was a somberness I could have found at any other cemetery. Was this even the spot where she had died? I doubted

that her fellow actors had been ordered to dig between the existing gravestones, and it wasn't at all clear to me where else her gang of refugees could
have been taken. We saw a couple of municipal workers making valiant efforts to pull up some weeds, but they had no further information. So we lit
a *yahrzeit* candle, left a stone on an unmarked grave chosen at random, and
moved on.

The next place we wanted to go was the site a few miles out of town
where the Nazis and their Lithuanian helpers had killed more than four
hundred people in October 1942. This was the roundup in which the victims were selected not by the Nazis, but by a visiting delegation of Jewish
policemen from the Vilna ghetto, an episode that haunted me in the early
days of my research because I worried that Franya had somehow been involved. Getting to the site was far from easy. Nobody, not even the workers
at the local history museum, could give us reliable directions. The historical amnesia was pervasive, it seemed. A cab driver let us pile into his car,
but didn't take us more than a few hundred yards before acknowledging
that he, too, had no idea where to go. He stopped again to find someone
who did.

We were on the outskirts of Ashmyany now, an area of old farmhouses
with splintered picket fences and outhouses painted odd shades of green and
pink. Behind the buildings were grassy fields, some planted with wheat, that
stretched out over rolling terrain toward distant stands of trees. We soon
came across a woman, the mother of the collective farm manager, who knew
the memorial site for which we were searching. She offered to accompany
us there.

While Regina was speaking with our new guide, I walked out into one
of the fields. There, in the distance, I could imagine Franya skipping and
dancing with her companions over a green hill. I could hear them singing
Yiddish songs and laughing, ever performers, even while searching for refuge in fear for their lives.

It was here, or somewhere much like it, that Franya was captured, had
struggled, and then sank her teeth into her Nazi executioner. It was here, I
thought, that she finally succumbed.

I knelt down and dug into the earth with my bare hands. The ground wasn't hard or stony or uneven like the cemetery, but soft, lush, and strikingly black. I'd been to other parts of Belarus and remembered the soil there being gritty, like sand mixed with clay. This was entirely different. It was moist, dark earth. It looked rich and abundant.

I was suddenly reminded of my conversation with my professor in Iowa, when he suggested that I write my family's story. I thought of the forbidden manuscript, found in the dust. I thought of the other invaluable writings that were saved by the Paper Brigade throughout the war, kept belowground. I thought of the Etingins, hiding beneath the earth in a hole barely large enough to fit them. I thought of my years of digging to extract buried truths from the past. I thought of Franya's beginning and, of course, her end. I thought about my family's history in this place, their roots still deep despite the attempt to make them disappear.

I lifted a handful of the soil to my nose so I could smell it. It had a rich, fertile aroma. And, surprising even myself, I opened my mouth to taste a bit on the tip of my finger. And it was good. It tasted of life. At that moment, a biblical passage struck me: "I have put before you life and death, blessing and curse—therefore choose life!" And I felt a weight lifting from me. In its place came something I'd been craving all my life: a sense of reconciliation with the past. I felt real peace. I had released a burden, but had kept the history that lived inside of me.

My family had lost so much, but in this process, there had been discoveries too. The scales tipped as I stood there, and the journey became as much about what we'd found as what we'd lost. Serge and his family, Léa and hers, even the archivists who had become part of a team working to honor the past—these were new precious relationships that had formed.

The Nazis had wanted to erase Franya, as they'd wanted to erase all Jews, but they hadn't succeeded. Too many people had worked to keep her spirit alive and honor her memory.

I was one in a long line of people who had refused to let Franya go unremembered. There were Serge Mogère and Aurore Blaise, and before them Aunt Mollie. Before her were Shabtai Blecher and Dora Rubina, and before *them* all the theater critics and newspaper columnists who fell under Franya's spell, moved to write about her during her heyday on the Yiddish stage.

Now, in the same dark soil where she'd perished, I'd finally found Franya. For the first time I was able to see her as a truly full human being, who loved life and enriched the lives of others, just as she now enriched this black earth. I did what I was meant to do. I faced the fear; I honored her memory. I released her, and, in doing so, she released me.

ACKNOWLEDGMENTS

OVER THE SEVEN YEARS THAT IT TOOK TO RESEARCH AND WRITE THIS BOOK I was surrounded by people who were tremendously supportive and enthusiastic about this project.

First and foremost, my husband, Steven Gabel, without whom this book would never have been possible. He is my rock. Although he didn't share my obsession with the subject, he was always there to listen, read copy, offer insight, and surround me with his love and devotion. I will never be able to repay him for all that he's done to support me.

I must also recognize my children, Isaac, Eli, Eve, and Belle, and their incredible spouses for their ability to question assumptions, challenge me, and poke fun at me whenever they had a chance. Through this process the experience of our family and the lessons of our tradition have found their way into their bone marrow too . . . memorial candles all.

My sisters, Carol, Cathy, and Charlene Frank, all deserve my gratitude for understanding that this is our family history, through my perspective, and offering their unconditional support and enthusiasm. I particularly want to thank my sister Cathy for her translation and transcription assistance.

I could not have completed this book without the support of a large group of family and friends, from those who provided encouragement to those who read drafts and offered advice. First of all, I owe a debt of gratitude to Sharon Krengel, whose expert editing made this a better manuscript, and Diane Weinberg, who listened nearly daily to my whining and whose wisdom got me through some tough patches. I must also recognize the contribution of my very dear friend Hakima el Haite for her tough critique, her unique international perspective, and her insistence that I write about my heritage and the trauma that is passed through generations. I would like to thank Joan Hocky for helping me successfully launch this project, and my sisters-in-law, Beth Perlman and Marianne Roosels, and friends Eetta Prince-Gibson, Gayle Brill-Mittler, Gloria Bachman, Lorraine Perlman, Martin Gliserman, and Gia Rosenblum who graciously read drafts, asked questions, and offered needed advice.

Serge, Christele, and Maiwen Mogère have become more like family than friends to me. And we must all recognize his mother, Madeleine Formentin Mogère, who risked her life to save the lives of her Jewish neighbors, but who considered her brave act nothing special.

To Aurore Blaise, the intrepid archivist at the Memorial de la Shoah, I offer my heartfelt thanks.

I will never find words enough to thank the inimitable researcher and guide Regina Kopilevich, who made this project a true adventure. She was a tremendous resource and key to this book.

Additionally, there were two Yiddish theater scholars, Debra Caplan and Alisa Quint, whose books on the subject and time discussing it is greatly appreciated, as well as Ina Pukelytė, for her insight into the interwar Yiddish theater.

I am indebted to Irina Guzenberg and Rachel Kostanian, who have worked diligently to keep the memory alive. I truly appreciate the research and translation assistance of Roza Bieliauskiene, Pamela Russ, Evgenia Lokis, Aleksandra Komorchenko, Camille Gillain, and Danka Szwajkajzer. And I am grateful to Andrew Gumble for his excellence in research, translation, and his use of the language.

I must also thank archivists from all over the world, particularly Leo Greenbaum and Stephanie Halpern at YIVO for their time, effort, and quick response to my many requests for information; the staff of the United States Holocaust Memorial Museum (USHMM); Bret Werb, Susan Evans, Liliya Meyerovich, Sarah Kopelman-Noyes, Allison Zhang, and Emmanuelle Moscovitz at Yad Vashem; and also David Mano and Lior Lalieu-Smadja at the Memorial de la Shoah for their personal attention to this project.

I would like to express my gratitude to Professor Lon Otto, my instructor at the Iowa Summer Writers' Festival, for allowing me to share Franya's fate with the class and for his encouragement to write this book, and Professor Saulius Sužiedėlis and Christoph Dieckmann, whose course and lecture at YIVO and their groundbreaking work on the Holocaust provided the historical context for the destruction of Lithuanian Jewry.

I am grateful to Rabbi Jeremy Kalmanofsky, Rabbi Eliyahu Kaufman, Rabbi Eliot Malomet, and Pastor Kit Swartz for their guidance and insight into biblical texts.

I will not easily forget the many synchronicities that were part of this project, particularly those that involved my friend Michael Murphy, who randomly encountered members of the Etingin family of Montreal, Karen and Kiki Etingin. I thank them all for their contributions.

It would not have been possible to find our living relatives without the help of Rebbetzin Esther Suissa, who dove into the research and refused to give up until she found living relatives. Her positive attitude and detective work were invaluable. She is a treasure.

I cannot forget my friends in Vilnius who taught me the history of the great city, Dovid Katz, and those who are committed to Vilnius today and in the future, Anna Avidan and Aušrinė Armonaitė.

I would be remiss if I did not remember Teresa Ginel-Gulbatzky, a witness of the massacre in Wasiliski (Vashiloshik), Belarus, for providing firsthand knowledge of the fate of my family and reconnecting me with my long-lost cousins Miroslav, Nella, and Vitaly Boyarsky. I would also like to thank Galina Bogdanovich, a witness to the Ashmyany Ghetto, for her tearful recollections; Yadviga Prosolovskaya, a public school teacher who is dedicated to the study of the Jews of Ashmyany; the staff of the Ashmyany Museum; and Dona, the mother of the collective farm manager, who was one of the few in the city who was able to lead us to the site of the massacre of the Ashmyany Jews.

I must also thank Josaine Broll for her assistance communicating and providing clothing for Marcel Rosenrot, Stephan Botbol for saving Marcel's poetry, Dr. Kissous for providing some background on Marcel's spiritual journey, and the staff of Hopital Rothschild Paris for arranging my visit with Marcel.

I will be ever grateful to my agent, Michael Signorelli at Aevitas Creative Management, who believed in this book, held my hand, and allowed me to cry on his shoulder, and who fought to make this the best possible manuscript. And to my editors at Hachette: Sam Raim, who saw a powerful story here and provided needed guidance, and Mollie Weisenfeld, who picked up where Sam left off to sharpen the narrative and make the story even stronger. I would also like to thank Nora Zelevansky, who artfully helped shape the story to make it clearer and more impactful, and Judith Bass for having my back.

I would like to acknowledge my deep appreciation to the survivors of the Vilna ghetto Fania Yocheles Brantsovsky, Marcus Petuchauskas, and Joshua Zak, who found tremendous strength and broke the silence to tell the stories that we all need to hear.

And finally, I would like to express my heartfelt gratitude to Léa Rosenrot Guinet, who—without knowing it—followed the same path I did. Separately searching for our family until we completed our task, reuniting a brother and his beloved sister in spirit and a family that was all but destroyed, keeping the memorial candle lit for generations to come.

NOTE ON SOURCES AND SELECT BIBLIOGRAPHY

THE TRAGIC HISTORY OF VILNA IN WORLD WAR II DOES NOT OCCUPY THE place it deserves in either the academic literature or the popular imagination. The city was at the center of a remarkable outpouring of Yiddish literature and culture before the war, and it was a focal point of the Nazi extermination machine from the moment the Holocaust started in July 1941. Yet the history of the Warsaw ghetto is far better known than the history of the Vilna ghetto. The horrors of Auschwitz are stamped into the consciousness of the contemporary world in a way that the lime pits at Ponary are not.

Partly, this is a matter of how the crimes were discovered. The liberation of concentration camps in Germany in 1945, and the fact that film crews were able to accompany Allied forces through their gates, gave the world indelible images of emaciated people in striped prison uniforms and piles of dead bodies. Later, when crews reached Auschwitz and the other death camps in Poland, the world learned the full horror of the gas chambers and crematoria. By contrast, when the Soviet army liberated Vilna in July 1944, there were almost no Jews left to be rescued and few physical signs of how the Nazis had killed the sixty thousand or so who did not make it. At that point, most of the killings were more than two years in the past, and the Nazis had taken care in the final months before their defeat to destroy most of the corpses. It did not help that the Soviets had no interest in highlighting the fact that the vast majority of civilian victims during the Nazi occupation were Jews. The dead were labeled only as amorphous "victims of fascist terror," to be mourned, maybe, but not remembered for who they were.

Vilna's relative obscurity also has to do with the linguistic challenges facing any researcher investigating what happened there. Before the war, Vilna had been an unusually cosmopolitan city where Polish, Yiddish, Hebrew, Lithuanian, Russian, and German were all native languages. Then in a few short years, the city bounced between Poland, Lithuania, Nazi Germany, and the Soviet Union. Anyone wanting to come to grips with the full range of source documents has an unusually large number of languages to master, and it's rare to find anyone who speaks more than two or three.

Because of these challenges, the history of Vilna remained for many decades a subject restricted to the small community of Jewish survivors and those able to read their eyewitness accounts, almost all of which were written in Yiddish or Hebrew. It didn't help that most Lithuanian and Russian documents remained off-limits until after the Cold War—and even then were not made available as quickly as researchers would have liked. To the extent that a handful of texts appeared in English before the turn of the millennium, it was largely thanks to the efforts of Israeli organizations like the Ghetto Fighters' House, which translated Yitskhok Rudashevski's diary in 1973 in the hope of emulating the international success of Anne Frank's diary, and Yad Vashem, which translated Yitzhak Arad's authoritative history *Ghetto in Flames* in 1982. Regrettably, these remarkable books went little noticed by nonspecialists in Europe and the United States.

The literature has become much richer and more available to English-language readers in recent years. Yale University Press published Herman Kruk's extensive diaries in 2002 and Kazimierz Sakowicz's chronicle of the killings at Ponary in 2005. It is now translating Christoph Dieckmann's exhaustive two-volume history of the Nazi occupation of Lithuania, first published in German in 2011. Abraham Sutzkever's highly readable diary came out in English for the first time in 2021, with an excellent introduction by Justin Cammy. With luck, some of the other invaluable eyewitness accounts—by Shmerke Kaczergynski, Mark Dvorzhetski, Grigorij Schur, and others—will follow in due course.

As more information has become available, the historiography has also changed. Dieckmann and other scholars of the region have helped sharpen our understanding not only that the Holocaust began in Lithuania, but also why. Newly available documentation makes clear that while exterminating the Jews was certainly a long-term goal of the Nazis, it was not something they had planned for but began, rather, in response to the realization that Germany's armed forces were not conquering the Soviet Union fast enough. If the killings started and stopped and started again, it was because the Nazis became enmeshed in conflicting interests. They believed, on the one hand, that Jews were to blame for their military setbacks and would continue to be a problem until every last one of them had been annihilated. But they also needed to build a supply chain to their soldiers on the front lines, and Jews held a near monopoly of the skills required to make winter boots and hats, to service military vehicles, and to provide any number of other essential services to a vast invasion force.

These new lines of academic inquiry were enormously helpful in my efforts to understand the story of Franya and the other family members described in these pages, and in particular helped make sense of an otherwise puzzling sequence of deadly events in Vilna in the summer and fall of 1941. I am likewise indebted to Deborah Caplan, a brilliant historian of the Yiddish theatrical avant-garde who helped me understand the trajectory of Franya's stage career and the reasons her talents were so treasured. I have done my best to acknowledge the influences on my thinking in the Endnotes. What follows is a list of the most valuable sources I drew on, most but unfortunately not all available in English.

SOURCE DOCUMENTS AND TESTIMONIALS

This is a partial list only. On the documentary origin of other individual pieces of factual information—for example, dates of deportation or death, or census information taken from the Lithuanian State Archives—see Notes.

Bayroff, Mollie. 1932 travel journal, letters, notes (including marginalia in books and comments on author's high school family history essay), from the author's personal collection.
———. Testimonial documents on Isaak Punski (May 5, 1991) and Franya Winter (May 12, 1991), available through Yad Vashem.
Blecher, Shabtai. *Twenty-One and One: Twenty-One Yiddish Actors Murdered by Nazis in Vilna, 1941–1942.* New York, 1962.
Bolesław, Boratyński, and Józefa Boratyński. File supporting their nomination as Righteous Among Nations, available through Yad Vashem. File includes July 8, 1991, letter

by Maks Etingin; December 14, 1991, letter by Henry Etingin; and February 25, 1992, account by Józefa Boratyński.

Daul, Hinda. Holocaust diary, part of the Ashmyany (Oshmyany) Yizkor published online in English by JewishGen.org.

Dobruszkes, Azario. Testimonial letter written to the Ghetto Fighters' House on December 15, 1964, available in Yiddish through the Ghetto Fighters' House.

Jäger, Karl. "Gesamtaufstellung der im Bereich des EK. 3 bis zum 1. Dez, 1941 durchgeführten Exekutionen" (the Jäger report).

Mogère, Serge. Collection of Punski and Rosenrot family photographs, with researcher's notes and an explanatory letter from Mogère, available at the Mémorial de la Shoah, Paris.

———. *Récit illustré*. Unpublished description with photographs and illustrated panels of his discovery of the Punski and Rosenrot family photographs, from the author's personal collection.

Punski, Rachmil. File on his battle to maintain residency in Germany. Russian refugee case files (1927–1938, Puk-Rad) of the Nansen Office for Refugees, High Commissioner for Refugees, Delegation in Germany (Berlin), folder C 1207.

Rosenrot, Abraham. Documents including marriage certificates, death certificates, September 1939 letter confirming his fitness to serve in the French Foreign Legion, March 1940 letter approving renewal of his French residence certificate following his application to join the French army, and handwritten letter dated July 31, 1989, to his granddaughter Léa, all from the author's and from Léa Guinet's private collections.

Rubina, Dora. "The Path of Suffering of Jewish Actors." Yad Vashem Tenenbaum-Mersik archive, document M.11.

Yizkor, Vasilishok. Available online via JewishGen.org.

Zaslavsky, Rudolf. "The Day I Died." Handwritten manuscript in Yiddish available through YIVO.

Zinger, Rochl. Testimony given at the US-run Feldafing displaced-persons camp in West Germany on August 11, 1948, available in Yiddish through YIVO, Record Group 104, series 3.

OTHER SOURCES

Adler, Hermann. *Ostra Brama: Legende aus der Zeit des grossen Untergangs*. Zurich: Helios, 1945.

Aleichem, Sholem. *Stempenyu: A Jewish Romance*. Translated by Hannah Berman. New York: Melville House, 2007.

Amichai, Yehuda. *Open Closed Open*. New York: Harvest, 2006.

Angrick, Andrej. *Aktion 1005: Spurenbeseitigung von NS-Massenverbrechen, 1942–1945*. Göttingen: Wallstein, 2018.

Arad, Yitzhak. *Ghetto in Flames: The Struggle and Destruction of the Jews in Vilna in the Holocaust*. New York: Holocaust Library, 1982.

Avraham, Tory. *Surviving the Holocaust: The Kovno Ghetto Diary*. Cambridge, MA: Harvard University Press, 1990.

Balberyszski, Mendel. *Stronger than Iron: The Destruction of Vilna Jewry, 1941–1945, an Eyewitness Account*. Jerusalem: Gefen, 2010.

Bart, Michael, and Laurel Corona. *Until Our Last Breath: A Holocaust Story of Love and Partisan Romance*. New York: St. Martin's Press, 2008.

Beevor, Anthony. *The Second World War*. New York: Little, Brown, 2012.

Broch, Ludivine. "French Railway Workers and the Question of Rescue During the Holocaust." *Diasporas* 25 (2015): 147–167.

Bryant, Louise. *Six Red Months in Russia: An Observer's Account of Russia Before and During the Proletarian Dictatorship*. New York: George H. Doran, 1918.

Caplan, Debra. *Yiddish Empire: The Vilna Troupe, Jewish Theater, and the Art of Itinerancy*. Ann Arbor: University of Michigan Press, 2018.

Curilla, Wolfgang. *Die deutsche Ordnungspolizei und der Holocaust im Baltkum und in Weissrussland*. Paderborn: Ferdinand Schöningh, 2006.

Dąbrowska, Agata Katarzyna. "Jewish Theatre in Poland as an Institution of Nationality, Education and Intercultural Dialogue." In *Communication Today: An Overview from Online Journalism to Applied Philosophy*, edited by Maria Micle and Claudiu Mesaroş. Budapest: Trivent, 2016.

Dawidowicz, Lucy S. *From That Place and Time: A Memoir, 1938–1947*. New York: W. W. Norton, 1989.

———. *The War Against the Jews: 1933–1945*. New York: Bantam, 1986.

Dean, Martin, and Geoffrey P. Megargee, eds. *The United States Holocaust Memorial Museum Encyclopedia of Camps and Ghettos, 1933–1945: Ghettos in German-Occupied Eastern Europe*. Bloomington: Indiana University Press, 2012.

Déom, Jacques. "Une voix du yiddish, Azario Dobruszkes." *Les Cahiers de la Mémoire Contemporaine* 8 (2008): 219–231.

Dieckmann, Christoph. *Deutsche Besatzungspolitik in Litauen, 1941–1944*. Göttingen: Wallstein, 2011.

———. "The War and the Killing of the Lithuanian Jews." In *National Socialist Extermination Policies: Contemporary German Perspectives and Controversies*, edited by Ulrich Herbert. New York: Berghahn Books, 2000.

Dieckmann, Christoph, and Saulius Sužiedėlis. *The Persecution and Mass Murder of Lithuanian Jews During Summer and Fall of 1941*. Vilnius: Margi raštai, 2006.

Donner, Rebecca. *All the Frequent Troubles of Our Days*. New York: Little, Brown, 2021.

Dvorzhetski, Mark. *Yerusholaym de-Lita in kamf un umkum: Zikhroynes fun Vilner Geto*. Paris: L'Union Populaire Juive en France, 1948.

Etkes, Immanuel, et al. *The Gaon of Vilna: The Man and His Image*. Berkeley: University of California Press, 2002.

Fishman, David E. *The Book Smugglers: Partisans, Poets, and the Race to Save Jewish Treasures from the Nazis*. Lebanon, NH: University of New England Press, 2017.

Flanzbaum, Hilene. "The Trace of Trauma: Third-Generation Holocaust Survivors." *Phi Kappa Phi Forum* (Spring 2012).

Garrin, Stephen Howard. "But I Forsook Not Thy Precepts: Spiritual Resistance to the Holocaust." In *The Routledge History of the Holocaust*, edited by Jonathan C. Friedman. London: Routledge, 2011.

Glantz, David M. *Operation Barbarossa: Hitler's Invasion of Russia 1941*. Stroud, UK: History Press, 2011.

Goebbels, Joseph. *Die Tagebücher von Joseph Goebbels: Diktate, 1941–45*. Edited by Elke Fröhlich. 15 vols. Munich: K. G. Saur, 1993–1996.

Golinkin, David. "'Kol B'ishah Ervah'—Is It Really Forbidden for Jewish Men to Listen to Women Singing?" *Responsa in a Moment* 6, no. 2 (2011).

Guzenberg, Irina, and Genrikh Agranovsky. *Vilnius: In Search of the Jerusalem of Lithuania*. Vilnius: Vilna Gaon State Jewish Museum, 2016.

Holmgren, Beth. "Cabaret Nation: The Jewish Foundations of *Kabaret Literacki*, 1920–1939." In vol. 31 of *Polin Studies in Polish Jewry*, 273–288. Liverpool: Liverpool University Press, 2019.

Jacobsen, Annie. *Operation Paperclip: The Secret Intelligence Program to Bring Nazi Scientists to America*. New York: Little, Brown, 2014.

Jewish Black Book Committee. *The Black Book: The Nazi Crime Against the Jewish People*. New York: Jewish Black Book Committee, 1946.

Judt, Tony. *Postwar: A History of Europe Since 1945*. London: Penguin, 2005.

Kaczerginski, Shmerke. *Khurbn Vilner*. New York: United Vilner Relief Committee, 1947.

Kadison, Luba, Joseph Buloff, and Irving Genn. *On Stage Off Stage: Memories of a Lifetime in the Yiddish Theater*. Cambridge, MA: Harvard University Library Judaica Division, 1992.

Kahan, Shoshana. *In Fayer un in Flamen: Togbukh fun a Yidisher Shoyshpilerin*. Buenos Aires: Central Union of Polish Jews in Argentina, 1949.

Kalisch, Shoshana, and Barbara Meister. *Yes, We Sang! Songs of the Ghettos and Concentration Camps*. New York: Harper & Row, 1985.

Katz, Dovid. "Lithuania's Museum of Holocaust Denial." *Tablet*, April 11, 2018.

Kostanian, Rachel. *Spiritual Resistance in the Vilna Ghetto*. Vilnius: Vilna Gaon State Jewish Museum, 2002.

Kruk, Herman. *The Last Days of the Jerusalem of Lithuania: Chronicles from the Vilna Ghetto and Camps, 1939–1944*. Edited by Benjamin Harshav. New Haven, CT: Yale University Press, 2002.

Lendvai, Paul. "The Old Austria and the New Nazis." *Commentary* (September 1967).

Lichtblau, Eric. *The Nazis Next Door: How America Became a Safe Haven for Hitler's Men*. New York: Houghton Mifflin Harcourt, 2014.

Longerich, Peter. *Heinrich Himmler: A Life*. Oxford: Oxford University Press, 2012.

Manekin, Rachel. *The Rebellion of the Daughters: Jewish Women Runaways in Habsburg Galicia*. Princeton, NJ: Princeton University Press, 2020.

Mendelsohn, Daniel. *The Lost: A Search for Six of the Six Million*. New York: Harper Perennial, 2006.

Miron, Guy, and Shlomit Shulhani, eds. *The Yad Vashem Encyclopedia of the Ghettos During the Holocaust*. Jerusalem: Yad Vashem, 2009.

Mishell, William W. *Kaddish for Kovno: Life and Death in a Lithuanian Ghetto, 1941–1945*. Chicago: Chicago Review Press, 1988.

Nuger, Abram. "Forgotten and Half-Forgotten Names." Translation from Yiddish and literary adaptation by Simon Kopelman. *Ebreiskaya Starina* (Jewish Antiquity) 70, no. 3 (2011).

Petuchauskas, Marcus. *Price of Concord*. Translated by Izolda Geniusiene. Vilnius: Versus Aureus, 2015.

Porat, Dan. *The Boy: A Holocaust Story*. New York: Hill and Wang, 2011.

Porch, Douglas. *The French Foreign Legion: The Complete History of the Legendary Fighting Force*. New York: Skyhorse, 2010.

Poznanski, Renée. *Jews in France During World War II*. Hanover, NH: University Press of New England, 2001.

Quint, Alyssa. *The Rise of Modern Yiddish Theater*. Bloomington: Indiana University Press, 2019.

Ran, Leyzer. *Jerusalem of Lithuania: Illustrated and Documented*. Jackson Heights, NY: Laureate Press, 1974.

———. "Vilna, Jerusalem of Lithuania." Lecture presented at the Oxford Centre for Postgraduate Hebrew Studies, October 1987. https://www.ochjs.ac.uk/wp-content/uploads/2011/09/4th-Stencl-Lecture-Vilna-Jerusalem-of-Lithuania.pdf.

Renan, Ernest. *What Is a Nation? and Other Political Writings*. Edited and translated by M. F. N. Giglioli. New York: Columbia University Press, 2018.

Rhodes, Richard. *Masters of Death: The SS-Einsatzgruppen and the Invention of the Holocaust*. New York: Random House, 2002.

Rudashevski, Yitskhok. *The Diary of the Vilna Ghetto*. Beit Lohamei Haghetaot, Israel: Ghetto Fighters' House, 1973.

Sacks, Rabbi Jonathan. "A Sense of History." https://www.rabbisacks.org/covenant-conversation/ki-tavo/a-sense-of-history/.

Sakowicz, Kazimierz. *Ponary Diary, 1941–1943: A Bystander's Account of a Mass Murder*. New Haven, CT: Yale University Press, 2005.

Sandrow, Nahma. *Vagabond Stars: A World History of Yiddish Theater*. New York: Harper Row, 1977.

Sands, Philippe. *The Rat Line*. New York: Alfred A. Knopf, 2020.

Schreiber, Marion. *The Twentieth Train: The True Story of the Ambush of the Death Train to Auschwitz*. New York: Grove Press, 2003.

Schur, Grigorij. *Die Juden von Wilna: Die Aufzeichnungen des Grigorij Schur, 1941–1944*. Edited by Wladimir Porudominskij. Munich: Deutscher Taschenbuch Verlag, 1999.

Service, Robert. *Stalin: A Biography*. Cambridge, MA: Belknap Press of Harvard University Press, 2005.

Snyder, Timothy. *Black Earth: The Holocaust as History and Warning*. New York: Crown, 2015.

———. *Bloodlands: Europe Between Hitler and Stalin*. New York: Basic Books, 2010.

———. "Memory of Sovereignty and Sovereignty over Memory: Poland, Lithuania and Ukraine, 1939–1999." In *Memory and Power in Post-War Europe: Studies in the Presence of the Past*, edited by Jan-Werner Müller. Cambridge: Cambridge University Press, 2002.

———. *On Tyranny: Twenty Lessons from the Twentieth Century*. New York: Crown, 2017.

Sutzkever, Abraham. *From the Vilna Ghetto to Nuremberg: Memoir and Testimony*. Edited and translated by Justin D. Cammy. Montreal: McGill–Queen's University Press, 2021.

———. *The Full Pomegranate: Poems of Avrom Sutzkever*. Selected and translated by Richard J. Fein. Albany: Excelsior Editions, 2018.

Taylor, Frederick. *Exorcising Hitler: The Occupation and Denazification of Germany*. New York: Bloomsbury, 2011.

Ullrich, Christina. "Der erste deutsche Prozess gegen Einsatzgruppentäter: Die Besonderheiten des Falls Martin Weiss." In *Naziverbrechen: Täter, Taten, Bewältigungsversuche*,
edited by Martin Cüppers, Jürgen Matthäus, and Andrej Angrick, 303–318. Darmstadt:
WBG, 2013.

Viktus, Zigmas. "Paneriai Under the Soviets: Between Abandonment and Commemoration." *Deep Baltic*, October 14, 2021.

Wardi, Dina. *Memorial Candles: Children of the Holocaust*. London: Routledge, 1992.

Weiner, Tim. *Legacy of Ashes: The History of the CIA*. New York: Anchor, 2008.

Wynot, Edward D., Jr. "'A Necessary Cruelty': The Emergence of Official Anti-Semitism in
Poland, 1936–39." *American Historical Review* 76, no. 4 (1971): 1035–1058.

Yerushalmi, Yosef Hayim. *Zakhor: Jewish History and Jewish Memory*. Seattle: University of
Washington Press, 1996.

ENDNOTES

The Amichai poem is from his collection *Open Closed Open.*

1: THE MEMORIAL CANDLE

The key text on history and Jewish memory is Yosef Hayim Yerushalmi, *Zakhor: Jewish History and Jewish Memory.*

See Rabbi Jonathan Sacks, "A Sense of History."

On pro-Palestinian terrorism in the 1960s and 1970s, see "When Plane Hijackings Were Palestinian Terrorists' Weapon of Choice," *Haaretz*, March 29, 2016.

The World at War, first broadcast in the United Kingdom in 1973–1974, was shown in a slightly edited version on WOR, New York's channel 9, which the author's family received in New Jersey. The Holocaust episode, titled "Genocide (1941–45)" was twentieth of the twenty-six. At about the same time, my high school social studies class viewed *Night and Fog* (French: *Nuit et brouillard*), a short 1956 French documentary directed by Alain Resnais made ten years after the liberation of Nazi concentration camps with devastating images of victims.

On children of the Holocaust, see Dina Wardi, *Memorial Candles: Children of the Holocaust.* The quote, attributed to a woman named Devorah, is on page 36.

2: THE BOOK

On the refugee crisis in Vilna after the Nazi invasion of Poland and the frantic attempts by many Jews to get out, see Yitzhak Arad, *Ghetto in Flames: The Struggle and Destruction of the Jews in Vilna in the Holocaust*, 14–20.

The story of *Twenty-One and One*'s origins is told principally in the introduction to the book itself, as published in New York in 1962. The same goes for the less than complete story of how Bolesław Boratyński retrieved it from the abandoned ghetto—although the detail about pages "rolling along the street" was added later and included in an exhibition about Vilna mounted by Yad Vashem, the World Holocaust Remembrance Center in Jerusalem. As of 2021, the phrase was still included in a summary of the exhibition on Yad Vashem's website.

The Etingins' story has been told a number of times in different forums. See, for example, Michael Bart and Laurel Corona, *Until Our Last Breath: A Holocaust Story of Love and*

Partisan Romance, 52, 275–279, and the following newspaper accounts: "Jewish Student Here Lived 10 Months in Wilno Grave," *Baltimore Evening Sun*, September 9, 1947; and Michele Gelormine, "Reliving History: GHS Students Hear Holocaust Survivors Tell Their Stories," *Greenwich (CT) News*, April 22, 1993. On July 8, 1991, Maks Etingin wrote a letter to Yad Vashem, since obtained by the author, describing the family's wartime escape and asking that the Boratyńskis be honored for what they did. On December 14, 1991, Maks's younger brother, Henry, wrote a similar letter to Yad Vashem, and on February 25, 1992, Józefa Boratyński, then recently widowed, added her own account. In 2017, Maks Etingin gave a half-hour television interview to the Jewish Broadcasting Service program *Witness*, since posted on YouTube. That same year, Maks's daughter Orli wrote an account, based on the family stories she'd heard her whole life. The accounts are substantially consistent but vary slightly in some of the details. Henry mentioned his father selling cars to Boratyński in about 1937 but not the farm loan; Orli mentioned the farm equipment loan but not the cars. Henry said the family escaped the ghetto by bribing a "guard." Other accounts indicate that members of the ghetto police had keys to the gate on Jatkowa Street, and it seems overwhelmingly likely that Henry meant a Jewish guard.

Additional information on Boratyński—including his past as a taxi driver, the fact that his wife was pregnant in September 1943 (mentioned by both brothers), his first marriage, and other details—was obtained from, or corroborated by, census records and other official documentation stored at the Lithuanian State Historical Archives.

For background on the deportations to Estonia and the last days of the Vilna ghetto, see Arad, *Ghetto in Flames*, 401–440.

The detail about the key being imprinted in bread dough was provided by Irina Guzenberg (author interview, Vilnius, October 24, 2021) and corroborated by the former resistance fighter Fania Yocheles Brantsovsky, who said she didn't know the details of this particular key but that the resistance copied other keys using the bread-dough method (author interview, Vilnius, October 26, 2021). If the key was not originally provided by Jakob Gens, the head of the Judenrat, it probably came from one of his lieutenants in the ghetto police.

On the circumstances surrounding Blecher's death in Estonia, see W. H. Lawrence, "Nazi Death Camp a Scene of Horror," *New York Times*, October 6, 1944. The biblical valley of bones is evoked by Lucy S. Dawidowicz in her memoir *From That Place and Time: A Memoir, 1938–1947*, 258. See also Ezek. 37. The detail about Blecher's death falling on Rosh Hashanah comes from a biographical sketch in *Twenty-One and One* by Leyzer Ran. The Jewish New Year indeed fell on September 17–19 that year; Blecher died on the nineteenth.

The three-volume history on my aunt's shelf was Leyzer Ran, *Jerusalem of Lithuania: Illustrated and Documented*. The PBS documentary about the partisans of Vilna first aired in 1986.

3: The Pilgrimage

News reports on Vilna reaching the United States: see "1,800 Jews Executed by Nazis in Vilna Region, 30,000 Jews 'Missing' in Vilna," *Jewish Telegraphic Agency*, February 8, 1942. On June 17, 1942, the same agency carried a story with the headline "60,000 Jews Executed in Vilna Last Month in Continuous Two-Week Pogrom." The author's family would most likely have followed the news in the *Yiddish Daily Forward*, or *Forverts*, which was published in Yiddish in New York City.

On the Gaon of Vilna, see, for example, Immanuel Etkes et al., *The Gaon of Vilna: The Man and His Image.*

For a standard telling of the legend of Napoleon calling Vilna the "Jerusalem of Lithuania," see Leyzer Ran's 1986 lecture "Vilna, Jerusalem of Lithuania." The true story of Napoleon's brief time in Vilna is told most authoritatively by Count Philippe-Paul Ségur, who was part of the emperor's entourage and wrote up his experiences in a famous memoir, available in English as *Napoleon's Russian Campaign* (London: Michael Joseph, 1959). The book was also heavily used by Leo Tolstoy in writing *War and Peace.* Benjamin Harshav convincingly dates the "Jerusalem of Lithuania" epithet to the mid- to late nineteenth century, decades after Napoleon's Russian campaign. See Harshav's introduction to Herman Kruk, *The Last Days of the Jerusalem of Lithuania: Chronicles from the Vilna Ghetto and Camps, 1939–1944*, xxx–xxxi.

For many years, the restaurant at the author's family address was an establishment called Felicie. In 2019, it was replaced with a first-class modern Lithuanian establishment, 12 Istorijų, or 12 Stories.

The story of the Jews given asylum from the Nazis at the Carmelite shrine of Our Lady of Ostra Brama is told, in German, in Hermann Adler, *Ostra Brama: Legende aus der Zeit des grossen Untergangs.* The priest there, Father Andrzej Gdowski, not only hid Jews but made a carefully concealed synagogue where they could worship or hide, as needed. He helped fake Lithuanian identity papers. And he was in regular touch with Anton Schmid, a remarkable Austrian Wehrmacht sergeant who saved hundreds of Jews before he was caught and executed in April 1942. My aunt used to say "Our Lady of Ostrobramska," but the more common appellation in English is "Our Lady of Ostra Brama."

On the different ways in which Jews died in the Holocaust: We have only approximate numbers, which vary from one estimate to the next, but a very rough accounting suggests about 2.5 million died in the death camps, about 2 million were shot, and about 1 million more died of hunger or cold or disease or otherwise perished in the ghettos. The iconic figure of six million dead Jews originated in a boast made by Adolf Eichmann in 1944 to an SS officer named Wilhelm Höttl, who relayed it in an affidavit presented at the Nuremberg Trials. See the trial transcript for December 14, 1945, available online via the Yale Law School's Avalon Project. Modern historians generally estimate the total number of Jews killed to have been between 5.4 million and 5.8 million.

Multiple books recount the details of the killing at Ponary and the subsequent burning of the bodies. Arad gives an excellent overview in *Ghetto in Flames*, 75–77, 444–445. On Lithuania as the place where the Holocaust started, Christoph Dieckmann writes in his authoritative *Deutsche Besatzungspolitik in Litauen, 1941–1944*: "The murder of Jews in the German-occupied Soviet Union began in the summer of 1941 on Lithuanian soil. There, for the first time, whole Jewish communities in rural areas, villages and small towns, were exterminated. No other area saw so many Jewish victims before October 1941" (792). On the importance of Ponary, Benjamin Harshav writes in his introduction to Kruk's *Last Days*: "When the underground in Warsaw Ghetto learned about Ponar[y], they concluded that this was the beginning of the extermination of all Jews in Europe, an ideological policy rather than a unique case" (xliii). For a much longer discussion of Lithuania and the origins of the Holocaust, see Chapter 7.

Some of the history of the monuments at Ponary is told in displays at the memorial itself. Separately, a useful rundown is Zigmas Viktus, "Paneriai Under the Soviets: Between Abandonment and Commemoration." Paneriai is the Lithuanian name for Ponary.

On the conflicting narratives of the Holocaust in Lithuania, see Dieckmann, *Deutsche Besatzungspolitik*, 15–17, 19–23. Dieckmann (156–177) also provides a comprehensive analysis of the Lithuanian Jews' "multi-faceted and mostly ambivalent" experience of Soviet annexation in 1940 and shows how Soviet rule gave rise to myths and stereotypes of Jews as money-grubbing capitalists or communist traitors, or both simultaneously, that fueled a surge of anti-Semitism among ethnic Lithuanians.

On the ethnic Lithuanian population of Vilna: The last prewar census, taken in 1931, found fewer than 2,000 Lithuanians out of a total city population of 195,100, or around 1 percent. A count in late 1939, after Vilna became Lithuanian, increased that number to 6 percent, but this included an influx of government officials and others moving in from Kaunas, the old capital, and elsewhere. There are also grounds for thinking the Lithuanians were exaggerating their own strength as part of a policy of "Lithuanization" of the new capital and that many Poles, including refugees from Nazi-occupied western Poland, chose to recategorize themselves as Lithuanian to avoid being treated as second-class citizens deprived of significant rights. These were certainly major factors by July 1941, when a new Lithuanian count in the wake of the Nazi invasion put the Lithuanian population at 65,000, almost 25 percent. See Arad, *Ghetto in Flames*, 27; Dieckmann, *Deutsche Besatzungspolitik*, 109–110, 280–281; and Timothy Snyder, "Memory of Sovereignty and Sovereignty over Memory: Poland, Lithuania and Ukraine, 1939–1999," 47.

During an interview with the author in 2016, Irina Guzenberg read out the "beloved above all" line from a Russian book from the 1920s but was later unable to find it again to provide the exact source. Also in 2016, in an expanded edition of her guidebook to Jewish life in Vilnius published in Russian and Lithuanian, Guzenberg uses the same phrase, "beloved above all," to describe Franya. The book, cowritten with Genrikh Agranovsky, is called *Vilnius: In Search of the Jerusalem of Lithuania*. An English translation is forthcoming.

4: IN THE CLAWS OF THE BEAST

On the Nazi invasion of June 22, 1941, see Arad, *Ghetto in Flames*, 29–38; Abraham Sutzkever, *From the Vilna Ghetto to Nuremberg: Memoir and Testimony*, 7–9; Mendel Balberyszski, *Stronger than Iron: The Destruction of Vilna Jewry, 1941–1945, an Eyewitness Account*, 3–15; Kruk, *Last Days*, 46–48; and Dieckmann, *Deutsche Besatzungspolitik*, 303–306.

On the first killings and Lithuanian lawlessness in the first weeks of the Nazi invasion, see Arad, *Ghetto in Flames*, 41–58; Kruk, *Last Days*, 50–51, 56–57, 61–66; and Dieckmann, *Deutsche Besatzungspolitik*, 9, 339, 342–344.

On the older generation holding on to hopeful memories of World War I, see Dieckmann, *Deutsche Besatzungspolitik*, 303–304. He cites a Jewish woman, Sima Skirkowitz, whose mother reassured her: "The Germans treated us well in the first war." Benjamin Harshav, in his preface to Kruk's diary, describes his neighbors' amazement when he (then aged thirteen) and the rest of his family packed small rucksacks and fled Vilna on the second day of the German bombardments. "The Germans are a cultured people, they will not touch the city of the Vilna Gaon!" he remembers the neighbors saying. To which his father responded: "I read Hitler's *Mein Kampf*, and I believe him." See Kruk, *Last Days*, xvi.

Even Mendel Balberyszski, who had viewed the Germans' arrival with such dread, came to believe a German civil administration would be an improvement: "We waited impatiently for the moment when a German administration would be organized, no matter what its character, so that the Lithuanian lawlessness could be put to an end." (This is in the original Yiddish version of his diary but not in the condensed English translation. Arad quotes it in *Ghetto in Flames*, 47–48.)

On Stalin's refusal to believe the evidence of an impending German invasion, see Anthony Beevor, *The Second World War*, 186–207. The German ambassador in Moscow, Graf Friedrich von der Schulenburg, would later be arrested and executed for his role in the June 20, 1944, plot to assassinate Hitler. On Stalin's belief that appeasing Hitler through favorable trading terms could forestall German aggression and on his intentions to attack Germany himself once the Soviet forces were ready, see Robert Service, *Stalin: A Biography*, 405–409. The intelligence from the German Air Ministry is detailed in Rebecca Donner, *All the Frequent Troubles of Our Days*, 345–348, as is Stalin's obscenity-laden scrawl on the report of the Luftwaffe battle plan. On the Soviets racing out of Vilna, see Arad, *Ghetto in Flames*, 29–32. Stalin's howl of regret on June 29 is cited in Richard Rhodes, *Masters of Death: The SS-Einsatzgruppen and the Invention of the Holocaust*, 105.

The narrative of German planning for Operation Barbarossa and the upending of those plans owes a significant debt to Christoph Dieckmann's groundbreaking work. His research, based on an exhaustive reading of primary sources from within the German war machine, among other things, shows convincingly that the Nazis did not plan the Holocaust before the invasion of the Soviet Union; they did not start their systematic killing of Eastern European Jews until their lofty ambitions for the invasion started to fall short in the first couple of weeks. See in particular Dieckmann, *Deutsche Besatzungspolitik*, 178–228, 267–279, 924–928, 1509–1513. Dieckmann sources the phrase "Geopolitik des Hungertodes" to Herbert Backe, a state secretary in the Food and Agriculture Ministry (198). An earlier, much less detailed version of Dieckmann's research can be found in English in his essay "The War and the Killing of the Lithuanian Jews." The term "death reservation" (*Sterbereservat*) originated with Adolf Eichmann. See Christoph Dieckmann and Saulius Sužiedėlis, *The Persecution and Mass Murder of Lithuanian Jews During Summer and Fall of 1941*, n.p., footnote 35.

Besides Hellmuth Stieff, other leaders Dieckmann cites on the army in crisis (*Deutsche Besatzungspolitik*, 924–925) include Field Marshal Wilhelm Keitel and Erich Hoepner, commander of the Fourth Panzer Division. General Hoepner and General Stieff were, like Ambassador von der Schulenburg, later executed for their role in the 1944 plot to kill Hitler; Keitel was tried for war crimes at Nuremberg and executed by the Allies in 1946.

For more on Nazi "decapitation" operations in Poland, see Peter Longerich, *Heinrich Himmler: A Life*, 428–430; and Timothy Snyder, *Bloodlands: Europe Between Hitler and Stalin*, 126–128. As both authors demonstrate, the Einsatzgruppen did target and kill Jews, but the driving purpose of these killings was to displace Jews in large numbers, not to kill them wholesale. The policy, as articulated by Hitler and Heydrich and as reflected in the overall numbers, was to destroy Polish leadership. For examples of the standard narrative of the opening months of Barbarossa, see, for example, Beevor, *The Second World War*; or the British television series *The World at War*, episode 5, "Barbarossa." For more on the military aspects of the invasion, see David M. Glantz, *Operation Barbarossa: Hitler's Invasion of Russia 1941.* Himmler's speech to SS and police leaders is quoted in Rhodes, *Masters of Death*, 17–18. In the speech, Himmler estimated that twenty to thirty million "Slavs and Jews" would perish from hunger and other causes in the coming war; the figures "thirty million" and "many tens of millions" appear in Nazi documents cited by Dieckmann that lay out the hunger plan. Rhodes also quotes Himmler (*Masters of Death*, 92) on the Soviet Union being "our India." Regrettably, there is no exhaustive edition of Goebbels's diaries in English. In German, see Joseph Goebbels, *Die Tagebücher von Joseph Goebbels: Diktate, 1941–45.* For more on the "stab in the back" theory (*Dolchstosslegende* in German, literally "dagger-blow legend") and how it played into Hitler's endorsement of exterminating the Jews, see Snyder, *Bloodlands*, 213–214.

On German plans for Vilna, their manipulation of the Lithuanians, and the development of an extermination policy over the summer of 1941, see Dieckmann, *Deutsche Besatzungspolitik*, 75–114, 246–261, 301, 313–317, 393–397, 416–430, 473, 527–528, 649–650, 742–745, 925, 1120–1121. On the pogrom in Kovno (Kaunas in Lithuanian): the head of Einsatzgruppe A, Franz Walter Stahlecker, put the number of dead at thirty-eight hundred in a report he submitted in October. There are grounds, however, for thinking that number is an exaggeration. Other sources suggest a number in the range of six hundred to one thousand. See Dieckmann and Sužiedėlis, *Persecution and Mass Murder of Lithuanian Jews*, n.p., footnote 108. Rosenberg is quoted in Arad, *Ghetto in Flames*, 37–38. Arad also quotes an LAF manifesto published on the day of the German invasion that said: "Lithuania must be liberated not only from the yoke of Bolshevism but also from the long-protracted burden of the Jewish yoke. . . . The new Lithuania will not give any Jew civil rights nor possibility of existence." The accusation of arson leveled against the Jews killed in Daugavpils is in a report filed by the commander of Einsatzgruppe A, Franz Walter Stahlecker, on October 15, 1941 (available in German and in a partial English translation via the US Holocaust Memorial Museum). Stahlecker echoes the policy established by Heydrich of encouraging local Baltic militias to carry out pogroms and other "self-cleansing actions." He also confirms that the militias were photographed and filmed to demonstrate who had carried out the mass executions. On the Einsatzgruppen in Vilna and the mass shootings at Ponary, see Arad, *Ghetto in Flames*, 64–79. For more on the Einsatzgruppen filming and blackmailing the Lithuanian killers, see Sutzkever, *From the Vilna Ghetto to Nuremberg*, 64.

On the bounty demanded of Vilna's Jews in early August 1941, see Arad, *Ghetto in Flames*, 95–97. Balberyszski's reflections on the difficulty many Jews had in accepting bad news are in *Stronger than Iron*, 105–160; Kruk's are in *Last Days*, 88. Kruk first wrote about Ponary on July 20 (66). The Polish journalist living near the forest was Kazimierz Sakowicz. See his *Ponary Diary, 1941–1943: A Bystander's Account of a Mass Murder.* Early discussions of the ghetto and Hans Hingst's fear of Jewish infection are chronicled in Dieckmann, *Deutsche Besatzungspolitik*, 967–971. While living Jews were no more infectious than the rest of the population, the shallowness of many Jewish mass grave sites across Lithuania would later prove to be a major source of typhus outbreaks; see Dieckmann, *Deutsche Besatzungspolitik*, 917–918. On the timing: Both Kaunas (Kovno) and Šiauliai (Shavli), Lithuania's two other major cities, had ghettos fully established by mid-August. On the "great provocation," see Arad, *Ghetto in Flames*, 101–104; Sutzkever, *From the Vilna Ghetto*, 29–30; and Grigorij Schur's ghetto diary, unavailable in English. German reference: Grigorij Schur, *Die Juden von Wilna: Die Aufzeichnungen des Grigorij Schur, 1941–1944,*

49–51. The first days of the ghetto are described in Arad, *Ghetto in Flames*, 108–113; Kruk, *Last Days*, 96–99; Sutzkever, *From the Vilna Ghetto*, 36–39; and Yitskhok Rudashevski, *The Diary of the Vilna Ghetto*, 31–34.

On the pace of killings in Vilna, see Dieckmann, *Deutsche Besatzungspolitik*, 1004. On the reshuffling of the ghetto populations, see Arad, *Ghetto in Flames*, 133–135. On Ponary as a "third ghetto," see Balberyszski, *Stronger than Iron*, 105; and Dieckmann, *Deutsche Besatzungspolitik*, 981. The September eyewitness accounts from Ponary are detailed in Kruk, *Last Days*, 89–93. His diary includes other later accounts—for example, on 223–225. On the clothing of the dead being sorted at Gestapo headquarters, see Sutzkever, *From the Vilna Ghetto*, 75–76. Some of the discarded clothing made its way back to the ghetto, where Sutzkever saw a pair of shoes that had belonged to his own mother. The story of the young woman who spat in the guard's face is in the Yiddish version of Balberyszski's diary and relayed by Dieckmann, *Deutsche Besatzungspolitik*, 998. On the *malines*, see Sutzkever, *From the Vilna Ghetto*, 119–123; Arad, *Ghetto in Flames*, 192–193; and Rudashevski, *Diary*, 37–38.

On the controversy over the Lithuanian genocide museum—now, in the awkward official English translation, the Museum of Occupations and Freedom Fights—see Jonathan Steele, "In the Jerusalem of the North, the Jewish Story Is Forgotten," *Guardian*, June 19, 2008; Dovid Katz, "Lithuania's Museum of Holocaust Denial"; and Rod Nordland, "Where the Genocide Museum Is (Mostly) Mum on the Fate of Jews," *New York Times*, March 30, 2018. After 2011, Katz reports, the new exhibit devoted to the Holocaust was in a basement cubicle and was still riddled with errors.

5: In the Archives

On Marcus Petuchauskas: The theater had such a strong impact on his young mind that his entire sixty-year career was dedicated to understanding and celebrating the power of art. As a professor and theater critic, he has published more than three hundred articles and a dozen books on the subject. See his autobiography, *Price of Concord*.

On the record of railway workers helping Holocaust prisoners to escape convoys to Auschwitz, see Ludivine Broch, "French Railway Workers and the Question of Rescue During the Holocaust." For more on the Belgian resistance's convoy attack, see Marion Schreiber, *The Twentieth Train: The True Story of the Ambush of the Death Train to Auschwitz*. For a short account of German deportation policy in occupied Belgium, see Laurence Schram, "The Transit Camp for Jews in Mechelen: The Antechamber of Death, Mass Violence & Résistance," published online at sciencespo.fr, February 6, 2008. For a longer account in French, see Maxime Steinberg, *La Persécution des Juifs en Belgique (1940–1945)* (Brussels: Complexe, 2004). Steinberg also wrote an exhaustive, three-volume history of the occupation titled *L'étoile et le fusil* (The star and the gun), published in the 1980s.

The Ghetto Fighters' Museum was unable to provide a photograph or other copy of the yellow stars that Dobruszkes mentions in his letter. Forty years after Dobruszkes sent them to the museum for safekeeping ("please guard the yellow patches so that they remain joined together"), staff told the author they could not locate them. One interesting coincidence: the name of the Mechelen barracks, Caserne Dossin, was named for the same Belgian World War I commander as the street where Lola and Naomi had been living, the Avenue Général

Dossin de St Georges. The information on Dubruszkes himself comes from Jacques Déom, "Une voix du yiddish, Azario Dobruszkes."

The paperwork on Rachmil's battle to maintain residency in Germany is included in the Russian refugee case files (1927–1938, Puk-Rad) of the Nansen Office for Refugees, High Commissioner for Refugees, Delegation in Germany (Berlin), folder C 1207. They are available through the UN archives in Geneva. The paperwork on Rachmil runs out in 1934, at the time he was retraining as a car locksmith. Most likely, he did not need the Nansen office's help thereafter because he found gainful employment and thus earned the right to stay in Germany—until the anti-Jewish laws created an entirely different set of problems. The office was named for Fridtjof Nansen, a Norwegian League of Nations official who championed refugees and prisoners returning home after World War I and was recognized with the 1922 Nobel Peace Prize. The office itself was awarded a second Nobel Peace Prize in 1938. Michael Hansson, who as president of the board of trustees accepting the 1938 award, noted the office's work in "reach[ing] down into the public, and especially amongst those most impoverished and unhappy, to those who are completely lacking in rights." Hansson cited at the Nobel Peace Center's website entry on the 1938 award; see https://peaceprizelaureates .nobelpeacecenter.org.

Rachmil's date of arrival at Dachau and his date of death are widely available through numerous online Holocaust archives including the International Center on Nazi Persecution (the Arolsen Archives, arolsen-archives.org). The date of his deportation to Auschwitz was provided by Ewa Bazan and Krystyna Lesniak of the Auschwitz-Birkenau state museum in an email to the author dated May 6, 2016. For one account of the death march from Auschwitz, beginning on January 17, 1945, see Marc Santora, "Before the Liberation of Auschwitz, a March of Misery," *New York Times*, January 27, 2020.

On Jewish population growth in the nineteenth century and the flourishing of Jewish political activism and culture around the time of Franya's birth, see Harshav's introduction to Kruk, *Last Days*, xxxii–xxxiii. The story of the Orthodox girls who ran away to seek an education is told in Rachel Manekin, *The Rebellion of the Daughters: Jewish Women Runaways in Habsburg Galicia*. On the impact of this rebellion on religious and educational leaders in Warsaw, see 186–190.

For a discussion of Talmudic prohibitions on women singing in front of men, see David Golinkin, "'Kol B'ishah Ervah'—Is It Really Forbidden for Jewish Men to Listen to Women Singing?" *Ervah*, per Golinkin, translates as "nakedness, unchastity, impropriety."

On the upheavals of World War I and the emergence of a cosmopolitan "cabaret of the intelligentsia" in Warsaw, see Debra Caplan, *Yiddish Empire: The Vilna Troupe, Jewish Theater, and the Art of Itinerancy*, 46; and Beth Holmgren, "Cabaret Nation: The Jewish Foundations of *Kabaret Literacki*, 1920–1939." The Buloff quote about the sufferings and endurance of Jewish performers is from Luba Kadison, Joseph Buloff, and Irving Genn, *On Stage Off Stage: Memories of a Lifetime in the Yiddish Theater*, 87. There is some evidence (from a playbill in the Center for Jewish History's collections featuring last names only) that a young Buloff and Franya shared a stage in 1917, in an operetta titled *The Wedding Day*, directed by Nahum Lipowski. Location unknown. The Dutch critic, Simon Koster, is cited in Caplan, *Yiddish Empire*, 119.

On Yiddish theater's absurdist elements: Eugène Ionesco, later the author of the play *The Lesson, The Bald Prima Donna,* and other classics of the Theater of the Absurd, was a fan of the Vilna Troupe. Much later, Buloff wrote: "By its nature, the infant Jewish theater had to be absurd because it grew out of the absurd situation of the Jews in Czarist Russia. . . . When Jewish actors recognized spies entering the makeshift theater and infiltrating the audience, they would send a signal to the stage. Then, abruptly, the actors would switch from the Yiddish script they were performing. An actor from Poland would begin declaiming in Polish. A Hungarian actress would answer him in Magyar. A couple of actors who only knew Yiddish would carry on a dialogue in meaningless gibberish. . . . There you have it: a dozen actors on a bare stage, each one speaking a different language. Alienation, failure of communication, absence of objective meaning—all the elements of the Theater of the Absurd. And it was invented a century ago by Jewish actors out of grim necessity." Quoted in Caplan, *Yiddish Empire*, 141.

6: *Un Trésor Familial*

Aurore Blaise's side of the story is based on her notes on the photos in the collection; on the email correspondence she initiated with the author on August 28, 2015, and continued thereafter; and on multiple meetings and conversations, including one taped on May 18, 2021, and a fact-checking phone call on December 7, 2021.

The French revolutionary Georges Danton moved into the house in Choisy-le-Roi shortly after marrying his sixteen-year-old second wife, Louise Sébastienne Gély, in July 1793. His first wife had died four months earlier while in labor with their fourth child, who did not survive either. Choisy-le-Roi, known just as Choisy at the time, was a country retreat popular with the revolutionary political class despite its association with one of the recently executed king's hunting estates. Danton, who had multiple properties of his own, continued living in Choisy until he was arrested, tried on corruption charges, and guillotined in April 1794. The subsequent history of the house is difficult to ascertain, but early-twentieth-century photographs indicate that it was already in disrepair then. Ordinarily, a building of this significance would have been earmarked for preservation, but by 1980 the French authorities deemed it too dilapidated to save.

Serge Mogère chronicled his discovery of the family photographs at the Maison Danton in a number of ways. He took Polaroids of the house on the day he broke in (pictures included in the collection now at the Mémorial de la Shoah in Paris); he wrote it up in a one-page document he submitted to the Mémorial along with his photos in 2015; he described it in a *récit illustré*, an illustrated account including text in ink, photographs of the Maison Danton, and seven watercolor panels, which he produced in 2017–2018; he also described it in multiple conversations with the author from 2015 to 2021, some of them captured on tape; in a formal pair of interviews conducted in Annecy on October 21 and 22, 2021; and in a fact-checking phone call on December 6, 2021.

The picture of the boy in the Warsaw ghetto first appeared in the Stroop Report, the Nazis' own seventy-five-page account of how they suppressed the 1943 uprising, with the caption "Pulled from the bunkers by force." For more, see Dan Porat, *The Boy: A Holocaust Story*.

On Nisen's cause of death: In their email to the author of May 6, 2016, Ewa Bazan and Krystyna Lesniak of the Auschwitz-Birkenau state museum provided the original German wording, which was *Darmkatarrh bei Körperschwäche*. The translation given is more accurate than "acute gastroenteritis," which is how the museum rendered it in English.

The stories about Madeleine Formentin, later Madeleine Mogère, during and after the war are based on the same conversations with Serge, and on a video interview with Madeleine that the author recorded in Choisy-le-Roi on May 12, 2017.

7: THE VILNA GHETTO

On the use of brass artificial limbs in the nineteenth century, see, for example, William Robert Grossmith's book *Amputations and Artificial Limbs* (London: Longman, 1857). The Science Museum in London has some of Grossmith's brass legs in its collection.

On Russian soldiers carrying spoons in their boots: Louise Bryant, in her book *Six Red Months in Russia: An Observer's Account of Russia Before and During the Proletarian Dictatorship*, writes, "We ate with wooden spoons, the kind the Russian soldiers carry in their big boots" (47). In Alexander Solzhenistyn's *One Day in the Life of Ivan Denisovich*, the protagonist, a former soldier consigned to a gulag shortly after the end of World War II, pulls a handmade aluminum spoon out of his boot to eat (16, 18 in the Farrar, Straus & Giroux paperback edition, 2005).

Mollie's Yad Vashem testimonial documents are dated May 5, 1991 (Isaak) and May 12, 1991 (Franya). In response to the question about "circumstances of death," she wrote for Franya: "See *21 and 1*." For Isaak, she put a question mark, followed by: "Read about him and wife in *Twenty-One and One*."

The account of the October 1942 *Aktion* in Ashmyany (Oszmiana) is taken from Arad, *Ghetto in Flames*, 341–348; Kruk, *Last Days*, 387–397, 394; Dieckmann, *Deutsche Besatzungspolitik*, 1256–1261; and the diary of Hinda Daul, an Ashmyany Jew whose testimony is including in a Yizkor, or memorial book, dedicated to the town and available in English online via JewishGen.org. The use of the nickname *Judenverrat* ("Yidn-farat" in Yiddish) is from Kruk, *Last Days*, 184. The same epithet attached itself to the Judenrat in Warsaw and other ghettos; see Lucy S. Dawidowicz, *The War Against the Jews: 1933–1945*, 239.

On Jakob Gens telling his wife his place was in the ghetto, see Dieckmann, *Deutsche Besatzungspolitik*, 1108. His views on the Kiemeliszki killings are in Kruk, *Last Days*, 406, 410. His statement on what would give him "a quiet heart and a pure conscience" is in Arad, *Ghetto in Flames*, 427. Arad comments: "Gens erred in his fundamental conception—that the German administration regarded the existence of the ghetto and its inhabitants vital for economic reasons, above all other considerations. This illusion was shattered with his murder." The ghetto diarist quoted is Sutzkever, *From the Vilna Ghetto*, 44.

Many writers have described the "spiritual resistance" of the Vilna ghetto, a phenomenon echoed elsewhere in Nazi-occupied Eastern Europe but nowhere on the same scale. Wiskind is quoted in Sutzkever, *From the Vilna Ghetto*, 93. Sutzkever said the conversations about a ghetto theater started the day after his mother was murdered, which was in December 1941. The writers, actors, and theater directors of Vilna were all highly secularized, and the religious objection to a concert did not come from them; it was, however, something on the minds of many Jews in ghettos where concerts took place; see William W. Mishell, *Kaddish for Kovno: Life and Death in a Lithuanian Ghetto, 1941–1945*, 131. For Kruk's writings on the theater and his changing views, see his *Last Days*, 173–174, 226–228, 239–240. Gens's line about helping to carry a heavy burden was reported by Israel Segal, who was himself skeptical at first but later served as director of the ghetto theater, quoted in Dieckmann,

Deutsche Besatzungspolitik, 1155. The opening concert of January 18, 1942, is described in detail in Shoshana Kalisch and Barbara Meister, *Yes, We Sang! Songs of the Ghettos and Concentration Camps*, 3–4. The Kalmanovich material comes from his diary and is quoted in English in Stephen Howard Garrin's essay "But I Forsook Not Thy Precepts: Spiritual Resistance to the Holocaust," 340.

Caplan's *Yiddish Empire* provides easily the most authoritative account of the birth of the Vilna Troupe and the Yiddish avant-garde, especially 44–83. The Peretz quote appears, along with others, on 24.

Some of the information on the plays Franya performed comes from an author interview with Caplan, *Yiddish Empire*, June 7, 2021. *Yankele* was a show cocreated by Molly Picon, an American-born comic actress who enjoyed considerable fame in the 1930s and 1940s but is probably best known now as Yente the matchmaker in the 1971 film *Fiddler on the Roof*. Picon and her European-born husband Jacob Kalich wrote *Yankele*; Picon starred.

On *Motke the Thief* as a model for Hollywood gangster movies: one direct connection was the American actor Paul Muni, born in Lemberg (later Lvov, now Lviv in Ukraine), with Yiddish as his first language. Muni starred as Motke on the New York stage in 1917 and later took the title role in *Scarface* (1932), based loosely on the life of Al Capone and directed by Howard Hawks.

The editor of *Vilner Tag* who praised Franya, Zalman Reisen, was reviewing a show called *The Duke* (sometimes translated as *The Magnate*) in the December 3, 1925, issue. The review of *The Virtuous Susanna* appeared in the Russian-language *Vilenskoye Utro* (Vilna Morning) on May 5, 1924. The front-page poem appeared a week later, on May 12, under the byline A. Rubinshteyn. (In 1927 Franya reprised her performance as Susanna in Riga and was similarly celebrated.) Publications calling Franya a "prima donna" include the Lvov daily *Chwila* on July 20, 1931, and the Kovno daily *Echo* on March 24, 1934. A poster for a production in Lublin in October 1932 called her "the prima donna of the Riga Royal Theater."

Some of the best stories about Rudolf Zaslavsky are told in Abram Nuger's "Forgotten and Half-Forgotten Names." His groundbreaking performance as Hamlet was in Łódź in 1913. Zaslavsky directed and starred, and Nahum Lipowski was one of the producers; see Agata Katarzyna Dąbrowska, "Jewish Theatre in Poland as an Institution of Nationality, Education and Intercultural Dialogue." The Edwin Booth line is from an article titled "Russian Tragedian Here, 'Edwin Booth of Russia' Tells of Rise of Bolshevist State Drama," *New York Times,* December 2, 1926. Zaslavsky was working in St. Petersburg (Petrograd in the article) at the time.

Maurice Schwartz's celebrated staging of *Yoshe Kalb* opened in New York in 1933 and ran for five hundred performances before he took it on the road to Europe. See Clive Barnes, "Theater: *Yoshe Kalb*," *New York Times*, October 23, 1972.

On *Lebensraum* and Manifest Destiny, see, for example, Timothy Snyder, *Black Earth: The Holocaust as History and Warning*, 13–16. On the emergence of political anti-Semitism in Poland after Marshal Piłsudski's death, see Edward D. Wynot Jr., "'A Necessary Cruelty': The Emergence of Official Anti-Semitism in Poland, 1936–39." On the deteriorating situation in Vilna and the rest of Poland, including the diplomatic standoff triggered by the German attempt to expel its Polish-born Jews, see Dawidowicz, *From That Place and Time*,

65–69, 71–73, 164–185. Turkow's manifesto is cited at length in Nahma Sandrow, *Vagabond Stars: A World History of Yiddish Theater*, 335–336.

On the lifting of university admission limits on Jews under Soviet occupation, see Dieckmann, *Deutsche Besatzungspolitik*, 157. Shoshana Kahan's diary, available in Yiddish only, is titled *In Fayer un in Flamen: Togbukh fun a Yidisher Shoyshpilerin* (In fire and flames: Diary of a Yiddish actress).

The Soviet census detailing Franya and Isaak's living situation, kept by the Lithuanian State Historical Archives, is dated April 23, 1941. On Sutzkever and Kaczerginski attending the premiere on June 21, 1941, see David E. Fishman, *Book Smugglers: Partisans, Poets, and the Race to Save Jewish Treasures from the Nazis*, 25. Kaczerginski, in his book *Khurbn Vilner* (The destruction of Vilna), published in Yiddish by the United Vilner Relief Committee (New York, 1947), describes Franya as "one of the finest artists of the Jewish theater."

The most extensive collection of Sutzkever's poetry in English is *The Full Pomegranate: Poems of Avrom Sutzkever*. The quoted poem is "On the Anniversary of the Ghetto Theater."

The story of Liuba Lewicka's death is told in Arad, *Ghetto in Flames*, 306; Sutzkever, *From the Vilna Ghetto*, 111–112; Kalisch and Meister, *Yes, We Sang!*, 8–9; Rudashevski, *Diary*, 126; and Dora Rubina's testimony. On German tolerance of ghetto cultural activities, see Dąbrowska, "Jewish Theatre in Poland." Sutzkever says Lewicka was caught with a bag of peas; Rubina says it was two kilos of beans. Arad consulted the German arrest record, which was almost certainly more accurate. On the ghetto residents' anxiety to clear the streets when Murer came near, see Dieckmann, *Deutsche Besatzungspolitik*, 970. The story about Gens offering up a sick old man to take Lewicka's place comes from Moshe Nadel, a member of the Zionist Underground who survived the war, quoted in Dieckmann, *Deutsche Besatzungspolitik*, 1119–1120n372. Different accounts have Weiss's girlfriend named Ellen, Helene, or Hilde. There are some grounds to be skeptical of Sutzkever's account (only some of which is relayed here), because it's unclear who, apart from Weiss and Degner, would have been privy to the details he provides.

Sutzkever's line about the Yiddish language is in *From the Vilna Ghetto*, 60. His reflections on his poetic output are from a 1991 lecture he gave at YIVO in New York, quoted in Justin Cammy's afterword to his diary (324).

The "Jewish grave" line is cited in Kruk, *Last Days*, 297. Kruk's own words ("A day will come . . .") are not from his diary but from a poem found among his final papers titled "For Future Generations." It appears in *Last Days* on v–vi.

On the Paper Brigade, see Fishman, *The Book Smugglers*, especially 27–32, 189–227; Sutzkever, *From the Vilna Ghetto*, 101–107; Kruk, *Last Days*, 212–214, 369–370; and Dieckmann, *Deutsche Besatzungspolitik*, 1043. Kruk writes: "The Rosenberg Task Force [the formal name of Johannes Pohl's team] purges the theater archive. Most of the documents go into the trash, and the Jewish workers take it out of the trash to sell it in the ghetto, which lacks paper. The Jewish actor, the ghetto bookbinder, cannot accept it, and the 'trash' wanders again into the archive of the ghetto" (*Last Days*, 369–370). The details about Uma Olkenicka come from a biographical sketch posted by the Vilna Jewish museum on its website, www.jmuseum.lt. YIVO's archives were not available online when the author first consulted them in 2016–2017, but much of the collection has since been digitized.

8: Revelation in Iowa

For details on the Yad Vashem file on the Boratyńskis, see notes to Chapter 1. The book to which Maks Etingin contributed interviews is Bart and Corona, *Until Our Last Breath*; for other sources, see the notes to Chapter 1.

The summary laying out the essentials of Dora Rubina's story is not at the Yad Vashem website but on a page maintained by EHRI (European Holocaust Research Infrastructure). As of December 2021, the *j* previously used to spell Franya's name had been changed into an *i*. For more on the purge of those without yellow work permits, see Arad, *Ghetto in Flames*, 149–152. See also the detailed description in Chapter 7.

For more on the cultural life of the ghetto, see Arad, *Ghetto in Flames*, 318–327; Dieckmann, *Deutsche Besatzungspolitik*, 1155–1160; Sutzkever, *From the Vilna Ghetto*, 93–94; Rudashevski, *Diary*, 76–77, 106, 109–110, 120, 132; Kruk, *Last Days*, 263–264, 271, 273, 342, 377–378, 421–422; and Dora Rubina's powerful testimony, titled "The Path of Suffering of Jewish Actors," part of Yad Vashem's Tenenbaum-Mersik archive (document M.11). The quote likening the ghetto theater to the Holy Temple is hers.

Class at University of Iowa Summer Writers' Festival, "The Novelist's Tools: Fiction and Narrative Nonfiction." Taught by Lon Otto, professor emeritus, University of St. Paul, MN, June 2016.

For an indication of what the average American knows about the Holocaust, see the multiple Pew Research Center polls conducted in recent years including "What Americans Know About the Holocaust" (January 22, 2020). The short version: almost everyone is familiar with the topic, which certainly compares favorably to what Americans know about their system of government, say, or who attacked the country on 9/11, but respondents struggle to say more than the fact that it involved Nazis killing Jews. For an example of higher-level errors and misunderstandings, see Katrin Bennhold, "80 Years Ago the Nazis Planned the 'Final Solution.' It Took 90 Minutes," *New York Times*, January 20, 2022, which overstates the importance of the Wannsee Conference in "planning the Holocaust" when the killing of Jews had been going on in chillingly well-organized fashion for months. The article does not discuss Hitler's earlier decisive endorsement and says that "mass killings in eastern territories had begun the previous fall" when in fact they began in July 1941.

9: *Twenty-One and One*

Many parts of Franya's life story are either taken from Blecher's account in *Twenty-One and One* or based on it. The author used the elements Blecher provided to research widely around the topics he raised and, in particular, found playbills, posters, and other evidence to trace Franya's theatrical career.

The interview in which Zaslavsky denounced *shund* appeared in the Vilna literary weekly *Literarishe Bleter* (1928, no. 40). The quotes from *Stempenyu*, the novel, are from 117 (Stempenyu) and 162 (Rokhele) of Sholem Aleichem, *Stempenyu: A Jewish Romance*. Aleichem wrote the stage version in 1907, but it was not a success until Maurice Schwartz mounted a production with the Yiddish Art Theater in New York in 1929. See Jan Lisa Huttner, "Everybody's Fiddler," *Forward*, September 5, 2003. The quoted extracts from act 2 are from a translation commissioned by the author. The Krakow engagements were in January 1931, as attested by a review printed on January 14 in the Zionist newspaper *Nowy Dziennik*. The critic who accused Zaslavsky of surrounding himself with mediocre actors was A. Fridkin in an essay titled "On Ibsen, Rudolf Zaslavsky and Tevye the Milkman," *Literarishe Bleter*, no. 39 (1927).

Zaslavsky handwrote a Yiddish-language account of his premature demise, titled "The Day I Died," and it includes a description of the amazement people expressed when they saw he was still breathing. The document is in YIVO's collections in New York. Zaslavsky claims to have been as surprised by the death announcement as anyone, but other sources cited by Nuger strongly suggest otherwise. According to the Jewish Telegraphic Agency, the date of the fake death notice was June 7, 1936. See "Zaslawski, Actor, Dies in Buenos Aires; Falsely Reported Dead Year Ago," *JTA*, September 21, 1937. The information about the memorial performance of *Day and Night* (which took place at 10:00 a.m. on October 31, 1937) is from a publicity poster, copies of which are in YIVO's collections and also at the New York Public Library.

On the Yom Kippur *Aktion*, see Kruk, *Last Days*, 122–123; Arad, *Ghetto in Flames*, 136–139; Dieckmann, *Deutsche Besatzungspolitik*, 991–995; Balberyszski, *Stronger than Iron*, 111–123; and, available in Yiddish only, Mark Dvorzhetski, *Yerusholaym de-Lita in kamf un umkum: Zikhroynes fun Vilner Geto*, 89–93. The title translates into English as "The Jerusalem of Lithuania in Struggle and Destruction: A Chronicle of the Vilna Ghetto." Kruk (*Last Days*, 285 and again on 360) gives a death toll of thirty-nine hundred for the Yom Kippur *Aktion*—twenty-two hundred people from ghetto one and seventeen hundred from ghetto two. The full name of the Jäger report, stamped "Secret Reich Business!," is "Gesamtaufstellung der im Bereich des EK. 3 bis zum 1. Dez, 1941 durchgeführten Exekutionen" ("Summary report of executions carried out in EK [Einsatzkommando] 3's area of operations up to December 1, 1941") and is widely available online both in the original and in a sometimes truncated English translation. In February 1942, Franz Walter Stahlecker of Einsatzgruppe A echoed Jäger's complaints, saying in a report of his own that the slaughter of two-thirds of Vilna's Jews and the complete eradication of Jewish communities in many rural areas—which he characterized as "liquidating a few Jews"—did not go far enough and made it "impossible to stabilize the areas behind the front line." Quoted in Dieckmann and Sužiedėlis, *Persecution and Mass Murder of Lithuanian Jews*. A month later, Stahlecker was attacked by Estonian resistance fighters and died of his wounds.

On the yellow-permit *Aktion*, see Arad, *Ghetto in Flames*, 143–152; Dieckmann, *Deutsche Besatzungspolitik*, 996–1000; Balberyszski, *Stronger than Iron*, 153–164; and Rudashevski, *Diary*, 36–41. On Herman Kruk's odd marriage: Kruk's assistant at the ghetto library, Dina Abramowicz, described her astonishment on seeing her boss in a short coat and beret walking arm and arm with "the ancient Pati Kremer who, with her gray hair and wrinkled face, looked like his grandmother." Cited in Benjamin Harshav's introduction to *Last Days*, xliv. Kremer was eventually selected for death on the day the Vilna ghetto was liquidated in September 1943; Abramowicz survived and had an illustrious postwar career as a librarian at YIVO in New York. In addition to increasing the number of permits, the Nazis also agreed in mid-October that several hundred workers at the Kailis fur factory (Arad puts the number at eight hundred to a thousand) should leave the ghetto and live at the factory instead, as a way of protecting them from roundups and killings. The total number protected ahead of the October 24 roundups, including family dependents, was thus around sixteen thousand, leaving more than nine thousand vulnerable. (By the end of October, when the last of the second ghetto had also been wiped out, that number was already down to four thousand.)

The details about Leib Shriftsetzer are taken from Balberyszski and from Dora Rubina's testimony. On Franya's options: Dora Rubina makes a point of writing that Franya knew how to get back in the ghetto, a line that appears tinged with some regret that she didn't. On the theory that the Byelorussian zone and Byelorussia were safer than Lithuania, see Hinda Daul's diary, part of the Ashmyany Yizkor, or memory book, available online through JewishGen.org, 59–74, and also the Yizkor for Olshan, or Gol'shany, available from the same source, 179. Both Ashmyany and Olshan were part of the Byelorussian zone at the time and were not integrated into the Vilna region until April 1942. On the reality of Byelorussia (modern-day Belarus) in this period, see Snyder, *Bloodlands*, which argues that no country suffered more during World War II. Snyder describes the capital, Minsk, where Franya had appeared many times onstage, as "a centerpiece of Nazi destructiveness" (225).

On Ashmyany in 1941, see Daul's diary; the testimony of Rochl Zinger, given at the US-run Feldafing displaced persons camp in West Germany on August 11, 1948, available in Yiddish through YIVO, Record Group 104, series 3; Dieckmann, *Deutsche Besatzungspolitik*, 1255–1256; the entries on Ashmyany (spelled the Polish way, as Oszmiana) and Olshan (ditto, as Holszany) in Martin Dean and Geoffrey P. Megargee, eds., *The United States Holocaust Memorial Museum Encyclopedia of Camps and Ghettos, 1933–1945: Ghettos in German-Occupied Eastern Europe*, 1056, 1098; and the entry on Ashmyany (also spelled Oszmiana) in Guy Miron and Shlomit Shulhani, eds., *The Yad Vashem Encyclopedia of the Ghettos During the Holocaust*, vol. 2, N–Z, 562–563. The schoolteacher quoted is Daul; the other witness quoted is Zinger. Data from the World Weather Records Clearinghouse at the federal government's National Oceanic and Atmospheric Administration show that temperatures in the Vilna area averaged an unseasonably low -3.9 degrees Celsius in November 1941, the coldest November of the war there. The average is based on mean temperatures per twenty-four-hour period, meaning it was generally warmer than -3.9 during the day and, typically, eight to ten degrees colder at night. The Sutzkever poem is "Frozen Jews," written while he was in the forest with the partisans in 1943–1944 and widely anthologized.

The accounts of Franya's death in *Twenty-One and One* and in Rubina's testimony differ slightly. Both agree she was buried alive. Blecher does not mention the biting and says it was Franya who begged the Germans not to shoot. "She grabbed their hands, knelt before them, and fell faint," he writes. But Rubina provides a source for her information—she writes that she heard her story from a man who'd been in Ashmyany at the time and later came to the Vilna ghetto—while Blecher does not say where he got his information. The biting also provides a better reason Franya would be singled out for such cruelty. The location of Franya's death, in the Jewish cemetery, is mentioned both by Blecher and by Shmerke Kaczerginski in a capsule entry on Franya in his book *Khurbn Vilner*.

10: THE AFTERMATH

On the distortion of Nazi names: Sutzkever, in an early chronicle of the ghetto, uses the names Schweingeburg and Maurer. When he testified at Nuremberg on February 27, 1946, he either got them wrong, or his words were mistranscribed as Schweichenberg, Muhrer, and Fincks (for Hingst). See Jewish Black Book Committee, *The Black Book: The Nazi Crime Against the Jewish People*, 320, 321; and Sutzkever, *From the Villa Ghetto*, 253. Kruk, throughout his diary, writes "Schweinenberg" instead of "Schweinberger." In another testimonial included in the Ashmyany Yizkor, by Lea Rudashevsky, yet another name is offered for the sadistic SS overlord of the ghetto, Keil.

On the fortunes of the war criminals who killed the author's family members: Martin Weiss's judicial journey is chronicled in Christina Ullrich, "Der erste deutsche Prozess gegen Einsatzgruppentäter: Die Besonderheiten des Falls Martin Weiss." See also Sutzkever, *From the Vilna Ghetto*, 76. Note that the Martin Weiss who operated in Vilna is not the same as Martin Weiss, the commandant at Dachau, hanged by the Allies in December 1945.

On Schweinberger, see Wolfgang Curilla, *Die deutsche Ordnungspolizei und der Holocaust im Baltkum und in Weissrussland*, 316–317; and, on the Schmitz trial, Tory Avraham, *Surviving the Holocaust: The Kovno Ghetto Diary*, viii, 407. Sutzkever, ever the keen observer, wrote of Schweinberger: "He was one of your 'handsome' German officers. . . . He was tall, elegant, with a delicate, girlish complexion. He never looked you in the eye when he spoke." He also enjoyed people addressing him as "father." See Jewish Black Book Committee, *Black Book*, 320.

On Murer, see Paul Lendvai, "The Old Austria and the New Nazis" and "An SS Murderer Is Enjoying His Old Age in Freedom in Austria," *Jewish Telegraphic Agency*, January 1, 1985. Murer lived thirty-one years after his Austrian trial, long enough to see his son rise through Jörg Haider's Far-Right Freedom Party to become a state secretary in Austria's agriculture ministry.

On Madeker and Krause together in Slutsk, see the official German documents reproduced and translated into English in *"Destroy as Much as Possible . . .": Latvian Collaborationist Formations on the Territory of Belarus, 1942–1944, Document Compendium* (Helsinki: Johan Beckman Institute, 2010), 30, 123, 126. On Madeker's career from 1942 on, see Barbara Orth, *Gestapo im OP: Bericht der Krankenhausärztin Charlotte Pommer* (Berlin: Lukas Verlag, 2013), 28n15, 49. Pommer was the doctor at the police hospital in Berlin where Madeker had nighttime terrors. On Waldemar Krause, see Andrej Angrick, *Aktion 1005: Spurenbeseitigung von NS-Massenverbrechen, 1942–1945* (Göttingen: Wallstein, 2018), 503–505.

On Kittel, see Zinger's testimony, Sutzkever, *From the Vilna Ghetto*, 131–132, 175–176; Kruk, *Last Days*, 587; Schur, *Die Juden von Wilna*, 200–301; and Dieckmann, *Deutsche Besatzungspolitik*, 1040n92.

The literature on the failure to prosecute more Nazi war criminals is extensive, but see, for example, Tony Judt, *Postwar: A History of Europe Since 1945*, 56–57, 61; Tim Weiner, *Legacy of Ashes: The History of the CIA*, 43–44, 46–49; Frederick Taylor, *Exorcising Hitler: The Occupation and Denazification of Germany*; Annie Jacobsen, *Operation Paperclip: The Secret Intelligence Program to Bring Nazi Scientists to America*; Eric Lichtblau, *The Nazis Next Door: How America Became a Safe Haven for Hitler's Men*; and Philippe Sands, *The Rat Line*. Adenauer's "dirty water" remark was specifically about his chief of staff, Hans Globke, who had helped draft the Nazis' Nuremberg race laws.

11: The Final Piece

Concerning the outside perception that Vilna was a safe place for Jews in 1939 and 1940, no less a figure than Vladimir Jabotinsky, then living in London, described members of his Polish youth organization who made it to Lithuania (including the future Israeli prime minister Menachem Begin) as "saved." See Snyder, *Black Earth*, 140. Nisen's arrest on May 14, 1941, is confirmed in French police documents obtained by the author. For more on the "green-ticket roundup" (in French: *la 75-65* residency papers), the little notice it received at the time, and the conditions at Pithiviers and at a neighboring internment camp, see Renée Poznanski, *Jews in France During World War II*, 56–61.

The narrative of Abraham's life is based largely on documents and photographs, most of them recovered by his granddaughter Léa Guinet, including his two marriage certificates; the "family booklet" (*livret de famille*) including details of Camille's death; the photograph from the early 1930s of Abraham, Camille, Jacques, and Nisen, which Léa obtained from her father after his death; a document from the Foreign Legion dated September 26, 1939, declaring that Abraham had passed a physical and was fit to serve "for the duration of the war"; a statement from a senior Paris police official (March 8, 1940) that mentions Abraham's application to join the French army and says that since there wasn't a single unfavorable item in his file his identity document was being renewed for another three years; and a handwritten two-page letter from Abraham to Léa dated July 31, 1989. The author also conducted phone calls and in-person interviews with Guinet, Esther Suissa, Naftali Suissa, and former synagogue elder Henri Moos, many of them while in Annecy, October 21–22, 2021. Guinet answered some additional questions by email on January 15 and 16, 2022, and again on February 24, 2022. The Foreign Legion training camp near Perpignan was a few miles up the Mediterranean coast in Barcarès, in a former prisoner-of-war camp previously used to house fighters from the Spanish Civil War. It's possible that Abraham later sent Jacques to a similar area, since the name of the Perpignan *département* is Pyrénées-Orientales (eastern Pyrenees). For more on the Legion and its foreign recruits at the start of World War II, see Douglas Porch, *The French Foreign Legion: The Complete History of the Legendary Fighting Force*, 446–456.

Aurore Blaise's research into Nisen's surviving wife and son is contained in an email to the author dated February 15, 2018. The Auschwitz-Birkenau museum's information about Midza is from the May 6, 2016, email cited above (see Chapter 4). For more on the French police roundups of July 1942, known in French as *la rafle du Vél d'Hiv* after the Vélodrome d'Hiver (winter cycling stadium) on the rue Nélaton, see Poznanski, *Jews in France*, 260–265. The information on Midza and the Igielmans is based both on information obtained by researcher Camille Gillain through conversations with Sandrine and others and conveyed to the author in writing on May 28, 2021, and also on a May 31, 2021, email to the author from Sandrine Ingelman's daughter. The "replacement child" observation about Henri comes not from these sources but from a magazine article written by a cousin. See Hilene Flanzbaum, "The Trace of Trauma: Third-Generation Holocaust Survivors."

12: The Taste of Dirt

On Jewish deaths in Vilna and Lithuania: the best overall estimate is somewhere between 200,000 and 206,000, out of a prewar population of 210,000, supplemented by several thousand refugees who fled east after the Nazis invaded Poland. See Dieckmann, *Deutsche Besatzungspolitik*, 792. The Jäger report puts the number killed before the end of November 1941 (almost but not quite all of them Jews) at 137,346, but this is not exhaustive. It omits the Yom Kippur *Aktion* in Vilna, for example, and does not include Jews killed by two Einsatzgruppen not covered in the report, EK2 and EK9, or those who continued to be killed in December 1941. Dieckmann (*Deutsche Besatzungspolitik*, 1009) puts the 1941 death toll in Lithuania at more than 150,000. In Vilna, where the Nazis chose to keep many workers alive to service their war machine, the proportion of Jews killed before the end of 1941 was closer to 60 percent. See Arad, *Ghetto in Flames*, 209–217, for a detailed breakdown. Many small-town communities, by contrast, were wiped out entirely. On the numbers across the eastern front, see Snyder, *Bloodlands*, ix–x. One proponent of the "two Holocausts" thesis is Benjamin Harshav; see his introduction to Kruk, *Last Days*, xxi–xxiv.

The Frantz Fanon quote is from *Peau noire, masques blancs* (Paris: Editions du Seuil, 1952), 98.

The Amanda Gorman quote is from her op-ed, "Why I Almost Didn't Read My Poem at the Inauguration," *New York Times*, January 20, 2022.

Brecht's poem "To Those Born After" was written in 1939 and has been widely anthologized—for example, in Bertolt Brecht, *Ausgewählte Gedichte* (Frankfurt: Suhrkamp, 1962), 56–58. *Harper's* has the poem on its website, with an English translation and a commentary; see Scott Horton, "Brecht 'To Those Who Follow in Our Wake,'" *Harper's*, January 15, 2008. Renan's lecture "Qu-est-ce que une nation?" delivered at the Sorbonne on March 11, 1882, is available in English in Ernest Renan, *What Is a Nation? and Other Political Writings*, 347–363.

On Lithuania's war criminals: The reappraisal of Jonas Noreika came largely at the initiative of his American granddaughter Silvia Foti, who broke through two generations of silence about who he really was and subsequently published a book, *The Nazi's Granddaughter: How I Discovered My Grandfather Was a War Criminal* (New York: Regnery, 2021). The line from Mayor Šimašius is from an American Jewish Committee news release, "AJC Hosts Vilnius Mayor Remigijus Šimašius in Washington," October 30, 2019.